JOURNEY
TO
PERFECTION

To Mary with
Love & Light
from John

24/11/08

JOURNEY TO PERFECTION

The Spiritual Evolution of
Individuals and Society

JOHN RILEY
M.B.E.

Glenstrae Press

First published in 2008 by
Glenstrae Press

© John Riley 2008

The right of John Riley to be identified as the Author of this
work has been asserted by him in accordance with the
Copyright, Designs and Patents Act 1988.

All rights reserved. No part of this publication may be reproduced, stored in a retrieval system or transmitted, in any
form or by any means, electronic, mechanical, photocopying,
recording or otherwise without the prior permission of both
the copyright holder and the above publisher.

A catalogue card for this book is available from
the British Library.

It is the belief of both the publisher and the author that all
necessary permissions have been obtained with reference to
copyright material, both illustrative and quoted. However,
should there be any omissions in this respect, we apologise
and shall be pleased to make the appropriate
acknowledgments in future editions.

ISBN 978-0-9560690-0-9

Printed in Great Britain by Biddles Ltd, King's Lynn

Acknowledgements

I wish to thank the following friends, colleagues and organisations:

To Mary Latimer, who has encouraged me throughout this project, expending much time and trouble in checking and re-checking my script, particularly from a spiritual perspective.

To Ian Craig, who has generously applied his expertise in publishing to checking and improving my wording and in particular for the hilarity created by his mimicking my 'rants' about bureaucracy during our meetings. To Kate Craig, for typesetting, designing and producing this book.

To Moira Robertson and Gavin Macnab for their guidance in enabling me to master my computer in producing both scripts and figures.

To a number of people and organisations who gave me permission to quote extensively from their publications, including: Norma Bordeaux Szekely (nicknamed Swallow) of the International Biogenic Society, British Columbia; regarding the works of her late husband Edmond Bordeaux Szekely: Carole Alderman of The British Institute of Sathya Sai Education in Human Values UK, regarding manuals and newsletters: Hugh McGregor Ross/Watkins Publishing, regarding The Gospel of Thomas: Glenda Green regarding her book *Love Without End* and Prosveta, regarding the works of the Master Omraam Mikhael Aivanhov.

To the host of other people, including Grant and Grace Clifford, Murray Dickie, Robert Gordon-Adams, Geoffrey Hardman, Jim Kinnell, Lionel McClelland, Joyce Russell, Sue Wyllie and the writers of the complementary articles presented in Part V: Anu Anand, Mary Latimer, David Walne, David Cowan, Colin Roxburgh, Moira Robertson, Chris Hughes, Diane Piette, Linda McCartney, and Lesley-Ann Patrick.

Lastly, to my wife Barbara who has stoically accepted that my creative energies have tended to surface often in the early hours of the morning during the last couple of years or more and who has also provided good advice on the structure, layout and wording of many parts of the book.

Contents

List of Figures   9
Introduction   11

Part I - *What are We and What is our Purpose?*   17

1. Our Amazing Potential   19
2. Our Soul's Journey   25
3. The Seven Bodies/Vehicles of the Soul   35
4. Our Life Energy Centres   43
5. Our Aura and Its Purpose   51

Part II - *Our Relationship with the Universe and the Divine*   65

6. Spiritual Masters-Religions-Misinterpretations and Misunderstandings   67
7. The Development of Orthodox Christianity   75
8. The Influence of Rediscovered Manuscripts   81
9. Controversies   97
10. The Rise of Agnosticism and Atheism   103
11. Core Teachings of Jesus   109

Part III - *Pathways to Enlightenment*   121

12. We Are All One   123
13. Yoga for the Ascetic   127
14. Meditation for Everyday Living   135

Part IV - *The Spiritual Evolution of Society*   147

15. Our Collective Journey   149
16. True Democracies   153

17. Are We Responsible for Climate Change?	161
18. Healing the Planet by Healing Ourselves	169
19. Education Based on Universal Love	185

Part V - *Complementary Articles*	*195*
20. Introduction	197
21. A Look at Life *Anu Anand*	203
22. The Gift of Colour *Mary Latimer*	209
23. From Tranquillisers to Tranquillity *David Walne*	221
24. Ley Lines, Ill-Health and Spirit Lines *David R. Cowen*	235
25. Community Futures *Colin Roxburgh*	261
26. Aromatherapy Massage *Moira Robertson*	267
27. Bio-Energy Therapy *Chris Hughes*	275
28. Kinesiology - Three in One Concepts *Diane Piette*	283
29. Reiki *Linda McCartney*	291
30. Sathya Sai School *Lesley-Ann Patrick*	315

Appendix	*325*
Bibliography	*329*

List of Figures

1.	Return Journey to Perfection	33
2.	Traditional Characteristics of Chakras	44
3.	Location of the Seven Main Chakras	46
4.	Evolution of the Chakra System	48
5.	The Auras of Successively More Evolved Beings	55
6.	Life Energy Bodies of the Soul	56
7.	Observing Life Energy Flow between Fingers	59
8.	The *'Chi-Rho'* Battle Standard utilised by Constantine	77
9.	Protein yields (kilogram per hectare) from various crops	181
10.	A simple and very efficient pair of divining rods made from fence wire	237
11.	The cup-marked stone at Connachan Farm with Foulford Inn in the background	240
12.	The cup-marked stone at Foulford Inn	241
13.	The dumbbell shaped petroglyph	241
14.	Plan view of a sinusoidal wave	242
15.	Ancient burial grounds	243
16.	The Druid's Cave at Glen Almond	244
17.	A beam of energy from a fault beneath a bed	245
18.	Spirit lines	248
19.	Energy spirals from each individual grave	249
20.	A spirit line spirals up from a graveyard	251
21.	Placing a cup-marked stone in its correct position, outside the wall of a house	254
22.	Putting a quartz crystal under pressure	256
23.	Quartz crystals used to protect a bed from negative energy	257

Dedication

To all people in the belief that these written words will inspire them to make progress on their own journey to perfection; thus bringing about peace on earth.

Introduction

I have been deeply interested in spiritual philosophy for many years, avidly studying the writings and teachings of some of the world's great masters and in the process undoubtedly expanding my inner awareness of life itself. Most importantly of all I have realised that our bodies' function is to be host to the soul throughout its sojourn on planet earth. In addition to assimilating the wise words of these masters, I have had to find my own pathway through life and as I progressed, I became only too well aware of the great inequalities which existed, and indeed which still do exist today; of the great importance placed upon material possessions, wealth and social standing, and of the lack of purpose and direction which prevails in our global society.

I became interested in politics in general, and of community politics in particular giving me a greater insight into the workings of society at large. My major realisation was that there is something very wrong with our 'democratic' way of life, and that far from it being democratic it tends to be 'autocratic', the people having minimal influence over factors affecting their lives. I realised that the 'something' which was missing throughout all of this was the spiritual aspect which seemed to be almost completely absent from any decision-making at a higher level, and indeed in all walks of life.

These issues have troubled me greatly for a very long

time, and to this end I have decided to put my thoughts onto paper, by writing this book addressing these adverse situations and offering corresponding solutions. I would ask you to have an open mind when reading this book, and whenever possible to effect a change for the better in yourself and so also change the world. To quote Mahatma Gandhi, *'We have to become the change that we want to see in the world'*.

This book carries a message of hope for all mankind that the negativity, which is infecting our global society, can be transformed by individual spiritual growth, which will have a cumulative effect: the whole is the sum of the individual parts and as each one of us embarks on our own journey to perfection there will be a corresponding expansion of global consciousness, which will ultimately lead to peace on earth.

Our leaders and representatives in governments, commerce and religions have tended to build centralised, top down structures, which have disempowered the majority of the people. This has caused frustration and resulted in negativity in society, such as violence, substance abuse and anti-social behaviour. Instead of being dominated in a top down manner, society can evolve spiritually from the bottom upwards, which in democratic terms will lead to Abraham Lincoln's ideal of *'Government of the people by the people for the people'*.

The book is divided into five parts, the contents of which are summarised below:

Part I - *What are We and What is our Purpose?* This explains the derivation of freedom of choice and claims that as we evolve spiritually we tend to make positive choices for universal benefit. It then describes the journey of our soul through many lifetimes and realities: in essence we are light beings who need to absorb light into our energy bodies and auras in order to be strong and healthy and to realise our full potential of God realisation.

Part II – *Our Relationship with the Universe and the Divine.* Sometimes, during the history of mankind, exceptional spiritual beings have incarnated as exemplars, whose teachings have been very similar and have led to the formation of religions, such as Buddhism, Christianity, Hinduism and Islam. Unfortunately both leaders and followers have tended to focus on differences between their religion and others rather than their similarities; claiming that theirs is the only route to God. For example, Christians have been told that Jesus was the only son of God; the Jews believe that they are the chosen people and many Muslims believe that infidels are their enemies. In other words, there is a focus on separation instead of the togetherness, which is the essence of all great spiritual teachings.

The teachings of Jesus are highlighted, as he was a well travelled man who had experience of many religions including Buddhism, Brahmanism, Hinduism and Parsism. Bearing in mind also that he was Jewish, that the Christian religion was formed around his life and that he became a prophet of Islam, surely his true teachings provide the best possible guide to the spiritual transformation of society.

It is suggested that orthodox Christianity, which was fabricated both during and after the Council of Nicea in 325AD, misrepresents both the life and teachings of Jesus. Instead, we should study a number of ancient manuscripts, such as The Gospel of Thomas and the Essene gospels,

JOURNEY TO PERFECTION

translated from the Aramaic, to understand the true philosophy of Jesus, which is explained by reference to the Beatitudes and The Lord's Prayer.

Part III - *Pathways to Enlightenment.* Explains our relationship with God, which is universal consciousness existing both inside and outside all life on earth. It describes two routes to enlightenment: firstly that of the ascetic who devotes his whole life to this quest, utilising yoga; which in its broadest sense, encompasses all other methods. Secondly, it describes the route appropriate for the majority of people who live conventional lives in society utilising various types of meditation, which opens all doors to the divine.

Part IV - *The Spiritual Evolution of Society.* Purports that the main reason for the devastation of our planet is that our way of life conflicts with the cosmic and natural laws of Love, Freedom, Cause and Effect, Balance and Karma. It criticises most democracies, arguing that many global societies are governed by autocrats and bureaucrats, disguised as democrats. It then analyses the issue of climate change and suggests that this trend will be reversed as we learn how to live in harmony with nature. The next chapter suggests that instead of relying solely on the medical profession and pharmaceutical industry, we should accept responsibility for our own health and well-being. The final chapter proposes that the reversal of planetary negativity will arise from a form of education based on universal love; the sole aim of teachers being to educate our children not only at an academic level, but to incorporate the highest possible level of spiritual understanding. Ultimately, this will bring about a scenario in which leadership roles in society will be undertaken by spiritually evolved people.

Part V - *Complementary Articles.* These articles have been especially written for this book by practitioners of various complementary therapies and people involved in other spiritual and democratic pursuits. This provides much greater depth than I could draw from my own experiences.

All references to men and mankind in this book apply equally to men and women.

PART I

WHAT ARE WE AND WHAT IS OUR PURPOSE?

1

OUR AMAZING POTENTIAL

The whole universe, outer space, the stars, our sun, the planet earth and all its inhabitants, whether animal, vegetable or mineral, are part of an energy field; a fact which is confirmed by scientists and concords with Einstein's theory of relativity. This universal energy field is also consciousness and has been identified with names like God, the Father, Brahman, Allah, the Great Spirit, the Oneness and the Divine. This provides an explanation of the evolution of life which differs from scientific hypotheses. Scientists are still unable to explain how life was formed; whether it originated on this planet or arose from material that arrived from space. There is however considerable scientific evidence that our planet was formed by a mighty explosion giving rise to a mass of extremely hot gases which slowly cooled down resulting in liquids and solids. What is regarded as a possibility is that, when conditions, such as temperature and atmosphere were suitable, life began by chance and evolved from single cells, with its rich variety evolving entirely due to the 'survival of the fittest' with the need to find food and shelter in order to survive. The contrary explanation is that the universe is omnipresent consciousness and therefore every individual particle of matter has the potential of life; the various species quite possibly, but not necessarily, evolving much as explained by Darwin's Theory.

Our ultimate potential is to realise and experience our relationship with the universe but in our body consciousness we are limited by our five senses, which only enable us to experience a relatively small range of universal energy frequencies. Instead of realising our universal nature, we perceive ourselves as separate beings, develop self awareness and can become self centred or selfish. In any situation, we have a choice of either acting for self, or for the benefit of the universe. The former choice is dictated by our ego and the latter arises as guidance from our conscience or soul. This perception of separation enables us to experience life in a physical body and interact with other people and life forms but our ego is in charge; the soul only being able to influence the ego as 'the little voice within' or conscience, which when ignored results in wrong decisions and actions. Utilisation of our freedom of choice thus creates polarisation into positive and negative decisions, actions and characteristics. However, negative decisions and actions can promote a positive outcome because if there was no negative, there would be no positive either; often, a very negative situation motivating a very positive reaction.

It is commonly claimed that human beings are naturally selfish and therefore there is no solution to the mounting chaos in our global society. The contrary assertion is that misuse of freewill results in selfishness, giving rise to greed, egotism and the wish to control others; such characteristics being the root cause of materialism, wars, cruelty in many forms, racial and religious intolerance, and destruction of the environment.

We have the potential to evolve beyond the limitations of our five senses and experience other dimensions of reality; a process which can be speeded up by various methods of spiritual exploration. As we evolve spiritually we tend to make positive choices which will be for the benefit of all; the cumulative effect of which is to reduce negativity in society; our emotions and characteristics tending to change from negative to positive; for example, negative emotions such as hatred, anger, revenge and despair evolve into positive ones of love, calmness, forgiveness and hope. Similarly, characteristics such as cruelty, stress, pessimism and victimisation move towards kindness, relaxation, optimism and self actualisation. Typically, when we are in a negative state of mind we will tend to bear grudges for a long time but as we evolve spiritually, we will tend to forgive others very quickly; realising that 'to err is human but to forgive is divine'.

The chaos in our society, which is endangering all life on earth, is caused by a misconception about our true nature and the purpose of our lives. We may think that we only have one life and then depending upon our decisions and actions, we pass into a permanent afterlife. Similarly, we may think that the purpose of our lives is to be wealthy, good looking and healthy. Instead we should realise that we are all part of an omnipresent spirit and our purpose is not only to understand this but experience it and dedicate our lives for everyone's benefit. This theme was explained by Sri Sathya Sai Baba as follows:

> *The purpose of life is to find out who we really are. Man, is like the prince who was stolen by the robbers when he was a baby. He has grown up to think that he is one of the robbers. But if he finds out and gets to know without doubt, that he is a prince with a wonderful inheritance, his life and outlook will be completely changed.*

> *Likewise, if we can reach direct, doubt-free knowledge of our true identity, then our lives will move onto a new level, and our outlook will change completely. Accompanying that change will be an abiding joy that is unaffected by the ups and downs of circumstance. For, discovering who we are, releases this joy, which is part of our true nature. We do not have to wait until we die, and move to some other zone of existence, before making the great discovery. In fact it is better that we make it here-and that it is the purpose of our human life on earth.*
>
> *When one has found one's real hidden Self, one has found God, for he is one with the Self. The inward journey to the Self and to God may have three stages.*
>
> *First, there is a feeling that God is the Master, a great Being out there somewhere and that the seeker is his servant. Then the seeker comes closer and understands that he is the son, the offspring of God; finally he realises that he is one with God.*
>
> *When the seeker realises that he is one with God, he will know also that he is one with all life. For God is all life. While he continues to live in the world, thereafter, his life will be governed by this sense of harmonious unity.*
>
> *He will not seek happiness and satisfaction through things of the world. Happiness will be always with him. He will seek only to serve his fellow men in order to bring them to the goal that he has, himself, already reached.*

From a spiritual perspective the purpose of life can be defined as finding our true identity and becoming God realised.

Within our being exists a blueprint of the perfect society; described by Jesus as the Kingdom of Heaven, which can be accessed during our spiritual journey. The inspirations of great scientists, musicians and artists arise from this infinite pool of wisdom. People who learn how to access this inner kingdom will become dissatisfied with the chaotic, self-seeking state of our civilisation and endeavour to change it for the better. Racism and religious intolerance will evolve into the realisation that there is only one race; that of humanity and only one religion, that of love. Similarly, competition in industry and commerce will move towards co-operation and autocratic, centralised styles of government will tend to become truly democratic in operation; providing the people with genuine influence over factors affecting their lives. Our ultimate potential is to re-create the Kingdom of Heaven on earth.

The article by Anu Anand in chapter 21 entitled *A Look at Life* expands on the themes of materialism, universal consciousness and the purpose of life.

This poem by Martin Armstrong beautifully expresses the limitations of our five senses.

THE CAGE

Man afraid to be alive
Shuts his soul in senses five,
From fields of uncreated light
Into the crystal tower of sight,
And from the roaring songs of space
Into the small flesh carven-place
Of the ear whose cave impounds
Only small and broken sounds,
And to his narrow sense of touch
From strength that held the stars in clutch,
And from the warm, ambrosial spice

*Of flowers and fruits of paradise
Into the frail and fitful power
Of sense and tasting, sweet and sour,
And toiling for a sordid wage
There in his self-created cage,
Ah, how safely barred is he
From menace of eternity!*

2

OUR SOUL'S JOURNEY

Medical scientists have concentrated their investigations on the physical body and mind of the human, providing very detailed information but our knowledge about the nature of our soul is very limited. We are well aware that the physical body is not our whole self, but rather a vessel which houses the soul throughout its earthly journey, and once the body dies the soul departs, leaving the body to decompose. Some of the questions which I will endeavour to answer in this chapter are: what is the nature of this being which provides the experience of life to all living creatures? Where does it come from? When does it enter the body? Where does it go to when our physical body dies? Is it still conscious after the death of the physical body, in other words, can death be regarded as a change in consciousness, rather than a tragic occurrence? Does it take on numerous bodies throughout its evolution? If it experiences multiple life times, why can't we remember past lives? In the context of our duality, as both a physical body and a soul, what is the purpose of our lives?

We are complex spiritual beings, having many parts, including soul, spirit, ego, physical body and personality. Our soul is a minute part of the universal conscious energy field (God) and witnesses our decisions and actions but is unable to interfere as this would remove our freedom of choice. Accordingly, it will only prompt and guide us when asked by sincere prayers and meditation. It is generally regarded as residing in the area of the body's energy field in the centre of the chest. Our spirit, like our soul, is omnipresent, and is therefore present in our whole being but unlike our soul, it is not bound by our previous actions. It is part of the universal spirit and can most easily be experienced in, around and above our head. Our ego, which is closely connected with our unique personality, is the decision maker and is regarded as operating from the solar plexus. Our body is a life experiencing vehicle for our soul, a generally accepted theory being that our body is given life when our soul enters at our conception or soon afterwards and leaves again just after our death, allowing us to travel into different spiritual realms.

Our soul is affected by our decisions and actions during our lives, this relationship being subject to 'The Law of Cause and Effect', which was defined by Sir Isaac Newton, as 'Action and Reaction are Equal and Opposite' in his 'Third Law of Motion', which is not just a law of motion but also a law of life. When we make decisions and take actions for our own benefit at the expense of others we create negative stress in our being, which is called karma in Eastern religions. Similarly if the decisions and actions are of a selfless nature a positive stress is created. A related law is 'The Law of Karma', which states that 'If karmic balance is not achieved in the current life then it has to be balanced in successive lives'.

In spiritual terms, all souls are equal but different individuals may have taken negative actions, the effects of which have not been balanced out during a particular lifetime. An example of the effect of karma on the successive lives of an individual soul is if in a particular incarnation the person carries out an act of great cruelty against another person because he is of a different race, then in another life he may be a member of that race. Thus a hater of Jews in one life may be born a Jew in another life in order to experience the effects of his hatred. Another example is that if you purposely blinded someone in one life then, as a learning process, you would experience another life in which you were treated in this cruel way. Thus, for example, the statement 'an eye for an eye and a tooth for a tooth'[1] can be regarded as a karmic warning, in that our punishment for committing acts, which we know in our hearts are wrong, may be experienced in a future life, if not in our current life.

Karma also affects whole communities and nations. For example America, Great Britain and many other countries are still being affected by negative karma resulting from the slave trade. One purpose of this process of action and reaction through successive lives is to teach us compassion for all living creatures. As Albert Schweitzer, the renowned missionary said, *'until he extends the circle of his compassion to all living things man himself will not find peace'*.

The teachings of many religions, including Christianity, state that we only experience one life in a physical body and then, dependent upon our behaviour, we either arrive in a permanent hell or a wonderful heaven. This concept is derived from the apparent reality of our body and permanence of its surroundings. If we only had one life wouldn't it be so unfair that one person is born in perfect health, lives a wonderful and happy life, whilst another is born to an African women suffering from AIDS and lives a very short and painful life? The truth is that we experience multiple lives on this planet and others through time and space. It is necessary for us to be only conscious of our current life so that the experience is real, enabling us to experience freedom to make right and wrong decisions and learn from these experiences.

The doctrine of reincarnation was fundamental to many world religions, including Christianity until the Second Council of Constantinople in 553 AD, when the Roman Emperor Justinian, contrary to the wishes of Pope Virgilius, forced the ruling cardinals to remove the doctrine by issuing a decree. An interesting account is provided by Holger Kersten, in his book, *Jesus Lived in India*^{2}. Apparently, Justinian's wife had previously been a courtesan and after marrying the emperor she had about 500 of her previous colleagues tortured and put to death. She was afraid that she would have to suffer the consequences of this evil deed in subsequent lives and in order to escape this punishment she persuaded her husband to have this doctrine abolished. To quote Kersten, '*The prohibition of the rebirth doctrine is therefore simply an error of history and lacking all ecclesiastical validity*'.

Despite this decision there are a number of statements still remaining in Christian literature which give the impression that reincarnation was originally included. One such statement from the Old Testament, King James Edition, Malachi 4:5, states 'Behold I will send you Elijah the prophet, before the coming of the great and dreadful day of the Lord', which is an apparent assertion that Elijah will be born again, when he will make positive changes. Another excerpt from the Apocrypha KJV1611 Edition, Ecclesiasticus 41:8-9 is 'Woe unto you, ungodly men, who have forsaken the Law of the Most High God; for if you increase it shall be your destruction. And if you be born, you shall be born to a curse', is surely a clear karmic warning by Solomon that if one sins then one will have to make amends.

Now, referring to the New Testament, also utilising the King James Edition, there are a few passages which give the impression that the doctrine of reincarnation was a normally accepted concept in Jesus' society. One can only assume that these statements were left untouched as they were important in the general context. Also, it may be that they were regarded as ambiguous, in that they could be attributed with alternative interpretations:

Matthew 11: 13-15
13. For all the prophets of the law prophesied until John
14. And if ye will receive it, this is Elias which was for to come.

This is a follow on from the statement in Malachi, in effect stating that John the Baptist is the reincarnation of Elias (or Elijah)

Matthew 16: 15-16
15. He sayeth unto them, But whom say ye that I am?
16. And Simon Peter answered and said, Thou art the Christ, the Son of the living God.

The question asked by Jesus clearly demonstrates his belief in reincarnation.

Matthew 17: 10-13
10. And his disciples asked him, saying, why then

JOURNEY TO PERFECTION

sayest the scribes that Elias must first come?

11. And Jesus answered and said unto them, Elias shall truly come, and restore all things.

12. But I say unto you, That Elias is come already, and they knew him not, but have done unto him whatever they listed. Likewise shall also the Son of man suffer of them?

13. Then the disciples understood that he spoke unto them of John the Baptist.

This is similar to that in Matthew 16; referring to the reincarnation of Elias as John the Baptist.

Luke 1: 13-17

13. But the angel said unto him, Fear not Zacharias: for thy prayer is heard; and thy wife Elizabeth shall bear thee a son, and thou shalt call his name John

14. And thou shalt have joy and gladness; and many shall rejoice at his birth

15. For he shall be great in the sight of the Lord, and shall drink neither wine nor strong drink; and he shall be filled with the Holy Ghost, even from his mother's womb.

16. And many of the children of Israel shall he turn to the Lord their God.

17. And he shall go before him in the spirit and power of Elias, to turn the hearts of the fathers to the children, and the disobedient to the wisdom of the just; to make ready a people prepared for the Lord.

The first sentence of '17' is a clear indication of John being Elias reincarnated.

Luke 9: 7-8

7. Now Herod the Tetrarch heard of all that was done by him: and he was perplexed because it was said of some, that John was risen from the dead;
8. And of some, that Elias had appeared; and of others, that one of the old prophets was risen again.

These two verses could be regarded as an acceptance of the concept of reincarnation was common at that time.

John 9: 1-3

1. And as Jesus passed by, he saw a man which was blind from birth.
2. And his disciples asked him, saying Master, who did sin, this man or his parents, that he is born blind?
3. Jesus answered, neither has this man sinned, nor his parents: but that the works of God should be made manifest in him.

This response by Jesus infers that the question was perfectly reasonable, referring to re-payment of karmic debt. On this occasion, there was a different explanation for the affliction.

There are more references to reincarnation in the writings of 'Origen of Alexendria', who was a highly regarded early Christian theologian; 185-254AD. One of his most important works was 'De Principiis' or 'On First Principles', in which he describes the souls journey in terms of their pre-existence, transmigration and eventual restoration to a state of dynamic perfection in proximity to the Godhead.

He also insisted that each soul has absolute freedom. Apparently, even after Constantine and Nicea, some of the more educated monks were utilising Origen's ideas as a basis for spiritual practices aimed at becoming God realised.

As previously explained we have the potential to evolve beyond the reality created by the limitations of our five senses by consciously embarking on a journey of spiritual exploration, and ultimately experiencing oneness with God. Our ultimate potential is to evolve beyond the need for rebirth or reincarnation and experience life in higher spiritual realms, in other words to return to our source. To reach this state of perfection all karmic debt has to be balanced out but we can be totally unaware of our spiritual nature and continue building karmic debt for numerous lifetimes. Eventually, we begin to realise that there must be more to life than this unhappy drama and start searching for greater meaning in life. The outward journey away from God is followed by an inward journey back to God, a trend which is undoubtedly a joyous experience for the soul, which will provide guidance when asked. As Jesus said `Ask and you will receive, seek and you will find, knock and the door will be opened [3]. At this later stage in our spiritual journey, we may tend not to pray to God for our requirements but instead surrender ourselves to his will; as the Lord's Prayer says 'Thy will be done'.

Our journey away from and back to our source is illustrated in Figure 1.

In essence, we are travellers through time and space, experiencing numerous lifetimes on our journey to perfection.

Evidence of reincarnation has been demonstrated by the practice of past life therapy, in which people are hypnotised,

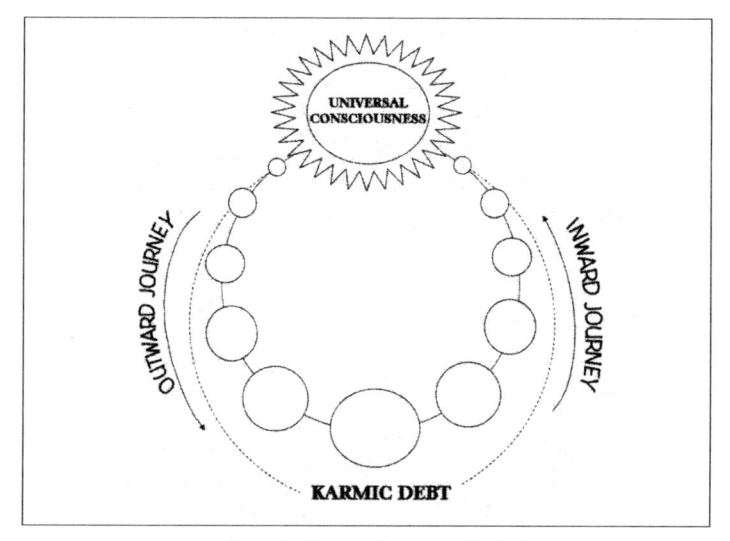

Figure 1. Return Journey to Perfection.

asked to travel back through time and describe their observations. It is based on the concept that some of the characteristics of our current life are related to dramatic experiences in a previous life, which are embedded deeply in our subconscious. For example, if one were drowned in a previous life one may experience a seemingly irrational fear of deep water in a future life. It is claimed that being taken back to re-live such negative experiences during hypnosis enables us to release deep stress in our nervous system, curing us of negative emotions and freeing us from the limitation of that particular fear This concept of past life therapy is explained by a Jungian psychotherapist, called Roger Woolger, in his book *Other Lives Other Selves*[4], in which he provides numerous descriptions of case studies.

Another common occurrence, reported in the media, is when somebody is able to describe the detail of events and places

33

which they have not experienced in their current lifetime. It is not my intention to dwell on this aspect, as such events have already been described in great depth in various books and television programmes and, in any case, anyone with a particular interest can locate a vast amount of information in libraries or on the internet.

3

THE SEVEN BODIES/ VEHICLES OF THE SOUL

Spiritually evolved people have explained that we have various bodies occupying the same space as our physical body, which in order of increasing spiritual refinement are the etheric, astral, mind, causal, buddhic and atmic bodies, the last two being constituents of our 'body of glory'. Each of these creates an aura, the combined effect being illustrated in Figure 6 in the next chapter, their role both during sleep and on the death of the physical body, is explained below:

Our `Ka' or Etheric Body is less dense than our physical body and occupies the same space, its function being to enable us to leave our body during sleep. It has infinite elasticity, and can be seen by clairvoyants and other multidimensional beings as a cord which remains attached to both the physical and the astral bodies, whilst the former is unconscious and the latter travels into other dimensional realities. Apparently the etheric body surrounds our nerves and gives sensation to our nervous system. An interesting observation is that when we are given a local anaesthetic the etheric body retreats from that area, so that there is no feeling. Similarly, when we are given a full anaesthetic our etheric body leaves the physical body, remaining attached by the cord. If we are given too much anaesthetic, the cord is broken causing death, which is the method used by veterinary surgeons to carry out humane euthanasia on animals such as dogs and horses.

The etheric body has no continuing function after our death but fearing its own demise, clings to the astral body as it tries to leave our corpse after death. Our soul, now existing in the astral body, has to shake itself free from the etheric body and sometimes is held back; being effectively trapped but when it eventually breaks free, the etheric body quickly disintegrates. In my capacity as a Reiki healer, I had a very strange experience when I visited the mortuary to see the body of someone to whom I had previously given healing, but had been aware that the Reiki energy was not being drawn by the body, but realised that the whole exercise was being given to provide psychological support. As I walked towards the room where the body was laid, I experienced Reiki healing energy being very strongly drawn. The explanation of this experience by three independent healers was that the astral was body-bound and needed healing energy to enable it to break free and ascend into finer dimensions. One of the advisers also explained that the soul would have experienced the flames of the cremation, had it still been trapped. Apparently, to be able to help someone in this way is a blessed experience, being of great service to the deceased.

Our Astral Body exists in the same space as the physical and etheric bodies and is less dense, with its purpose, during our life, to enable our soul to experience life in higher dimensions, whilst our physical body sleeps. We often remember fragments of these experiences as confusing dreams. Apparently, we can learn how to remain conscious during sleep, this practice being called astral projection or travelling. This exercise can be extremely dangerous and should only be practiced under close supervision by experienced teachers. Sometimes, people have 'out of the body experiences' (OBE's) by chance and are aware of floating in the air whilst fast asleep. This often happens whilst people are anesthetised during an operation and they are able to recall the conversations which had taken place between surgeons and their assistants during their operations, or observe and describe the dust on top of the light shades and the contents on high shelves.

I have experienced only two conscious OBE's, which I believe were given to me to demonstrate that our body is not our whole being. On the first occasion, I was awakened by the noise of a near neighbour starting up his motorcycle early in the morning, and sat up in bed, propped up on my elbow. The noise was extremely loud, as if the motorcycle was in the bedroom, and seemed to continue for a very long time as the motorcycle was driven down the road. When I decided to re-continue my sleep I realised, to my amazement, that my body was still fast asleep. On another occasion, I became aware of floating in the air and when I tried to propel myself to the end of the bed found no resistance to the movement of my arms, having to jerk myself forward ending up floating above the end of the bed, bouncing up and down like a balloon. I turned round and realised, to my astonishment, that my body was still fast asleep. Apparently, this type of experience is very common but people are often reluctant to talk about it in case they are regarded as odd. Such experiences can also happen when people are extremely fatigued, on drugs, suffering from sensory deprivation, in life threatening situations and during the practice of relaxation or meditation exercises. For example, one of my friends described how during the practice of Transcendental Meditation he rose from a chair on which he had been sitting, walked across the room into another room, and on returning observed that his body was still sitting on the chair. On another occasion, he had an OBE 'when he was driving his car and his shocked reaction propelled him straight back into his body.

Our astral body has experiences in other spiritual planes, which are just as real as those in the physical dimension. When we die, it becomes the vehicle for the soul to rise into these higher planes, where further learning experiences take place and we often meet relatives, friends and pet animals who have either preceded us in this lifetime, or previous ones.

There are seven levels of conscious experience in the astral plane ranging from low to higher frequencies from bottom to top with the soul being sent to the appropriate level relative to its spiritual development. Life in the astral plane is similar to our earthly life, except that we can materialise by thought whatever we like, whether, for example, a house or a garden or anything else which we might desire. We can even choose who we wish as our neighbours! Our surroundings tend to be much more beautiful than those on earth and we can propel ourselves to other locations at will. We don't need sleep, are perfectly healthy and can continue to learn subjects of interest.

Our Mind and Causal Bodies Eventually we experience death of our astral body and move into a yet higher level called the mental plane, which also has seven levels of reality, rising successively in spiritual refinement. Highly evolved souls often rise straight into this mental plane after their death; returning to the level from whence they came to incarnate. The upper levels of the mental plane are called the causal level and it is here that we prepare for our next incarnation on earth or another planet. We choose our own parents, by mutual consent and, subject to the lessons we need to learn during the coming lifetime, we choose our geographic location, culture and state of health. As explained before, the ultimate purpose of our multiple lives is to experience everything, balance our karmic debt and return permanently to the higher levels of reality.

The spiritual transformation of humanity is accelerating and many souls are moving directly into the causal plane when the physical body dies.

Our Buddhic and Atmic Bodies As we evolve spiritually we reach a stage when our karmic debt is balanced, and we begin to experience instant karma whilst finding it increasingly difficult to make negative choices, and when we do, experiencing most unpleasant effects. Sai Baba is referring to this state of affairs in the following message to his followers:

YES

When you said 'yes' to me, you gave up the right to be like everyone else. That is why you draw experience to yourself, to cleanse yourself of that which does not fit who you are.

Over and over, again and again, until I make you see that

> *the past no longer works, I challenge you and tempt you every day with your past so that you may see that the past is the ultimate delusion.*
>
> *When you said 'yes' to me, gave me your body, your thoughts, your actions, when they don't suit the new you, the uncomfortableness is unbearable. It will be so every time and until you realise this folly, then and only then will you completely give up your desire, for this is the only way that man will learn. Very seldom does he learn by quiet reminders.*
>
> *Man's desires and pitfalls are placed there so that I may do my work. When you give up totally, then your desires will fade. I will never give up on you.*
>
> *Every slip will become harder to bear and less easy to remedy. You will tire of your foolishness because I love you, and although not completely aware of it, you did say 'yes'.*

During this period our astral body reduces and eventually disappears, enabling the development of our Buddhic and Atmic bodies. Our Buddhic body develops as we evolve spiritually by tending to make unselfish choices with its formation often being stimulated by experiences of pain and suffering, which leads to a feeling of compassion for all living beings. At a later stage, the development of our Atmic body is associated with experiences of expanded awareness and the realisation of the oneness of the whole of creation.

The Body of Glory [5a] Our Buddhic and Atmic bodies are part of our 'Body of Glory', which is the Christ principle within us, but only as a seed, which has to be nurtured and developed by right thoughts and actions. When we experience elevated consciousness, for example during times when our whole being resonates with scenes of great beauty, wonderful music or words of great wisdom, we attract luminous particles made of pure light, which stay with us permanently, through life and death for eternity. The 'Body of Glory', takes many life times to develop to its full potential but it eventually imbues us with great spiritual powers, like animals recognising this power and obeying us just by reading our thoughts. The esoteric basis of Free Masonry is not the building of an earthly temple but the building of the temple within our being in which God can reside. When Christ told his disciples that he would be with them always, he meant that although his physical body would die, his 'Body of Glory', which is omnipresent, would always be with them.

These various bodies or vehicles of the soul emit successively more powerful energy fields, the etheric being very close to the physical, the astral extending to about one metre; dependent on the spirituality of the person and the 'body of glory' ultimately being omnipresent.

4

OUR LIFE ENERGY CENTRES

All life forms have a life force energy field, which is both within and around their physical body. Life energy is distributed through the etheric body via a network of vortexes, which operate in a similar manner to electricity transformers, altering frequencies to enable the energy to be absorbed in the necessary positions, without damaging sensitive systems. This distribution system operates in a similar manner to the cardiovascular system. Just as the heart pumps oxygenated blood around the arteries of mammals, this network of energy transformers ensures the distribution of life force energy to various parts of the etheric and astral bodies; our health and quality of life being dependent on its efficient operation. These vortexes, which are named chakras in Eastern philosophies, are located in areas of our etheric and astral bodies, which correspond to the position of the main nerve plexuses and endocrine glandular system in the physical body. Traditionally there are seven main chakras, which are located in a vertical column stretching from the top of the head to the base of the spine, their characteristics being summarised in Figure 2 and illustrated in Figure 3. There is considerable evidence that the human chakra system is undergoing a major transformation, which is associated with our spiritual evolution. This is the reason for describing this information as traditional.

We have many other chakras, some of which can appar-

Trend	Number	Name	Sanskrit Name	Healthy Colour
↑ Spiritual Issues / Increasing Frequency	7	Crown	Sahasrara	Violet
	6	Third Eye	Ajna	Indigo (Red + Blue)
	5	Throat	Vishuddha	Sky Blue
	4	Heart	Anahata	Emerald Green
	3	Solar Plexus	Manipura	Yellow Sunlight
Material Issues / Decreasing Frequency ↓	2	Sacral	Svadisthana	Orange
	1	Root	Muladhara	Ruby Red

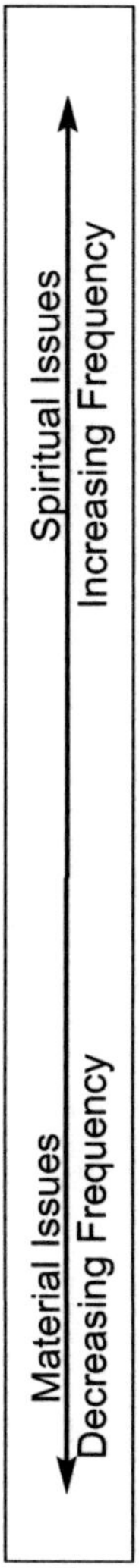

Figure 2. Traditional Characteristics of Chakras.

Position	Gland	Organs Controlled	Sense	Affects
Top of Head	Pineal	Upper Brain Right Eye	One-ness	Omnipotence God Realisation Total Freedom Trust
Between Eyebrows	Pituitary	Lower Brain Left Eye Ears Nose Nervous System	Sight Smell	Spirituality Clairvoyance
Throat	Thyroid	Alimentary Canal Vocal Chords Bronchia Lungs	Hearing Taste	Truth Communication Depression Judgement Wisdom
Centre Chest	Thymus	Heart Circulation Immune System Endocrine System Upper Back	[Love]	Universal Love Will Forgiveness Divine Guidance
Solar Plexus		Pancreas Spleen Stomach Gall Bladder Liver		Relationships Personal Power Self Interest Emotional Sensitivity
Above Pubic Bone		Reproductive Ovaries/Testes Sexuality Immune System		Creativity/Emotions Cravings Addictions Appearance
Base of Spine	Adrenal	Kidneys Spinal Column		Physical Vitality Body Position Movement Fight or Flight Response

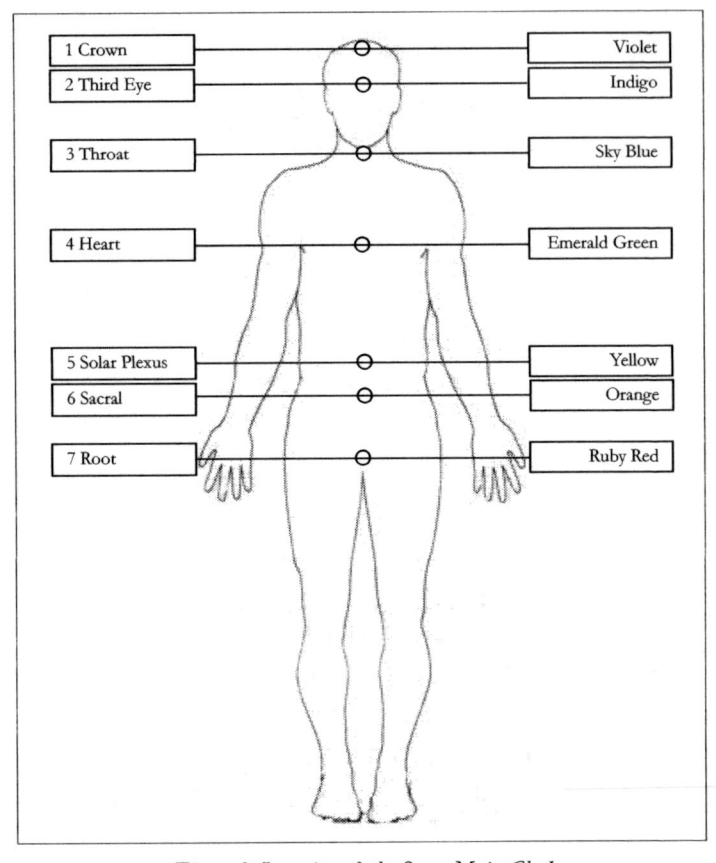

1 Crown	Violet
2 Third Eye	Indigo
3 Throat	Sky Blue
4 Heart	Emerald Green
5 Solar Plexus	Yellow
6 Sacral	Orange
7 Root	Ruby Red

Figure 3. Location of the Seven Main Chakras.

ently, when correctly developed, imbue us with seemingly magical powers, such as being able to move through space at will.[5b]

Earth energies vibrate at a relatively low frequency similar to our heart beat and are located in our base chakra, which traditionally appears to us as the colour red. Universal energies vibrate at a much higher frequency, which we observe as the colour violet emanating from our crown chakra and becoming white light some distance above our heads. One function of the seven main chakras is to progressively modify the frequencies of energy entering via our crown so that it harmonises with earth energies located in our base chakra. Traditionally, we have perceived the colours emanating from our chakras as the colours of a rainbow changing from red at the base, through the spectrum, to violet at the crown, as shown in Figure 3.

However, there is strong evidence that our chakra system is changing as we undergo a spiritual mutation; all the chakras joining together to create a vertical column of light, from our earth chakra below our feet, to our universal chakra above our heads, as illustrated in Figure 4.

People experience this transformation in different ways; this illustration showing one way in which it can happen. Sometimes the heart chakra expands first and sometimes the crown; the head and its surroundings being bathed in bright light extending outwards into the universe. These blissful experiences of expanded awareness can last for varying times from a few seconds to several minutes but when in this state one is oblivious to the passage of time. One can have numerous experiences of expanded awareness and then months or even years pass by before they recur.

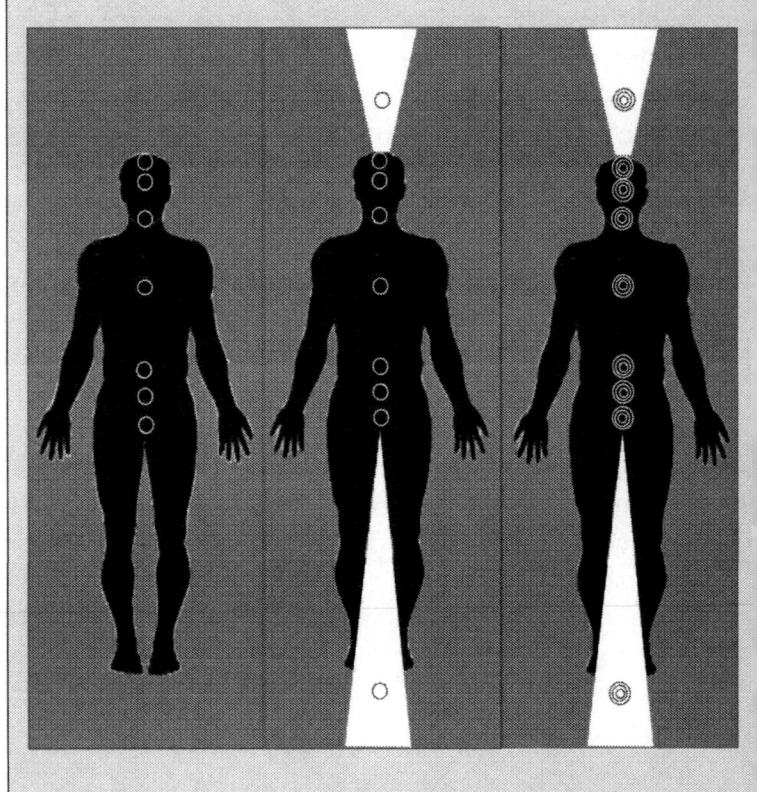

Figure 4. Evolution of the Chakra System.

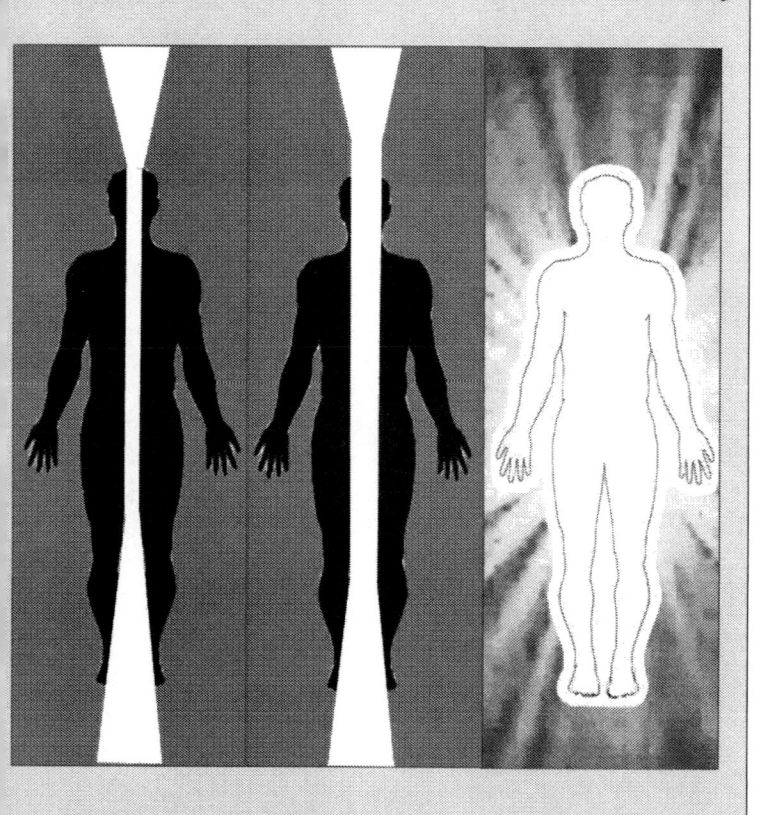

| Column of Light | Wider Column of Light | Enlightenment |

5

OUR AURA AND ITS PURPOSE

Each chakra is surrounded by its own energy field, the energy fields of all our chakras merging together to form an aura, which emanates from within all living beings reflecting their physical, mental and spiritual characteristics. Human auras generally change in appearance from moment to moment, dependent on the thoughts and emotions. Also they vary in size, colour and brightness depending on the spiritual advancement of the being. The purpose of the aura is to protect the soul from negative cosmic energy and also to enable communications with other human souls and higher spiritual beings in the universe. It is also a sense organ, which enables us to judge the character and health of other beings

From a spiritual perspective, all life forms are knowingly or unknowingly on a spiritual journey towards perfection; relative to their stage in this journey, minerals are at the lowest level, followed by plants, the lower animals and the higher animals, including human beings. The aura of a mineral emanates solely from its etheric body and can be seen by clairvoyants as a light surrounding the body. Crystals are a mineral type, which have a very even atomic lattice structure, which gives them the immense storage capacity, which we utilise in computers. Some crystals have beautiful colours and can be used to magnify the effect of various types of healing.

The aura of plant life also emanates solely from the etheric body but is generally much more vigorous and wider than that observed around minerals. All plant life, which is nurtured by nature spirits, exists in a different stream of life from animals, its evolution being entirely governed by the laws of nature. Nature spirits exist in a range of frequencies beyond detection by our five senses; although some clairvoyants are well aware of their existence. They operate in harmony with nature and experience a state of permanent bliss, as they apply themselves to their duties. Trees are the most highly evolved form of plant life on our planet and we can gain great peace of mind as we walk through their combined auric field, which exhibits great brilliance, particularly in natural hard wooded areas. Sometime, when walking through the woods, locate an old oak tree with a straight trunk and you can try this beneficial exercise. Stand with your back and the palm of your left hand touching the tree and the palm of your right hand on your abdomen, just above the naval. Try to still your mind and tune into the energy of the tree. This is a very relaxing experience and is a beautiful form of meditation. If you are really attuned to the spirit of the tree, you will experience a wonderful deep green energy flowing through your whole being. Ask it to remove all your stresses and strains and your wish will inevitably be granted. Give thanks to the tree before leaving.

The lower animals are the next in the scale of spiritual ascendancy and their aura emanates not just from their etheric but also from their astral body, these two layers being much more intense and wider than that exhibited by the lower life forms. The astral energy vibrates at a higher frequency than that from the etheric or physical bodies. In effect, the successive layers of the aura vibrate at finer frequencies, relative to their distance from the body. Many people are able to see a glow around animals and plants, which is the reflection from their etheric body but generally only clairvoyants are capable of seeing the light reflected by the astral body.

The aura of the higher animals, including, for example, elephants, monkeys, horses and dogs as well as human beings has another layer, which is a reflection of the mental body, the total energy field being much brighter and wider than that of the lower animals and plants. Similarly, the aura of spiritually evolved souls who have either completed or almost completed their karmic cycle has a further layer, which emanates from the causal body. The auras of some spiritual masters have been observed extending way beyond their physical body; as they have reached the stage of God realisation or cosmic consciousness. It is very beneficial to sit in the aura of a spiritual master and experience great peace and healing. This transfer of energy is called dharshan in Eastern philosophies, often devotees travelling long distances to receive this type of spiritual blessing. According to Omraam Mikhael Aivanhov, who was a member of the Universal White* Brotherhood, we can awaken not only our causal body but also our buddhic and atmic bodies on

---

*The 'Editor's Note' *at the beginning of* Man's Subtle Bodies and Centres *explains that the word 'white' in the name of the brotherhood is not a discriminatory reference to the colour or race of its members. On the contrary: just as white light is the sum and synthesis of all of the colours, so the Universal White Brotherhood concerns all human beings of every race, nation or creed and invites them to unite in creating a new world brotherhood and harmony.*

our pathway to enlightenment.[5b] These add other brighter and more luminous colours and powerful vibrations to the aura; these emanations, forming the 'Body of Glory', referred to by St Paul in his writings. This explained Jesus' transfiguration, on Mount Thabor, in the company of Elijah and Moses, which was witnessed by Peter, James and John. To quote Paramahansa Yogananda, in his book *The Second Coming of Christ*[6a], *'When Jesus was praying on the mountain top, consciously communing with Cosmic Consciousness, the delusive human consciousness in him and his disciples, through which the lifetronic (prana) essence of the universe appears as matter, completely vanished. The body of Jesus, its very atoms shorn of the mask of delusion and consciousness of solidity, appeared luminous and ethereal'.*

The aura of an unenlightened human being expresses the character of the whole being, with all its strengths, faults and foibles, whereas the body of glory expresses only the most intense level of spirituality and purity, enabling spiritual masters to heal the sick. The aura of a spiritual master can be a display of dazzling brilliance and can extend for a relatively long distance, healing and protecting all those who are lucky enough to be in its presence. The relationship of the various layers and the width of the aura in successively more evolved spiritual beings is shown in Figure 5 and illustrated in Figure 6a and b, the lines between the layers being drawn for the sake of clarity; as the various layers actually merge into one another. The base and crown chakras create vertical vortexes, which explain the conical patterns emerging from the bottom and top of the physical body. The aura of an unenlightened person will generally only extend to include the causal body, as shown in Figure

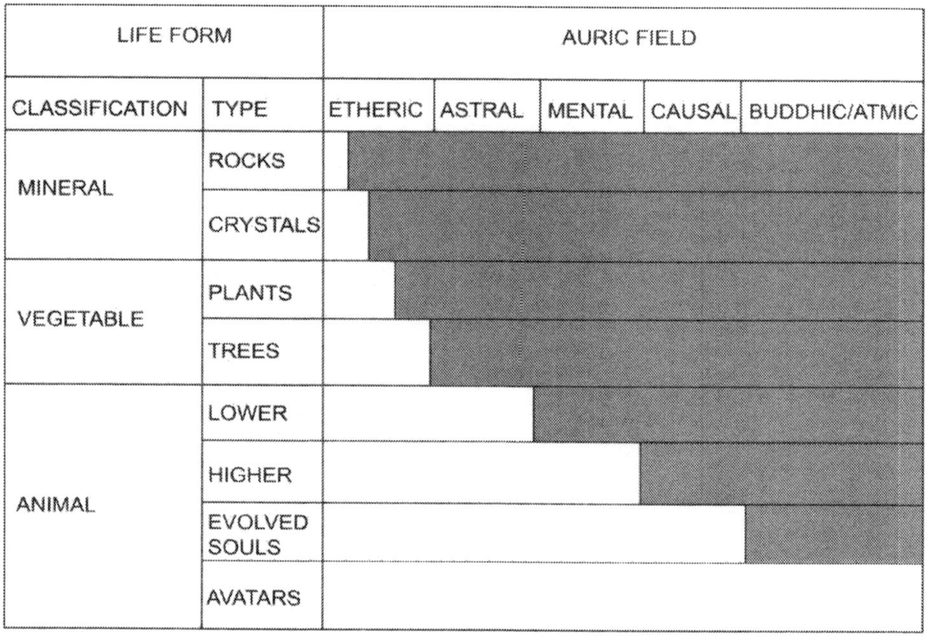

LIFE FORM		AURIC FIELD					
CLASSIFICATION	TYPE	ETHERIC	ASTRAL	MENTAL	CAUSAL	BUDDHIC/ATMIC	
MINERAL	ROCKS						
	CRYSTALS						
VEGETABLE	PLANTS						
	TREES						
ANIMAL	LOWER						
	HIGHER						
	EVOLVED SOULS						
	AVATARS						

Figure 5. The Auras of Successively More Evolved Beings.

Figure 6a. Human Aura

Figure 6b. Spiritually Evolved Aura

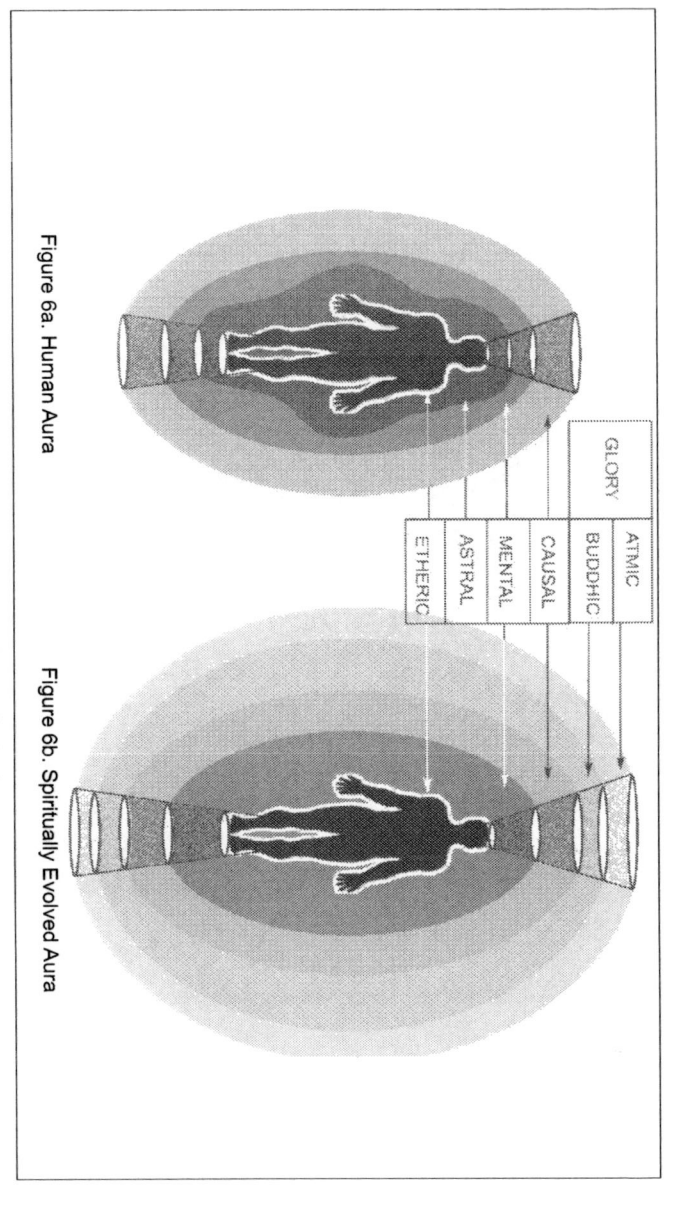

GLORY
ATMIC
BUDDHIC
CAUSAL
MENTAL
ASTRAL
ETHERIC

Figure 6. Life Energy Bodies of the Soul.

6a, whereas the astral body will not be present in the aura of a spiritually evolved person who has balanced their karmic debt, as shown in Figure 6b, which illustrates the full potential of a human being. The body of glory, which includes both the Buddhic and Atmic bodies, gradually develops over numerous lifetimes.

There has been much controversy about the existence of the aura, particularly regarding the interpretation of Kirlian photographs. The process of Kirlian photography is named after Seymon Kirlian, an amateur inventor and electrician, from Russia, who, in the early 1940s, noticed an orange glow, radiating from his fingertips in a colour photograph of his hand. He, and his wife who was a biologist, photographed a whole range of objects, originally in black and white and later in colour, and claiming that the corona effect was caused by the aura. Scientists, who have studied this subject, claim that the coloured halo is not a manifestation of the spiritual aura but a corona discharge produced by stimulating an object electrically, in various conditions, of temperature and humidity. The truth is that both of these effects are valid, occur quite naturally and are more easily observed in particular conditions.

There have been many historical references to the universal energy field. For example between 3000 and 500BC life energy was discovered in India, as prana, in China as chi, and in Greece (by Pythagorus) as vital energy. In 1911, Walter Kilner used coloured screens and filters to show that three different layers of the human energy field were related to disease. Between 1916 and 1960, Dr Harold Burr studied the relationship between many life forms and electromagnetic fields, which could be measured and mapped using voltmeters. He showed that these energy fields are closely related to various diseases.

More information on scientific aspects of these life energy fields is provided by Chris Hughes in his article on 'Bio-Energy Therapy', in chapter 27.

A vast amount of information about these energy fields and centres has also been derived from the teachings of both spiritual masters and the observations and descriptions by clairvoyants, who have trained themselves to see the aura. Clairvoyance is a spiritual gift, which is related to the opening of the third eye, which is an energy vortex situated between the eyebrows.

Anybody who is interested in observing some aspects of their own aura or that of their companions can experiment in various ways. One exercise involves putting the fingers of the two hands together against a neutral background in dim light and then moving the hands apart and up and down and observing energy flowing between the hands, as shown in Figure 7. This is a useful way of demonstrating these lines of force to friends: Some people can see the energy lines and others cannot.

A person's etheric body can also be seen against a dark/neutral background with a dim light shining from behind the observer. Similarly, one can often experience light shining around people's head and shoulders, which is a reflection of the aura.

The aura can also be observed by people who have been born with the ability to see the aura clairvoyantly or have developed the technique. It does require patience and practice, but if the desire is there then it can be achieved by standing naked in front of a full-length mirror in a room

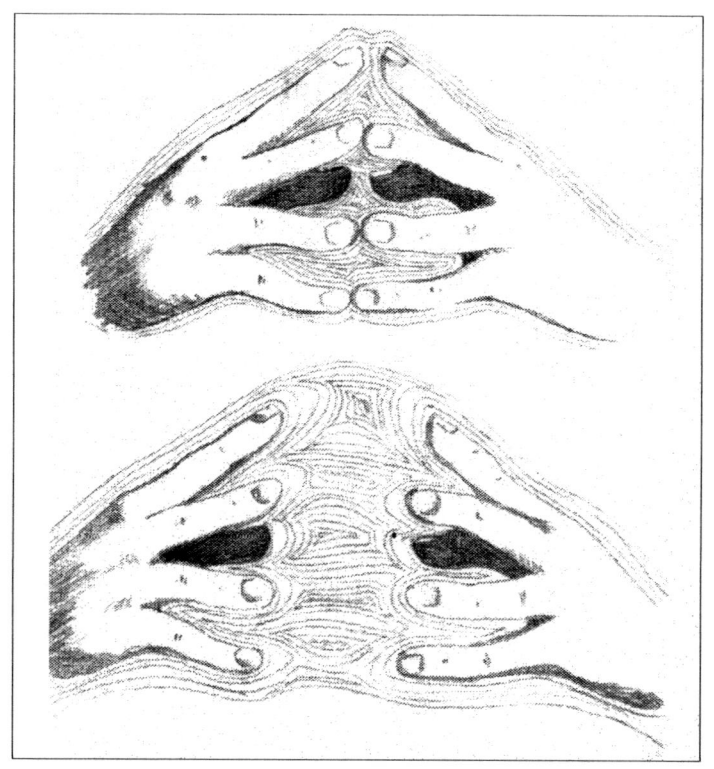

Figure 7. Observing Life Energy Flow Between Fingers.

which is dimly lit, with your back to either a wall or darkish curtains. Try to relax as much as possible and gaze at your reflection in the mirror, where you should see a bluish tinge emerging around the body. This image may seem distorted because you are actually observing this through your own aura. It is sometimes more discernible to look through half-shut eyes, where you are almost shutting out the light and making the image slightly darker. This exercise can also be done by viewing only the head area where the effect should be the same as that of the entire body. The more often you practice, the more you will see, until eventually you may be able to observe people's auras in their full colour.

Strangely enough, I am sometimes able to observe a person's aura when speaking to them on the telephone. I don't consciously look for their aura but become aware of it and am able to describe my observations. Similarly, a friend has described my aura during a telephone conversation. On one occasion I was sitting in the bath and she remarked that she saw me surrounded in water. On another occasion she remarked that my aura was very green when I was wearing green trousers and a green sweater. This is all, of course, subjective and therefore impossible to prove to people with logical scientific minds. The only way to progress is to practice. Nobody else can prove to another person the reality of our spiritual nature. It is an individual journey, which will be supported, often in strange and unexpected ways, such as by the occurrences of coincidences. A determined and sincere spiritual seeker could decide to find a guru or teacher but no genuine guru will give demonstrations of their powers or abilities; preferring to guide the student into appropriate situations to enable them to learn from their own experiences.

Some years ago, I got involved with dowsing using both pendulums and dowsing rods and was astonished when I realised that these devices were reacting to changes in energy but I wasn't consciously making it happen. The ability to successfully utilise these tools varies considerably from one person to another. My friends were greatly amused when, on one occasion, I asked my pendulum to tell me whether I should drink a pint of lager and the answer was positive but when I asked if I should have a second pint, the answer was negative. The point in explaining these experiences is that both dowsing rods and pendulums can be utilised to show the edge of an energy field, such as that surrounding a piece of fruit or a human being. Fruit or plants, which are still on the tree or in the ground, show a noticeable energy field, which dissipates soon after the fruit is collected or the plant removed from the ground.

There are numerous books on dowsing, in which instructions are provided on the utilisation of pendulums and dowsing rods, which could be of interest to some readers. A particularly good book, which I recommend is *Pendulum Dowsing* by Tom Graves.[7] Instructions on making and using a dowsing rod are given in an article by David Cowan, in chapter 24.

The aura can provide a great deal of information about the physical, emotional and spiritual characteristics of an individual. Relevant characteristics are its size, colours, brightness, intensity and texture, which continuously change, with thought patterns, stresses and strains. The aura, can best be studied whilst the person is in a peaceful state of mind and against a neutral background in a dimly lit room, as already shown in Figure 6a.

By studying the aura, information can be obtained about both diseases and their location in the body. Many complementary healing techniques are based on removing imbalances and blockages in the aura, which is regarded as the blueprint of the physical body. Healing often takes place some time after the treatment during the continual and natural process of cell replacement. Typically, defects in the aura can be healed by bio-energy therapists, who are able to draw out energy blockages, often utilising empathic skills even when they are unable to see the effect on the aura. This technique is described in an article in chapter 27, written by Chris Hughes.

In this context it is a great pity that scientists and particularly the orthodox medical profession limit all their treatments to the physical body and mind and deny the existence of the aura, although there is strong evidence that it has been used for thousands of years both for observation and cure by medical monks in Tibet and other far Eastern countries. Hopefully occidental scientists will eventually be able to detect, explain and work with these finer energies, in effect gaining from oriental knowledge and experience. Currently, the rigid appliance of science combined with a large dose of self interest by pharmaceutical corporations has frustrated the advancement of medical knowledge into these possibilities. Instead of being open minded and logically trying to explain many of the skills demonstrated by practitioners they seem to be determined to undermine or disprove many reported achievements often explaining away cures as temporary remission or placebo effects.

In addition to providing information on the health and vigour of a person, the aura also reflects qualities of character such as perseverance, willpower, truthfulness. In this latter respect, it is possible for a person to tell lies face to face but untruths would be immediately detected by a clairvoyant, who has developed the skill of reading the aura, as it reflects both thoughts and feelings.

The aura can be affected by being in the presence of other energy fields. For example, we can often feel weakened or drained after spending time with some people (or in some places). One explanation of this type of negative experience is that the other person is either physically or mentally depleted, and often unconsciously drains another person's life force energy to enhance their own aura. Vampires do exist but they utilise other people's life force energy rather than sucking their blood, as depicted in various horror stories. It is important that we realise that this type of energy depletion is likely to happen and that we are able to protect our aura from this type of attack. William Bloom, in his book *Psychic Protection*, provides both an explanation and means of protecting our aura from such negative effects.[8] For example, we can imagine ourselves surrounded by a bubble of white light, and ensure that it extends around every part of our aura and particularly at the top and bottom and we can utilise the emblem of our spiritual master, such as a crucifix, if we are Christians, to protect the outside of the bubble, in various positions. This type of symbolic protection can be very effective but only if we have total faith in its power. Such protective shields can be set up so that they allow access of positive energy.

It is worthwhile learning how to enhance our aura because it is a sense organ, which not only protects us from negative forces but also improves our perceptions way beyond the limited range of our five senses. Examples of techniques which can be used are suggested below:

● By eating food which is rich in life energy. In particular, we should eat organic fruits and vegetables, which are freshly gathered and if possible raw and reduce the consumption of food containing chemical preservatives and colouring, as the human body is not designed to be able to metabolise man-made chemicals, which often have unpleasant side effects. The life force energy field of food can be greatly enhanced by giving it healing utilising such techniques as Reiki, by blessing food with a sincere prayer or by imagining it being enveloped in a field of white energy. Conversely, the energy field of food is totally destroyed by cooking in a microwave oven and severely depleted by other methods of cooking.

- By acquiring the virtues of purity, patience, forgiveness, generosity, hope, faith, faith, humility and justice.
- By refusing to be bound by rigidly enforced disciplines, such as moral codes and religious doctrines and instead seek guidance from within.
- By meditating daily on pure bright colours; for example those produced by passing sunlight through a prism[5b].
- By practicing or receiving natural healing utilising such techniques as Reiki and colour therapy.
- By endeavouring to keep good company. In particular to spend time in the presence of evolved souls; the energy field of a spiritual master, effectively protecting and enhancing the auras of all people in its vicinity.

The article, in chapter 22 on *The Gift of Colour*, which was written by Mary Latimer especially for this book, suggests many ways in which our aura can be enhanced.

PART II

OUR RELATIONSHIP WITH THE UNIVERSE AND THE DIVINE

6

SPIRITUAL MASTERS- RELIGIONS- MISINTERPRETATIONS AND MISUNDERSTANDINGS

Scientists, and in particular astronomers, explain the universe; the stars, planets and other celestial bodies, in purely physical terms. They hypothesise that our galaxy is so immense that even if we could travel at the speed of light of 186,000 miles/second, it would take 100,000 years to travel from one side to the other, emphasising the insignificance of our planet relative to the universe which comprises numerous galaxies. This explains the nature of the universe relative to our perceptions, which are affected by the limitations of our five senses but, as previously explained, the universe is in fact consciousness. Once we have realised our full potential of oneness with God or cosmic consciousness, we will be capable of traversing the universe instantaneously, at will. Sometimes during our meditations we may observe that not just our planet but the whole universe is present in our heart centre, which provides an explanation of our being made in the image of God: we are light beings and an intrinsic part of the light which pervades the whole universe.

From time to time, in the history of the human race, evolved spiritual beings that have either almost balanced their karmic debt or had completed their karmic cycle, decided to incarnate on Earth as exemplars. The difference between them and us is that they were multi-sensed and multi-dimensional, in that they had already realised their oneness with the whole of creation. Often, they were capable of performing actions, which appeared to us as miracles, because they utilised advanced laws of nature, which haven't yet and may never be discovered by science. The lives of these advanced souls have quite often led to the formation of a religion, usually after their death. In fact the majority of world religions have been formed in this way.

Often, these spiritually advanced beings are regarded by their followers as sons of God. However, we are all children of God, having been created by Him. Jesus is regarded by Christians as the only Son of God; an assertion, which is eloquently discussed, by the Master Omraam Mikhael Aivanhov, in the passage below [5c]:

> *'The belief that God sent 'his only son' to earth two thousand years ago to demonstrate his love for human beings has perhaps helped some of them to evolve over a period of time. Now, however, we must abandon such an outrageous belief, because it does not represent a proper understanding of God's love, which is immense, inexhaustible, and infinite. God has had many sons and daughters and he will have many more. For millions of years he has sent these exceptional beings to earth to enlighten their brothers and sisters, and he will continue to send others. He has no use for Christians who have forbidden him to send anyone, under any circumstances, after Jesus, or who claim that before the coming of Jesus human beings were deprived of the true light. As if the salvation of human beings depends on the epoch in which they lived: before Jesus or after Jesus! The Church may*

insist on fixing a beginning and an end to the divine revelation, but the Lord himself is not impressed by such decrees. He is beyond this and takes no notice.'

Daily Meditations 15th November

A relatively small number of other people have experienced this state of perfection, some before Jesus' time and some since. People who were born in this state of oneness with God are described as avatars, a state of consciousness, which is the ultimate potential of all forms of life, when they complete their journey to perfection. As Jesus said, *'On that day ye shall know that I am in the Father, and ye are in me and me in you'*.[9]

All world religions arose out of the lives of spiritually advanced souls, whose teachings were very similar; though expressed in different ways. They all believed in love, truth, right conduct, non-violence and peace and various aspects of these values such as compassion, sympathy, forgiveness and freedom. Also, they incarnated for the benefit of all of mankind and not just for one group or nation.

Christian, Muslim and Jewish religions have the same roots; Noah, Abraham and Moses, being regarded as prophets of all three religions and Jesus being a prophet of Islam.[10] In this context, it is disappointing that fundamentalist interpretations by some followers of these religions are a major cause of current global conflicts. Undoubtedly this antagonism arises out of misinterpretations by the leaders and followers rather than from some intrinsic difference in religious philosophy. A particular relevant aspect of these conflicts is a tendency to stick rigidly to false (or narrow) writings and beliefs, which have either been passed down through generations or stated as the absolute truth by their religious leaders or school teachers, a common theme being that our religion or belief is right and everybody else is wrong. This polarisation of religious beliefs, or fundamentalism, is a very worrying aspect of our modern global society, effectively removing the God given freewill of both children and adults.

Typically, young people are being indoctrinated into believing that they can achieve spiritual salvation by committing acts of violence against other races and followers of other religions. Such atrocities will not provide them with a special welcome in heaven but result in them having to reincarnate in other lifetimes until they learn that they themselves are part of society as a whole, and that whatever misdeeds they inflict on others will surely return to them. Those who knowingly lead people into committing such atrocities are either misguided or have their own evil agenda. Such people are probably building up an enormous karmic debt, which they will have to repay through numerous lives, in which they will suffer the consequences of their previous evil deeds.

Some common misconceptions, promulgated by various religions, which claim special relationships with the Divine, are false. For example, anybody who believes that their God is different from that recognised by any other religion is deluding themselves, as there is only one God. Also, there are no chosen people as we are all of equal importance and we already have everlasting life and therefore no religion can claim that it has a benefit derived from joining their ranks. Similarly and contrary to the teachings of many religions, God is not jealous, vindictive or cruel and never has been;

such statements, which are common in the Old Testament, being interpretations by mankind and not God.

The way to change the world for the better and obtain fair treatment for ourselves, our families and friends and our nation is to go within and obtain inspiration, or in other words to follow our hearts. When we do this, we all eventually reach the same place, which is the kingdom of heaven. If we act according to our conscience and refuse to be led into committing deeds, which are contrary to our inner guidance, it will not create conflict, because we all receive the same message of peace. Try to understand when you manufacture or use weapons, or when you strap a bomb onto your body with the intention of destroying a bus or a marketplace, that the people that you are trying to kill or maim are your brothers, sisters, children and parents for in the eyes of God, we are all one; all his children. Buddha, Jesus, Krishna, Mohammed and many others, although different human personalities were all spiritual reflections of the divine: they didn't want us to focus on our differences but on our togetherness. We have all incarnated to learn the lessons of life and ultimately not just realise but experience our oneness with the divine. Don't blame others for making silly mistakes as we all have lessons to learn-'To err is human but to forgive is divine'. Your God is my God-there is only one God, which is the totality of everything: the universe, the stars, our planet, the plants, the trees, all the animals but in particular you and me. We are the most spiritually advanced forms of life on this planet and our amazing potential is not just to understand this but to actually experience it during our current incarnation. This ultimate truth can be visualised in a beautiful meditation, which can be practiced individually but preferably in groups by imagining white light as divine essence:

> *White light within*
> *White light without*
> *I hold no fear, I have no doubt*
> *White light within and all around*
> *I am protected, love abound*
> *I feel God's power within my breast, and know that I am truly blessed.*
> *I give my thanks for this I know that in God's aura I do glow*

White light within

Imagine your heart centre, in the centre of your chest filled with white light.

White light without

Imagine the white light spreading upwards from your chest, through the top of your head, through the roof of the house, through the earth's atmosphere and out into the universe. Then follow it down, back into your body and down into the ground and see it filling up the earth and coming out onto the surface of the earth, into all forms of life.

I hold no fear, I hold no doubt

Release all fear and darkness into the light taking with it all negativity and darkness into the ground.

White light within and all around

Focus on white light at your heart centre and all through

your body and then see it spreading out and filling everybody in the room, in your community, your country, all countries, all religious believers of all faiths, all nature, the whole planet and see it spreading out into the universe. See yourself as a conductor of love and light into the planet and all forms of life and see love and light spreading out from the surface of the earth, in every direction and filling the universe.

I am protected, love abound

Feel immense joy and peace and realise that you are protected by the white light, which is the essence of the Divine.

I feel God's power within my breast and know that I am truly blessed

Realise and experience that God is always with you and can be experienced as white light in your heart centre.

I give my thanks because this I know that in God's aura I do glow

Give thanks for knowing that you are protected and that your light is part of the great light which pervades the whole universe.

NOTE: You can replace the word 'God', in the last two statements, with the name of your word for God, your guru or teacher. For example, if you are a Christian, use Christ's power. Alternatively, if you are a Muslim, replace 'God' with 'Allah' and so on.

7

THE DEVELOPMENT OF ORTHODOX CHRISTIANITY

This chapter is focussed specifically on the development of Christianity because Jesus had experience of virtually all the religions, which existed during his lifetime and therefore his true teachings must surely be a way of addressing the negative issues in our modern society. The main theme is that religious conflicts, and in fact all conflicts, will ultimately be resolved, not at the level of the mind, but by successively more people taking responsibility for their own lives and seeking spiritual enlightenment.

It is accepted by historians that the Roman Emperor, Constantine, was responsible for the development of Christianity into a world religion. Previously, Christianity had been gradually spreading through the Empire against a tide of persecution and martyrdom but it was still an illegal religion. Constantine has been depicted as a shrewd and ambitious leader, who re-united the Roman Empire. According to this version of history, which is confirmed by modern day historians, Constantine was drawn to Christianity by three significant events.

Firstly, in 312 AD, he was leading his army to a battle against the Emperor Maxentius, who had dominium over Rome. When during the march a meteor hurtled through the sky and landed nearby a Christian priest, called Lactantius, who was accompanying the army, claimed that this was a sign from the one Christian God.

Secondly, Lactantius persuaded Constantine to paint a Christian sign on his soldier's shields to assure his victory. The sign, which was also utilised on the battle standard, was made up of the first two letters of Christ's name in the Greek alphabet, as shown in Figure 8. Constantine later explained that he saw this 'Chi-Rho' symbol in a dream during the night before the battle. He proceeded to a victory at the Battle of Milvian Bridge, although considerably outnumbered and became the Emperor of the Western part of the Empire. Soon after this, he arranged the marriage of his sister to one of the Emperors controlling the Eastern part of the Empire, called Licinius and they agreed to unite against the other Emperor. Constantine and Licinius drew up the 'Edict of Milan', which ended the persecution of Christians by accepting the freedom of people in the Roman Empire to worship in a religion of their choice. In AD 313 Licinius defeated, the other Emperor of the Eastern Empire, Maximinus II Daia, resulting in the Empire being split into a two parts; the Western Empire controlled by Constantine and the Eastern by Licinius.

In 315 AD the 'Arch of Constantine' was erected in the 'Valley of the Coliseum' to commemorate the victory over Maxentius. During the opening ceremony Constantine declared that there was now one Empire, with one religion and one Emperor, a statement, which broke the terms of the 'Edict of Milan' and alienated both the senate and Licinius. As a result of this dispute, Licinius started persecuting Christians and sacking their churches in the Eastern Empire which resulted in a war with Constantine.

The third event took place some years later at an evenly matched battle between the armies of Constantine and Licinius. The turning point came when a very large battle standard depicting the *'Chi-Rho'* sign was raised, causing Licinius' army to flee in terror, as they thought that the sign had magical powers.

Having made Christianity the official religion of the Empire, against considerable resistance from both the senate and Roman society, Constantine was disturbed by the controversies existing in the Church particularly regarding the various interpretations of the nature of Christ and his teachings. One particular difference concerned the opinions of a priest, called Arius and his followers, who believed that Jesus was not fully divine, that Jesus was certainly a supernatural figure, but was not God, in the fullest sense. The opposing view proposed by Anthanasius, the Bishop of Alexandria, was that Jesus was of the same being or substance as the Father. In other words, was Jesus an exemplar of the ultimate potential of the human race or was he the

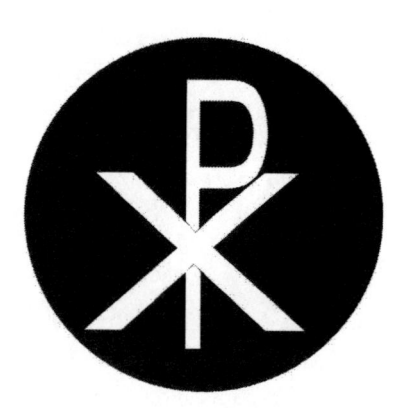

Figure 8. The 'Chi-Rho' Battle Standard utilised by Constantine.

only son of God and thus quite different from other people?

Accordingly, Constantine arranged an assembly of all Christian bishops in 325AD at Nicea, which continued for two months, its most significant conclusion being that Arius and his followers were wrong. The wording of a document was agreed by the council as the fundamental definition of the Christian religion; which is called the Nicean Creed. Both Arius and one of his supporters called Eusebius refused to sign it and as a result were banished. Some years later, in 331 AD the official version of the bible, called the ecumenical version was issued, which is the basis of all future versions.

The Nicean Creed, which became the core belief of organised Christianity, is copied below:

> *We believe in one God the Father Almighty, maker of all things both visible and invisible, and in one Lord, Jesus Christ. The Son of God, Only begotten of the Father, that is to say, of the substance of the Father, God of God and Light of Light, very God of very God, begotten not made, being of one substance with the Father, by whom all things were made, both things in Heaven and things on earth; who, for us men and for our salvation, came down and was made flesh, was made man, suffered, and rose again on the third day, went up into the heavens, and is to come again to judge both the quick and the dead; and in the Holy Ghost'.*

It is important in considering whether the correct decision was made, that we should bear in mind the prevailing circumstances; that the council had been convened by Constantine, an absolute dictator, who had been drawn to

Christianity by a series of events, which he would have regarded as magical and miraculous. He presumably insisted that the council and its resulting creed should include a magical or miraculous content. Also, bearing in mind that a number of other religions, which were influential in his Empire, that he would want Christianity to be exclusive, by instituting it as the only one that gave access to the one God. This is all, of course, conjecture but this theme could possibly, in part, explain the decisions of the Church: to declare that Jesus was the only son of God, was crucified, died and on the third day was resurrected. To insist that the Nicean Creed and the ecumenical version of the bible, issued six years later, were the only authorised beliefs. To condemn all teachings or writings which were contrary to the Nicean Creed as heresy and issue a decree that all heretical manuscripts must be destroyed. To form a top down centralised authoritarian Church, which gave both the ecclesiastic brethren and the Emperor dominion over the spiritual lives of all of the people. To persecute all those who dared to think and act differently, through the ensuing centuries; for example during the Crusades and the Spanish Inquisition. To endeavour to destroy or hide all religious manuscripts, which came to light, such as archaeological discoveries, to assert that the orthodox teachings were the absolute truth and refuse to debate or accept any contrary evidence. In addition great wealth in both land and property was accumulated, whilst much of the world was affected by poverty.

8

THE INFLUENCE OF REDISCOVERED MANUSCRIPTS

A number of religious manuscripts and scrolls exist, many of which have been discovered in the last eighty years, which provide versions of the life and teachings of Jesus which are different from those expressed in orthodox Christianity. The Church insists that its traditional teachings are absolutely correct, in effect, closing ranks and rejecting any contrary information, thus frustrating serious debate. It has been claimed that, when any new documents are found, the Roman Catholic Church endeavours to prevaricate and delay their translation, such tactics have been used on the translation of both the Dead Sea and Nag Hamedi manuscripts.

If the representatives of the Church are aware that the orthodox teachings are not the whole truth and refuse to take part in debates, which could potentially clarify the true meaning of Jesus' teachings, then they should be aware of the karmic consequences. We should never make decisions and take actions, which are contrary to the promptings of our conscience. Also, we should never be afraid of facing and accepting the truth, regardless of perceived detriment. This advice applies to people in all walks of life because there is no greater religion than the truth and to deny it is to deny our reason for being and so deny our creator.

It is particularly important that we should now take the opportunity of debating the meaning of all such manuscripts as they may enlighten us on methods of overcoming the chaos in our society, which is endangering all life on earth. Our way of life is flawed, including our so called democracies and many of our religions. Are they part of the problem rather than of the solution?

In this chapter, three manuscripts are discussed, which have particular significance in our modern society, all of which conflict with the theme of orthodox Christianity.

Jesus Lived in India

One of the strangest aspects of the orthodox Christian bible is that there is no record of the life of Jesus between the age of twelve and thirty. It is hard to believe that a person who embodied the soul of the universe spent eighteen years of his life working as a carpenter with his father. One very well documented explanation of this mystery is that Jesus travelled with a merchant's caravan into India at the age of twelve, where his teachings were remarkably similar to those described in the bible. Apparently, in 1887 a Russian traveller, called Nicholas Notovitch whilst in Kashmir, heard stories about a Saint Issa, who he became convinced was Jesus. He also heard that copies of some ancient documents, recording the life of Jesus in India, were preserved in various Buddhist monasteries and decided to visit the Himis monastery near Leh; the capital city of Ladakh. His request to see the manuscripts was denied but he was told that he would be able to see them if he ever travelled that way again. Those of us who know that we are on a spiritual journey, will not be in any way surprised to hear that

Nicholas had a serious accident soon after leaving the monastery, breaking a leg, and was taken back to the monastery to recuperate and given access to the manuscripts. God works in a mysterious way and when we yearn for something, for the right reasons, then the opportunity to receive it will often occur, seemingly by coincidence.

Nicholas Notovitch, with the help of an interpreter, meticulously copied the contents of the pages pertinent to Jesus as they were read to him by the head lama.[6a] A brief summary of his findings is presented below:-

From his earliest years the divine child, called Issa, began to speak of the one God, and people came to hear and marvel at his words of wisdom. The general opinion was that the Eternal Spirit dwelt within him.

At the age of twelve years, when it was the custom for an Israelite to take a wife, Issa (Jesus) joined a wealthy merchant on his journey along the trade routes into India.

His fame spread during his travels and he was particularly welcomed by the common people.

His teachings were virtually the same as those described in the orthodox bible, including, equality, helping the poor, assisting the weak, non violence and not coveting the possessions of others.

At one stage, he openly denounced caste bigotry, priestly rituals and the worship of many idols rather than the sole worship of the Holy Spirit. These teachings annoyed the Brahmin orthodoxy, who decided to have Issa killed.

Issa left and travelled into the Gothamide Country, which was the birthplace of the great Buddha, Shakiamuni. He spent many years learning scriptures and studying and mastering yoga.

He achieved high accomplishment in the classical science of Raja Yoga, which explains his ability to carry out miracles, via spiritual powers or siddhis, which are natural to a fully enlightened yogi, as described by Patangali, the father of yoga.

He travelled back via Persia, where the priests forbade the people to listen to him, as his teachings were contrary to their orthodox religion. He was arrested and brought before the high priest, who released him under the cover of darkness.

Continuing his journey, he travelled back first to Greece and arrived in Palestine at the age of thirty.

It went on to describe his life in Palestine and his eventual crucifixion.

Apparently, on his return home, Nicholas' revelations were rejected by the Orthodox Church and in 1894 he wrote a book, called *The Unknown Life of Jesus Christ*, which is still available. Nicholas's claims were strongly challenged by critics in both America and Europe but have since been authenticated by various people.

In 1922, Swami Abhedananda, who was vice-president of Ramakrishna Math from 1921 to 1924, visited the Himis Monastery, made his own translation and confirmed all salient details of Nicholas's book.[6a]

Nicholas Roerich, a renowned Russian explorer and archaeologist, saw and copied verses from the manuscripts, which also confirmed Notovitch's main claims.[6a]

There is a compelling account obtained from the Akashic Record, which is a record in time and space of all events since time began, which can be accessed by appropriately experienced people. The most comprehensive account was transcribed by Levi H. Dowling in forty years of study and meditation and presented in his book, *The Aquarian Gospel of Jesus the Christ*, which is a fascinating account of Jesus' life from birth to death and resurrection, the theme being very similar but much more comprehensive than Notovitch's account.[11]

These manuscripts are presumably still in existence and available for research by any ardent seeker. So in this context, why have the Church decided to ignore this information and continue to utilise the orthodox versions of the bible, which are deeply flawed? Surely, in this modern age, particularly bearing in mind the diminishing influence of Christianity, it would be beneficial if the Church were to admit previous mistakes and seek and find the true meaning of the teachings of Jesus. We should never be frightened of facing and accepting the truth. Would not the Church fathers be well advised to realise that at the time of their passing, they will look in the mirror face to face[12] and realise that they lied to themselves and knowingly misled their followers?

The Essene Gospel of Peace

This manuscript, which was found by Edmond Bordeaux Szekely (EBS) in the hidden archives of the Vatican demonstrates the Essene origins of Christianity and show that Jesus was a member of the Essene Brotherhood (Copies are also held in the Royal Library of the Habsburgs in Austria and are now the property of the Austrian Government).

The Essene Gospel of Peace was translated from the original Aramaic by EBS twenty years before the discovery of the Dead Sea Scrolls in 1947. EBS was educated in a Catholic monastery, where he specialised in Greek, Latin and ecclesiastical literature. Whilst at university he wrote an essay titled *Saint Francis Sings in My Heart*, which was noticed by his head teacher and led to his introduction to Monsignor Angelo Mercato, the Prefect of the Archives of the Vatican, who allowed him to study some of its ancient manuscripts. EBS reports in his book *The Discovery of the Essene Gospel of Peace*, that the Vatican has 25 miles of shelves containing ancient scrolls and manuscripts.[13f] He eventually gained access to a hidden archive, which contained a number of apocryphal gospels such as those of Matthew, James, Peter and Thomas. In particular he studied and translated the *The Essene Gospel of Peace*[13b], which was written by the disciple John. We may wonder why these original gospels, apparently written by some of Jesus' closest disciples, should be hidden away from the world by a Church based on his teachings.

EBS explains in his book that Jerome, who eventually became a saint, was brought up by wealthy parents in Yugoslavia, in the fourth century, but preferred to live in the desert. He gained a knowledge of Latin, Aramaic, Greek and Hebrew and gathered together a number of fragments of ancient manuscripts, including *The Essene Gospel of Peace*. He became the private secretary of the Pope Damascus, who eventually became Saint Damascus, who set him the task of translating the New Testament from original manuscripts. When the Pope died, Jerome's work was denounced, his work scattered and much of it eventually being sent to the Vatican, where presumably it is still kept.

Apparently, a monk named Benedict, stumbled across

some of these documents, which described the lives of first century Essenes and based on their teachings founded twelve Benedictine monasteries, which are based on the Essene way of life. The main difference between the lives of Benedictine monks and that of the Essenes is that the monks were celibate whereas the Essenes lived family lives in isolated communities.

There have been a number of deliberate alterations to the bible made by the Christian Church often directed by various Roman Emperors, such as Justinan who insisted on the removal of the doctrine of reincarnation. A most interesting insight into the number of alterations is obtained by comparing the text of the Gospel of St John, in current editions of the bible with *The Essene Gospel of Peace* by the disciple John[13b]. In the foreword to this book EBS explains that the words of Jesus were not collected till some generations after they were uttered and that they have been misunderstood, wrongly annotated, hundreds of times rewritten and transformed. Accordingly, the New Testament which is utilised by all the Christian Churches provides a deeply flawed version of the words of Jesus. For this reason EBS decided to publish the pure, original words of Jesus, translated directly from the Aramaic tongue spoken by Jesus and his beloved disciple John, who alone among Jesus' disciples noted with perfect accuracy his Master's personal teachings.

I have decided to include the complete fragment from the Essene Gospel of John, which is similar in some respects to parts of St John's Gospel, King James Edition has also significant differences:

John 1.1 *'In the beginning was the Word'*, whereas the fragment refers to the *'Holy Law'*, which is very significant in Essene teachings.

John 1.18 mentions *'the only begotten son'*, whereas the fragment states that *'every man who cometh into the world——-is given the power to be Sons of God'*. Also, *'By this shall all men know that ye too are brothers, even as we all are Sons of God'*.

In John 3.1-7, Jesus answers Nicodemus with the words *'Except a man be born of water and the Spirit, he cannot enter into the kingdom of God'*, whereas in this fragment he says *'except a man be born of the Earthly Mother and the Heavenly Father, and walk with the Angels of the Day and the Night, he cannot enter into the Eternal Kingdom. That which is born of the flesh is flesh; and that which is born of the Spirit is spirit. And the flesh of thy body is born of the Earthly Mother, and the spirit within thee is born of the Heavenly Father'*. This mention of the Earthly Mother and the Angels of the Day and Night is most significant in Essene teachings but to my knowledge never mentioned in orthodox texts.

John 3.15, Jesus says *'That whosoever believeth in him should not perish but have eternal life'*. Authors Note- We already have eternal life and it should not be regarded as a reward for believing in Jesus.

John 3.16, Jesus says *'For God so loved the world that he gave his only begotten Son'*. The relevant context of the fragment was quoted above in John 1.18.

The statement *'In my Father's house are many mansions'* in John 14.2 is in the context of Jesus preparing a place for us after death, which is presumably why it is utilised in Christian funeral services. Conversely in the fragment the statement by Jesus is explaining that everyone can be successful in life if they live in accord with the *'Holy Law'*.

In John 14.6 Jesus says *'no man cometh unto the Father, but by me'*. This is one of the best known statements of Jesus, in orthodox translations of the bible but is missing from both this fragment and from the whole translation of the Essene Gospel of Peace. In any case, it's hard to imagine that Jesus would make a statement which would mean that Christianity would be the only correct religion; causing so much conflict in future centuries:

> *'In the beginning was the Law, and the Law was with God, and the Law was God. The same was in the beginning with God. All things were made by him; and without him was not anything made that was made. In him was life; and the life was the light of men. And the light shineth in the darkness; and the darkness comprehended it not.*
>
> *From the far place in the desert came the Brothers, to bear witness of the Light that all men through them might walk in the light of the Holy Law. For the true light doth illumine every man that cometh into the world, but the world knoweth it not. But as many do receive the Law, to them is given the power to become the Sons of God, and to enter the Eternal Sea where standeth the Tree of Life.*
>
> *And Jesus taught them, saying 'Verily, verily, I say unto thee, except a man be born again, he cannot see the kingdom of heaven.'*
>
> *And one man said, 'how can a man be born when he is old? Can he enter a second time into his mother's womb, and be born?'*
>
> *And Jesus answered, 'Verily, verily I say unto thee, except a man be born of the Earthly Mother and the Heavenly Father, and walk with the Angels of the Day and the Night, he cannot enter into the Eternal Kingdom. That which is born of the flesh is flesh; and that which is born of the Spirit is*

spirit. And the flesh of thy body is born of the Earthly Mother, and the spirit within thee is born of the Heavenly Father. The wind bloweth where it listeth, and thou hearest the sound thereof, but canst not tell whence it cometh. So it is with the Holy Law. All men hear it, but know it not, for from their first breath it is with them. But he who is born again of the Heavenly Father and the Earthly Mother, he shall hear with new ears, and see with new eyes, and the flame of the Holy Law shall be kindled within him.'

And one man asked, 'How can these things be?'

Jesus answered and said unto him, 'Verily, verily, I say unto thee, we speak that we do know, and testify that we have seen; and ye receive not our witness. For a man is born to walk with the Angels, but instead he doth search for jewels in the mud. To him hath the Heavenly Father bestowed his inheritance, that he should build the Kingdom of Heaven on earth, but man hath turned his back on his Father, and doth worship the world and its idols. And this is the condemnation, that light is come into the world, and men loved darkness rather than light, because their deeds were evil. For every one that doeth evil hateth the light, neither cometh to the light. For we are all Sons of God, and in us God is glorified. And the light which shineth around God and His children is the Light of the Holy Law. And he who hateth the light, doth deny his Father and his Mother, who have given him birth.'

And one man said, 'Master, how can we know the light?'

And Jesus answered, 'Verily, verily, I give unto thee, a new commandment: that ye love one another, even as they love thee who work together in the Garden of the Brotherhood. By this shall all men know that ye too are brothers, even as we all are Sons of God.'

And one man said, 'All they talk is of the brother hood, yet we cannot all be of the brotherhood. Yet we would worship light and shun darkness, for none there is among us who desireth evil.'

And Jesus answered, 'Let not the heart be troubled: ye believe in God. Know ye that in our Father's house are many mansions, and our brotherhood is but a dark glass reflecting the Heavenly Brotherhood unto which all creatures of Heaven and earth do belong. The brotherhood is the vine, and our heavenly Father is the husbandman. Every branch in us that beareth not fruit he taketh away: and every branch that beareth fruit, he purgeth it, that it may bring forth more fruit. Abide in us, and we in thee. As the branch cannot bear fruit of itself, except it abide in the vine, no more can ye, except ye abide in the Holy Law, which is the rock upon which our brotherhood stands. He that abideth in the Law, the same bringeth forth much fruit: for without the Law ye can do nothing. If a man abide not in the Law, he is cast forth as a branch, and is withered; and man gather them, and cast them into fire, and they are burned.

And as the brothers abide in the love one for another, as the Angel of Love doth teach them so we do ask that ye love one another. Greater love hath no man than this, to teach the Holy Law one to another, and to love each other as oneself. The heavenly Father is in us, and we are in Him, and we do reach out our hands in love and ask that ye be one in us. The glory which he gavest us we do give to thee: that thou mayest be one, even as we are one. For thy Father in Heaven hath loved thee before the foundation of the world.'

And in this manner did the Brothers teach the Holy Law to them who would hear it, and it is said they did marvellous things, and healed the sick and afflicted with diverse grasses and wondrous uses of sun and water. And there are also many things they did, that which, if they should be written, every one even the world itself could not contain the books that should be written.'

The Gospel of Thomas

Some of the documents which were supposed to have been destroyed were those which were found in 1945 in at Nag Hamedi, in Egypt, by Arabs, who were searching for manure. The monks must have decided to bury the documents, rather than following the instructions of the authorities and having them burnt. Amongst the scrolls contained in an earthenware jar, sealed with bitumen, was *The Gospel of Thomas*, written by one of Jesus' disciples and thus an eye witness. Why would an established Church, based on the teachings of Jesus, decide to destroy the gospel of one of his closest disciples? The answer might be that it contained statements that contradicted those then being regarded as absolute truth. Thomas had started a Church, based on these teachings, the members of which were persecuted by the established Christian Church in the Roman Empire but it continued in India where Thomas was buried. This Gospel is most important giving us deep insight into the true teachings of Jesus, which has retained its original wording. Its first three logia state the whole message and the rest of the gospel is an expansion on this theme. These three logia are copied below, with comments, interleaved:

Note this translation has been copied from the book written by Hugh McGregor Ross called *The Gospel of Thomas*.[14]

> *1 These are the hidden logia*
> *2 which the living Jesus spoke*
> *3 and Didymos Judas Thomas wrote*

Comments - It would be a great mistake to regard the word 'hidden' to mean secret, esoteric, or from some cult. In the turbulent times in which Jesus lived it was normal practice to hide treasures, the inner meanings of which could be found by the ardent seeker. It seems relevant to comment that Thomas' name may have been deliberately dishonoured by the Church fathers utilising the 'Doubting Thomas' story, to support their decision to have his gospel destroyed.

1.
1. And he said
2. He who finds the inner meaning of these logia
3. will not taste death.

Comments - Hugh McGregor Ross suggests that the phrase 'will not taste death, means 'and find the Life which is independent of the body'. An alternative explanation is that it means, 'will complete his karmic cycle and find everlasting life in Heaven'.

2.
Jesus said:
Let him who seeks not cease from seeking
until he finds
and when he finds,
he will be turned around,
and when he is turned around,
he will marvel,
and he shall reign over the All

Comments - The seeking and finding wording is similar to that contained in the orthodox bible. In my opinion being 'turned around' refers to the spiritual transformation from self awareness and control by the ego to universal awareness and guidance from the soul. Therefore, when we evolve into enlightenment, we become one with the Father, who is omnipresent, omnipotent and omniscient. As Jesus said *'lift up a stone and you will find me there'*.[14]

>   3.
>   *1. Jesus said:*
>   *2. If those who guide your being say to you:*
>   *3. 'Behold the Kingdom is in the heaven,'*
>   *4. Then the birds of the sky will precede you;*
>   *5 if they say to you: 'It is in the sea,'*
>   *6. Then the fish will precede you.*
>   *7. But the Kingdom is in your centre*
>   *8. And is about you.*
>   *9. When you know your Selves*
>   *10. then you will be known,*
>   *11. And you will be aware that you are*
>   *12. the sons of the Living Father,*
>   *13. but if you do not know yourselves*
>   *14. Then you are in poverty*
>   *15. And you are the poverty*

Comments - Lines 7 and 8 mean that the Kingdom of God resides in your heart centre but it is also all around you.

Lines 9 to 12 mean that when you become enlightened, you will know that, like Jesus, you are a son of God and ultimately will experience oneness with the whole of creation.

Line 13 refers to self awareness, its negative aspect being self interest, which is effectively destroying our civilisation.

The state of poverty, in lines 14 and 15, could include a number of aspects of our lives, in that we don't realise our value and our incredible potential, being trapped in a delusory world of materialism. For example, we should not be allowing ourselves to be influenced by biased people, bodies or doctrines but rather finding out for ourselves by going within and listening to that still small voice which will never delude us. Poverty could also equate to agnosticism and atheism; as discussed in chapter 10.

The Influence of Rediscovered Manuscripts

The Roman Catholic Church has defended and continues to defend orthodox Christianity from criticisms arising out of manuscripts, which have come to light through history. For example, through the 'Ecole Biblique', they have frustrated the translation and publishing of a large proportion of the Dead Sea Scrolls for many decades; presumably because they fear that information may be found, which will challenge their orthodoxy. One of their policy statements is that '*All enquiry and investigation, regardless of what it might turn up or reveal, must be subordinated and accommodated to the existing corpus of official Catholic teaching*'. In other words it must be edited or adjusted or distorted until it conforms to the requisite criteria. Similarly, '*anything which can't be subordinated or accommodated to existing doctrine must, of necessity, be suppressed*'. This demonstrates that the Roman Catholic Church does not afford God given freedom of choice to its members to enable them to learn from their mistakes, pay off our karmic debt and ultimately achieve a state of God realisation.

Similarly in a document published by the 'Congregation for the Doctrine of the Faith' in June 1990, Cardinal Ratzinger, who is now Pope Benedict XV1, is quoted as stating: *'The freedom of the act of faith cannot justify a right to dissent. This freedom does not indicate freedom with regard to the truth, but signifies the free determination of the person in conformity with his moral obligations to accept the truth'.* In other words, one is perfectly free to accept the teachings of the Church, but not to question or reject them. Freedom cannot be manifested or expressed except through submission. It is a curious definition of freedom.[15]

In this context, we can understand why the Church was not interested in following up the findings of Nicholas Notovitch in 1887, why *The Essene Gospel of Peace* and other manuscripts are hidden away in the archives of the Vatican, and why they prevaricated and frustrated the translating and publishing of the Nag Hamedi Gospels and the Dead Sea Scrolls. However, the truth will come out in the end. It always does. The decision by the Church to condemn as heresy all teachings or writings, which were contrary to the Nicean Creed in 325 AD and to endeavour to have all heretical manuscripts destroyed, was thus the first of many taken by the Church, throughout history and into modern times. Unfortunately for the Church, their critics decided to disobey their instructions and instead of destroying many manuscripts, they hid them in the hope that they would come to light in the future.

9

CONTROVERSIES

Let's imagine that the decision made at the Council of Nicea was wrong and Arius and his followers were correct in their understanding that Jesus was an extraordinary man rather than the only son of God. In this scenario it is unlikely that Constantine would have supported or promoted Christianity and it may never have developed into a world religion. Presumably, in this situation, there would have been no need for a host of manuscripts to have been hidden in the hope that they would come to light at an appropriate time in the future. Also, there would be no need for a Dutch auction to take place every time a fragment of an ancient manuscript is found or for the Roman Catholic Church to be fiercely protecting their orthodox scriptures and policies against criticisms arising. With free access to the vast array of information, which was presumably available to the Christian bishops at Nicea, we could reach our own conclusions about Jesus, his life, his teachings and his death. Some of the questions which we may wish to answer are briefly discussed below:

Was Jesus the only son of God?

No - It is abundantly clear from reading both *The Gospel of Thomas* and *The Essene Gospel of Peace*, that we are all children of God.

Was Jesus an avatar, like Rama and Krishna?

Yes - He was an exemplar; an example of the ultimate potential of all human beings.

Was Jesus born in magical circumstances, of a virgin, in Bethlehem?

Similar stories are associated with the birth and early life of many of the spiritual masters around whose lives religions have evolved. Such beliefs make wonderful children's stories and there seems to be merit in continuing to accept that such things may have happened. The Creator could, of course, arrange virgin births and may well have done so if he thought it necessary; for example to protect genetic characteristics.

Did Jesus live in Nazareth and work for his father, who was a carpenter?

EBS in his book, *Essene Origins of Christianity*,[13c] explains that the descriptions, in the bible, of the location of Jesus' home are not supported geographically. It's more likely that he was born and brought up in Qumran or another Essene community and that he lived a strict physical, mental and spiritual life.

Why are there no records in the bible about Jesus' life between the age of twelve and thirty?

Presumably because Jesus travelled to India and was associated with other religions. He was thought to have been a Buddhist saint (Issa), but this part of history was deleted from orthodox teachings. Constantine and the Nicean Creed decreed that Christianity was an exclusive religion being the only route to the one God; thus the supposed statement by Jesus that *'no man cometh to the Father but by me'*.

Did Jesus perform miracles, as they are described in the bible?

Yogis who have developed the spiritual powers or siddhis are able to perform the miracles attributed to Jesus in the bible. Jesus would be well aware of the karmic balance of everybody who he decided to heal, as a demonstration of the power of God, working through one of his spiritually evolved children. As an Essene brother, Jesus primarily showed people how to heal themselves by fasting, diet and the utilisation of herbs. We are ultimately responsible for our state of health and we need to learn how to achieve and maintain balance with nature.

Was Jesus a member of the Essene Brotherhood, residing at Qumran or a similar Essene community?

Almost certainly.

Was Jesus crucified, did he die on the cross and was he resurrected?

This has been a most debated subject. Orthodox Christians believe that the crucifixion and resurrection are essential aspects of their religion. A contrary assertion in *The Essene Origins of Christianity* is that it was Barabbas, the zealot, who was crucified; (Barabbas meaning son of God) and that the gentle Essene teacher was set free.[13c]

Did Jesus survive the crucifixion and travel into India, where he died?

In his book, *Jesus Lived in India,* Kirsten Holger maintains that Jesus was crucified but taken down before his death, resuscitated and travelled to India, where he is buried[2]. A similar assertion is made by Richard Andrews and Paul Schellenberger in their book *The Tomb of God*, in which they claim that the 'Church' changed the wording of the works of the Roman historian Josephus, presumably to mislead future investigators. Fortunately an older manuscript was discovered, which stated that Jesus was alive, three days after the crucifixion.[16]

I have no intention of endeavouring to discuss these questions in any greater detail as such a task could fill several volumes. Certainly, some of the answers might be derived by studying Eastern spiritual philosophy but the answer to all these questions, and many others, lies in our own beings. Jesus wanted us to seek the kingdom within rather than seeking answers in the scriptures, as he explained in the following excerpt from *The Essene Gospel of Peace*.[13b]

> *'And Jesus himself sat down in their midst and said: 'I tell you truly, none can be happy except, he do the Law' and the others answered: 'We all do the Laws of Moses, our lawgiver, even as they are written in the Holy Scriptures.' And Jesus answered: 'Seek not the Law in your scriptures, for the Law is life, whereas the scripture is dead. I tell you truly, Moses received not his laws from God in writing, but through the living word. The law is living word of living God to living prophets for living men. In everything that is life is the law written. You find it in the grass, in the tree, in the river, in the mountain, in the birds of heaven, in the fishes of the sea; but*

seek it chiefly in yourselves. For I tell you truly, all living things are nearer to God than the scripture which is without life. God so made life and all living things that they might be the everlasting word teach the laws of the true God to man. God wrote not the laws on pages of books, but in your heart and in your spirit'.

10

THE RISE OF AGNOSTICISM AND ATHEISM

For the sake of clarity, before continuing with this chapter, I wish to define these beliefs: according to *Chambers Dictionary*. An agnostic is '*one who holds that we know nothing of things beyond material phenomena*' and an atheist is '*one who disbelieves in the existence of God*'.[26] A better definition of an atheist would be someone who believes that there is no God, no after-life and no ultimate justice. It could be argued that both agnosticism and atheism are good examples of the state of poverty, mentioned in logian 3 of *The Gospel of Thomas*, referred to in chapter 8.

Some religions, for example Christianity, Islam and Judaism, can be described as authoritarian or 'top down', because they have, to a large extent, taken control over the worship of their followers, insisting on conformity with rigid doctrines and rituals. The influence of Christian teaching and dogma on Western societies was challenged by the increasing effect of new scientific discoveries during and since in the eighteenth century. Most communities had their own churches and the preachers were highly respected members of their community. Church services were originally conducted in Latin, which was unintelligible to the majority of the parishioners, a practice which could well have been changed due to the difficulties, experienced by the Church, in recruiting priests after the ravages of the 'black death'. People tended to live well ordered, parochial and devout lives by the application of Christian philosophies. Over zealous Christians, or what may now be called Christian fundamentalists, persecuted and even killed off people who were accused of being witches, many of whom were actually complementary therapists and a great deal of knowledge was lost.

Early scientists tended to be ostracised by the Church but gradually new discoveries led to irrevocable changes in society. For example, electricity gave rise to numerous labour saving devices, and steam engines enabled transport over relatively long distances. People who had previously been confined to relatively small communities were able to travel cheaply and efficiently, thus widening their whole perspective of life. Previously it had been very unwise to challenge the authority of the Church or its man-made teachings and rituals as such challenges were regarded as heresy and severely punished, often by torture leading to death. However, the iron grip of the Church was gradually weakened and people were enabled to apply commonsense; in other words they regained their God given freedom of choice. Many Roman Catholics are still obeying the dictates of the centralised Church, as stated in their 'The Catechism of the Catholic Church'; the official formulation of tenets in which all Catholics are obliged to formally believe. This condemns, for example, divorce, homosexuality, masturbation and sexual relations before or outside marriage. Islam also holds an iron grip over the minds of its followers, who are not allowed to think for themselves.

In addition to the alterations, described above, a vast

array of different interpretations of Christianity, in the form of denominations, cults and sects, have arisen, all with their own version of the truth. However, there can only be one truth and finding it through studying Christianity can be a most confusing journey for seekers, which is probably one reason for the development of agnosticism. This confusion is beautifully expressed in the following poem:

The Agnostic's Prayer

1. Oh Lord above, if thou art there,
Please hear a poor agnostic's prayer.
I'm just a mortal man, and so
I simply don't presume to know.
So if indeed you do exist
Then reassure this pessimist.

2. Instruct them in thy ways, oh Lord
And let them not deny thy word.
"Thou shalt not kill" is set in stone,
But war brings death if lost or won.
Chide the hawk and spare the dove,
For art thou not the God of love?

3. In ways of man I have no faith;
The greed, the torture and the death
Of innocents and children who
Were brought up to believe in you.
Give to them their place above
And to the rest the gift of love.

4. The God of love, but God of whom,
The Suni Muslim or the Jew?
The God of all, but yet men fight
And kill each other for the right
To murder in thy name and say
That their true path's the only way.

5. God-fearing men, the wise men say
Have naught to fear on Judgment Day.
But why should others be afraid
When man is in God's image made?
And even if from grace they fall;
The bible tells, "God loves us all!"

6. Of holy war, may I opine;
It's fought with words of love divine.
I'll follow not the bigot's creed;
My war I'll wage on war and need
War, on war and hate, is holy.
Killing men is human folly.

7. And saints and sinners all were men
Therefore, they all were once children.
The path to grace or path to sin
Is possible to each within.
The way of mortal man is plain;
A lifetime ever changing lane.

8. Forgive me my impiety.
But let me keep my thinking free.
Then prophets false I will not follow,
Nor hail their heterodoxy hollow;
Pragmatists in robes and collars,
Blessing bullets, counting dollars.

9. Is any man all good or evil?
Mortal saint or living devil?
For monks have sinned against their brothers
And murderers been kind to mothers.
From darkness, our mortal state,
What makes a man degenerate?

10. But though despair is all around
Of thy existence, hope I've found
Hope in nature's morning light
And love prevailing darkest night.
Children's' laughter, human kindness;
Of thy concept does remind us.

11. Lord, save us all from evil madness
Bitter twisted inner sadness.
Show us somehow a way to find
And heal the sick malignant mind.
Those tortured souls with vengeful will,
Let us them cure, before they kill.

12. This knowledge I sincerely crave,
Who shall be damned? Who shall be saved?
Will evil men be heaven sent?
If on their deathbed they repent,
And godless human kindness be
A certain path to purgatory?

13. God save us from hypocrisy
And men who kill professionally,
And politicians world-wide;
Please, tell them you're not on their side.
From legal murder let them cease
And help us all to live in peace.

14. I hope thou can forgive my doubt,
I don't know what it's all about.
I can't repent my mortal sins
With no devout belief within.
I live in hope, Thy will be done!
For hope I have but faith I've none.

Lionel McClelland -1996[17]

The doubts and issues raised by Lionel McClelland are difficult to debate from the perspective of orthodox Christianity but in the context of the theme of this book, negative actions by individuals, religious sects and nations result in karmic debt, which ultimately has to be repaid: perceived differences between religions and races are illusory, so when we harm others we are effectively harming ourselves and our brethren. Lionel McClelland also raises the issue of faith, which has been challenged by Richard Dawking, for example, in his book *The God Delusion*.[18] How can we have faith in the existence of divine carer, helper, when it can't be explained by science? Some typical supporting arguments are that there is no scientific explanation of the existence of God and 'prove it to me'. A response is, on the one hand, that there is no proof that God doesn't exist and on the other hand, finding the Kingdom within is an individual journey, although guidance can be sought from a guru or teacher and it is also useful to be involved with a group of seekers. Another answer is that we are designed with these limited perceptions to enable us to experience freedom of thought and action and therefore faith evolves usually due to some type of dramatic personal experience, as allegedly experienced by St. Paul on the road to Damascus, or by going within. Another convincing answer to philosophic and scientific critics is provided in the following statement by the Master Omraam Mikhael Aivanhov.[5d]

'The knowledge acquired from books provides us with building materials, with resources, so why not acquire it? But beware of the conclusions drawn by scholars and philosophers from all these materials they have at their disposal. When they tell you after years of study and research that they have come to the conclusion that the universe is the work of chance, that there is no order in creation, that the soul and religion are inventions to be rejected, that life is absurd, that the earth is a battleground where each of us must fight tooth and nail not to be devoured by his neighbour, and so on...listen to them out of curiosity if you want, but do not let yourself be influenced by them. Over the centuries, how many times have the conclusions of scientists and philosophers changed! Why base your life on such unstable foundations? All the knowledge you can acquire must lead you towards God, towards an understanding of the meaning of life. Beware of all other conclusions.'

'Daily Meditations' 15th September

It is often argued that if there is a God, he wouldn't allow negative events like earthquakes, tsunamis, floods, genocide and ethnic cleansing but we have freewill and thus we, the human race, must take responsibility for most negativity affecting our civilisation. Some such disasters have resulted from excessive consumption of the planet's resources and others may be karmic. In this respect, it is interesting to make a comparison between ourselves and most of the other species on the planet in that we have freewill but they are governed entirely by the laws of nature.

There are no short cuts in our spiritual journey back to God and often people who have been indoctrinated with narrow religious beliefs may mistakenly believe that they have found the one true path and ultimate source: in fact, they are effectively delaying their spiritual journey, possibly into successive incarnations.

The majority of seekers have a long journey ahead from seeking, to belief, to knowledge and ultimately to direct experience and this progression is not necessarily straight forward, as there are many pitfalls and traps along the way. It is similar to a game of snakes and ladders. After making great progress, we can plunge back into darkness and poverty if we are tempted to stray from the path of love and light.

11

CORE TEACHINGS OF JESUS

Jesus was an avatar, in total communion with the soul of the universe. There have been other avatars that incarnated at times of great turmoil but Jesus had a unique relationship with most world religions in that the Christian religion evolved from his life, he was a Jew, and he was a prophet of Islam, studied Hindu scriptures, became a yoga master and is a Buddhist saint; named Issa. Surely, his teachings are the best available guide to resolving the problems of our dysfunctional society and bringing about peace on earth. It seems reasonable to state that the essence of Jesus' teaching is summarised in 'The Lord's Prayer', more guidance being included in 'The Sermon on the Mount' and specifically in the Beatitudes.

In his book, *The Search for the Ageless*[13d], Edmund Bordeaux Szekely (EBS), explains that a remarkable teaching has existed, for eight to ten thousand years, which is universal in its application and ageless in its wisdom. Traces of the teaching, which have appeared in many countries and religions, for example in Persia, Egypt, India, Tibet, China, Palestine and Greece, are transmitted in its purest form by the mysterious Essene brotherhood, which lived in the last two to three centuries BC and the first century AD in Palestine. The teaching appears in the Zend Avesta of Zarathustra, who translated it into a way of life that was followed for thousands of years. It contains the fundamental concepts of Brahmanism, the Vedas and the Upanishads; and the Yoga systems of India sprang from the same source. Buddha later gave forth essentially the same basic ideas, his Bodhi tree corresponding with the Essene Tree of Life. Similarly, in Tibet the teaching found expression in the Tibetan Wheel of Life'. EBS goes on to explain that 'The Pythagoreans and Stoics in ancient Greece also followed the Essene principles and much of their way of life. The same ancient teaching was an element of the Adonic culture of the Phoenicians of the Alexandrian School of Philosophy in Egypt, and contributed greatly too many branches of Western culture, Freemasonry, Gnosticism the Kabala and Christianity. However, it was translated in its most sublime and beautiful form in the Beatitudes expressed by Jesus'.

The Beatitudes were originally translated from the ancient language of Aramaic, an earthy language, used by the common people, in which particular words may have numerous meanings dependent upon their context. A number of different people, such as William Barclay and Yogananda, have suggested interpretations of the Beatitudes but in composing my interpretation of these statements by Jesus, I have particularly referred to the book by Glenda Green, *Love Without End*[19]; because her words resonate with my being. In this book, Glenda explains how Jesus appeared to her in visions, on numerous occasions, when she was painting a picture of him and during these sessions Jesus explained the meaning of many of his teachings, including the Beatitudes.

'Blessed are the poor in spirit, for theirs is the kingdom of heaven'
The word *'poor'* should be understood as *'simple'*, in this

context thus the statement can be translated as *'Blessed are the simple in spirit'*. This is equivalent to saying that God is within your own being and can be contacted directly by both meditation and prayer, as explained in Part III. Jesus made a similar statement in *The Essene Gospel of Peace*,[13b] *'God wrote not the laws in pages of books, but in your heart and your spirit'*. This raises a most important question: did the early translators deliberately change the meaning of this statement to claim that God must be approached via the Church? It is a tantalising thought and leads one to wonder whether Christianity would have evolved into a world religion had the correct interpretation been made. If the Church fathers had advised everyone to find God within, they would effectively be removing the need for a Church hierarchy or organised religion. In this context, would Constantine, successive Roman emperors and the strong connection between the Christian Church and the State, ever have developed? Another aspect of this paradox is that the creation of a hierarchy gives rise to separation, which is the antithesis of the oneness, which exists in the kingdom of heaven and was at the core of Jesus' teaching. Reference to the New Testament in *The New English Bible*,[20] gives the wording *'How blest are those who know that they are poor; the kingdom of heaven is theirs'*, is surely an example of how far a translation can stray from the true meaning of Jesus' teachings: presumably there was a genuine attempt to express the saying in modern language but it effectively misses the main point of one of Jesus' most important messages.

'Blessed are they that mourn, for they shall be comforted'

This saying also tends to be misunderstood as we should not dwell on our sorrow when someone dies but resolve to let them go to continue with their journey into higher levels of consciousness. This beatitude is about letting go or releasing the past on the understanding that as one door closes another opens. In this context, there are two aspects of love; attachment and letting go and for mutual benefit we should endeavour to let go as soon as possible. To quote a passage from Glenda Green's book; *'This process is relevant to the loss of anything, not just the loss of a loved one. The loss could be a dream or a hope——Such purging opens a space in which to celebrate a newly emerging stage of life——In releasing and honouring what has been, there may be tears, but there will also be doors opening to future possibilities——-accepting this process is great therapy and can result in many blessings——-when hoarding ceases there is plenty for all'.* A most important aspect of this saying is that of forgiveness, in that in realising that all human beings make mistakes, we should try to let go of the hurt, which has been caused, learn from the experience but move on to new experiences. Just consider how many conflicts between families and nations fester away for years or even generations because people are unable to forgive.

'Blessed are the meek, for they shall inherit the earth'

The true meaning of *'meek'* is *'moderate',* accordingly, we should only take what we need from nature to survive and be reasonably comfortable. Reference to a thesaurus provides numerous meanings of the word 'meek', such as humble, docile, unassuming, resigned, tame, timid and submissive and its opposites are arrogant, assertive and rebellious. In this context, it is tempting to think that the early Church fathers, particularly after the Council of Nicea, decided to use meek instead of moderate to quell any opposition to their imposed man-made religion, which conflicted with many prevalent teachings and philosophies. Conversely, confusion could have arisen due to a mistranslation.

This saying concurs with the natural law of balance; which states that 'All natural systems continually move towards a state of equilibrium or perfect balance'. If all people, communities and nations only took what they needed from nature and shared the excess then there would be plenty for everybody. In this context, Jesus recommended moderation not only in the food that we eat but also in physical comforts, mental pursuits, habits and work.

'Blessed are they who hunger and thirst for righteousness for they shall be filled'

Righteousness is universal love in action, equating to, for example, unity, respect, truth, justice and kindness. It emanates from our heart chakra or heart centre, which is traditionally regarded as the dwelling place of our soul. When we regularly focus on this centre, it expands to fill the whole of our being and eventually the whole of creation resulting in the blessed state of realising that we are all part of God. When we yearn for righteousness, in our every moment, we attract all that we need in our lives: *'The heart centre is a powerful magnet which generates life energy for the body and the soul and draws to you all the requirements of your life'.*[19] When we have evolved to this level of consciousness, we don't even need to ask, because all that we need to fulfil our purpose in life will be provided. The statement by Jesus *'Ask and you will receive'* is based on *'The Law of Magnetic Attraction'*, which is an expression of universal love. Another much quoted statement describing love is made by Saint Paul in 1 Corinthians 13.

'Blessed are the merciful for they shall receive mercy'

This is really an expression of the Law of Karma, which was discussed in chapter 2. If we extend mercy then we receive mercy. Conversely, if we live by the sword, we will die by the sword. One expression of mercy is forgiveness and if we forgive then we are forgiven and in so doing we grow spiritually; as we have said previously 'to err is human but to forgive is divine'.

'Blessed are the pure in heart for they shall see God'

Meditating on the heart centre can ultimately provide the experience of oneness with the Divine but before we can realise this blessed state we need to release all judgement of ourselves and others. Our spiritual journey can be greatly delayed when we stick rigidly to fixed ideas or teachings; such as those of a particular type of religion, instead of finding out for ourselves what is in our heart centre, in other words 'listening to the small voice within'. This will always take us on the right journey. Accordingly, we should strongly resist the urge to conform to mental preconceptions and judgements as this will deplete our life force. In society we do, of course, need to have rules and regulations and be seen to be punishing criminals but it is far preferable to endeavour to replace condemnation and punishment with correct education and encouragement to improve, if this is at all possible. The ultimate ideal is for us to restore the brotherhood of man and thus encourage criminals to rejoin a mutually supportive society; living in harmony together but never at the expense of individuality. The following poem, called *Follow Your Heart*, expresses a similar theme:

> *Follow your hearts*
> *The heart that is free*
> *Unburdened by*
> *Spoils of society*
>
> *Open your eyes*
> *The eye that can see*
> *And surely you'll find*
> *What is troubling thee.*
>
> *Do not be judge*
> *Make not this a test*
> *Show your mind peace*
> *Grant your body some rest*
>
> *For all that is true*
> *Will not forsake thee*
> *Follow your heart*
> *The heart that is free*

Linda McCartney
December 1996

Jesus related to Glenda Green, that his apostles were constantly asking him how to pray, seeking for words and formulas and his advice was that they should repeat his prayer and be sure to linger over the words for a while in silence and peace.[19]

'Blessed are the peacemakers for they shall be called the sons of God'

This is about evolving spiritually until we leave duality behind and realise the oneness of all creation. It was explained in chapter 1, that because of the limitations of our five senses, we develop self awareness, seeing ourselves as separate beings, separate nations, separate religions and so on. We become focussed on our differences rather than our togetherness but as we evolve spiritually; beyond the limitations of our five senses into higher states of consciousness we start having experiences of expanded awareness; which eventually evolve into enlightenment and ultimately God realisation. In these states we will realise and experience the truth of Sai Baba's saying that *'There is only one race, that of humanity'*, and in this sense we will become peacemakers. Also, as we progress we will find it increasingly difficult to make negative decisions and take negative actions; negative and positive polarity ceasing in our lives. In effect, we lose the need for freewill, being limited to right action, non-violence, non-violation of ourselves and others, resulting in peace of mind, peace between nations and ultimately peace on earth. Being a peacemaker means putting universal love into all aspects of our lives; love in speech and writing equating to truth and so on.

'Blessed are those who are persecuted for righteousness sake for theirs is the kingdom of heaven'

Persecution has a different meaning in the English language from that in Aramaic. In the former it means being harassed or punished whereas in the latter it means suffering. It is through hardship and difficulties that we grow in strength. The strongest and most durable steel has been forged, annealed and re-forged many times before it is suitable for making 'Excalibur'. Our relationship with God on our spiritual journey can be very difficult as we are tested time and time again until we are able to overcome our weaknesses and become worthy of being called sons and daughters of God and ultimately experience unity with God. Even Jesus was tested by Satan, whilst fasting and praying during his forty days in the wilderness. God is everything; both negative and positive aspects of our lives and we must learn to accept the bad as well as the good in our lessons of life, to build great resilience and know in our hearts that if we persevere we will eventually be fit to enter the kingdom. The ultimate prayer to God is therefore not to ask but to surrender and accept that his will be done. Eventually all illusions such as right and wrong, good and bad and positive and negative, will fall away and we will both realise and experience that God is in everything, is everything, knows everything and is all powerful. In other words God is omnipresent, omniscient and omnipotent.

Jesus' teachings are also expressed in the Lord's Prayer, which is interpreted below

The Lords Prayer

Our Father who art in Heaven
Lord God, who is our Father in Heaven, where we will join you for ever, when we have balanced all our karmic debt.

Hallowed be your name.
We visualise you, in the form of your son, Jesus, surrounded in an aura of all the beautiful colours of the rainbow, spreading out to infinity.

Thy kingdom come
The kingdom of peace and goodwill, which Jesus laid down his life to create, will come to pass, as inspirations and actions arising from our heart centres and will transform society.

Thy will be done, on earth as it is in Heaven
We are always aware that you have given us free will and we will use it to help to bring about a state of peace on earth, as it already exists in Heaven.

Give us this day our daily bread
Please fill the hearts of all your people with love and compassion so that they will ensure that everybody in the world knows how to contact you, has sufficient food, adequate shelter and can become self sufficient.

Forgive us our debts
We are well aware that we have freedom of choice and that we have sometimes made wrong decisions and taken wrong actions. Please help us to change our ways and make right decisions and take right actions in the future.

As we forgive our debtors
We, here and now, use our freewill to forgive all those who have acted in a negative manner towards us, our religion, our families and our nation.

Lead us not into temptation but deliver us from evil
Lord please guide us into always acting from our heart centres and therefore not be tempted by evil thoughts and situations

For thine is the Kingdom the power and the glory

OUR RELATIONSHIP WITH THE UNIVERSE AND THE DIVINE

In principle, we reject the control over us and our families and friends by unrepresentative, self-interested governments, institutions and corporations which have the power and the glory in our society. Instead, we accept that all power and glory is yours. (Jesus was opposed to the establishment, particularly of the Jewish Church, as he regarded it as seeking the power and the glory, which should be God's alone.)

For ever and ever
We repeat these words to emphasise our determination to live our lives according to the principles taught by your son, Jesus Christ.

Amen
We solemnly confirm all that has been stated, above.

In the *The Essene Gospel of Peace* Jesus asked us to then pray to our Heavenly Mother[13b]:

*'And after this manner pray to your earthly Mother:
Our Mother which art upon earth, hallowed be thy name.
Thy kingdom come and thy will be done in us, as it is in thee.
As thou sendest every day thy angels, send them to us also.
Forgive us our sins, as we atone all our sins against thee.
And lead us not into sickness, but deliver us from evil, for thine is the earth, the body and the health. Amen.'*

We should learn how to open our heart centres and channel the Holy Spirit through our thoughts and actions, absolutely refusing to ever act against our inner guidance or conscience. The future of our society, and in fact our whole civilisation is our responsibility. We cannot, in truth, blame unrepresentative bodies for leading us astray, to satisfy the cravings of their egos and to profit at our expense. We have the ultimate authority to individually take control of our own lives and collectively to oppose evil and precipitate the kingdom of heaven on earth. To do this, we must wake up and set forth, individually and collectively, on our journey towards perfection. The kingdom will not come about by violent revolution and war but by going within and enabling the Holy Spirit to channel through our heart centres. The nature of the kingdom is described in the following excerpt from *The Gospel of Thomas*, logion 20.[14]

> *'The disciples said to Jesus: Tell us, what is the kingdom of the heavens like? He said to them: It is like a grain of mustard, smaller than all seeds; but when it falls on tilled earth, it sends forth a huge stem and becomes a shelter for the birds of the sky.'*

PART III

PATHWAYS TO ENLIGHTENMENT

12

WE ARE ALL ONE

The Universal Consciousness, which we call God, has knowledge of all things, is all powerful and is present everywhere all the time. Our soul realises that it is part of God, whereas we, with our limited perceptions tend to be unaware of our true nature. Originally, when we decided, of our own freewill, to experience life in a material reality, we were well aware of our relationship with everything but during successive bodily incarnations we have forgotten who we really are; we have, in effect, become a two part being; one part conscious and the other unconscious. One part is experiencing absolute bliss and clarity, in oneness with the Divine, and the other is living in a state of delusion, believing itself to be separate, having freewill, making many wrong choices and effectively creating our dysfunctional global society. This was wonderfully expressed by Saint Paul in the following words *'Now we see only puzzling reflections in a mirror, but then we shall see face to face. My knowledge now is partial; then it will be whole, like God's knowledge of Me'*.[21] Our ultimate purpose, therefore, is to find ways of clearing the delusion and realising our true nature of oneness with our soul and thus God.

Various methods of seeking and finding our true self are described in this part of the book, our development being determined both by our present state of spiritual evolution and our determination to make progress. We are able to accelerate our spiritual journey if we are prepared to make the effort, a major motivating factor being our increasing awareness that our selfishness has created the crisis in which all life on earth and even the earth itself are endangered. Over-consumption of the planet's resources is creating such a massive imbalance that even the force of nature is being overwhelmed. Mother Earth needs our help to regain balance and harmony. Many of us understand this situation and experience a deep yearning to play a useful role to allow the balance of nature to be restored which will ultimately help to create a state of peace on earth. We may often feel powerless thinking that our individual striving is unlikely to affect this immense trauma. However, we must carry on regardless and be aware that we don't need to see the big picture: we may be producing just one tiny thread in a mighty tapestry but this is enough because the God within and without is well aware of our aspirations, and it is a law of life that when we genuinely ask for help, particularly for others, then we will receive. Often we can only see the whole picture as we look back and realise how much we have evolved.

This is an adventure for both individuals and our whole society, as we strive to bring about harmony with nature and recreate the Brotherhood of Man, the Motherhood of Nature the Fatherhood of God. The journey can be most puzzling; it's like driving along a country road on a misty night, sometimes experiencing bright moonlight and sometimes descending into a hollow and being blinded by a dense fog. Sometimes, we receive clear inspirations, like scientists finding new discoveries, artists creating masterpieces and musicians composing wonderful symphonies, but at other times we feel totally disconnected. We should try to be patient, as we need to assimilate our experiences, learn our lessons, maintain our balance but have faith that our progression is inevitable and when we are ready, full consciousness will return.

Much help is available from spiritual beings in this and other dimensions, who are well aware of our yearning and will prompt and guide us as we progress through many trials and tribulations. When the student is ready, the master will come. This advancement will not come to satisfy the ego. It will come when we apply ourselves to our lessons of life and yearn for it not just for our own benefit but for the benefit of all. Opportunities will present themselves, often seeming to be coincidences or synergy. There are numerous pitfalls on the way during our journey to perfection; for example many people and organisations may believe that their way is the only true path, but there are many ways of making progress and what's right for one person may not be right for another. The very fact that you have decided to read this book is an indication that you are ready to continue your journey, but please be patient as progress will eventually be made.

It is important to always remember that we are not trying to find or create something new but to find something that we already have, within us: it isn't somewhere else but within us, here and now. Many people spend a great deal of time and effort hoping to find salvation with various teachers or exemplars, all over the world. Whilst such experiences can be very stimulating and inspiring, we should always be aware that we already have the kingdom of heaven within our beings, but to access it we have to transcend the experiences derived from our five senses. When we master the art of absolute stillness of the mind everything will be revealed. Other people can help us, in various ways, but our salvation will arise from our own efforts. Some seekers may prefer to dedicate their whole lives to this quest and enter a monastery or live in the ashram of an appropriate teacher or guru, as described in chapter 13. Others may prefer to live a conventional life in society and utilise various spiritual techniques to transcend, as explained in chapter 14. The ultimate purpose of all our lives on this planet and in other realities is to complete our journey to perfection.

13

YOGA FOR THE ASCETIC

Yoga is a fully comprehensive pathway to spiritual salvation, in which there are many interpretations and different perspectives, described in numerous books, presenting the seeker with a confusing scenario. This chapter summarises the fundamental principles in the hope that it will help the ardent seeker to choose an appropriate way of proceeding.

The word yoga means yoke or union, a good definition being that it is a method of achieving spiritual union with the Divine. In yoga the God within is called the Atman and the God without Brahman, there being no real difference between this and our occidental idea of the soul being part of the omnipresent spirit or God. The Atman, like the soul, is regarded as being bound to the personality through its multiple life experiences, this perpetual cycle being pictured as a karmic wheel, which symbolises Buddhism. There are many different techniques of yoga depicted as the spokes of the wheel, leading to the state of Samadhi, or experience of oneness with God, at the hub. A prerequisite and on going ideal in taking the path of yoga is the practice of a number of abstinences and observances, called, respectively, yamas and niyamas, which are reminiscent of the moral codes of many religions, such as to Ten Commandments of Judaism. These practices shouldn't be regarded as rigid disciplines, as they could, in that context become an obstacle to advancement: rather than being regarded as walls, which we must climb before progressing, they should be regarded as bridges, which will lead us towards the goal. They are both an ideal requirement and a by-product of undertaking the journey.

Abstinences and observances are the first two steps on the eightfold path to realisation, as defined by Patanjali, who is regarded as the founder of yoga. These first two steps provide self control and mental calmness, which are ideal conditions in which to practise the various methods of yoga.

The yamas include abstention from violence, falsehood, stealing, greed, covetousness and incontinence. The meaning of the first five yamas is quite obvious, whereas the meaning of incontinence is more obscure. Non-violence or abstaining from injury to others can also be described as compassion for all living creatures. Truthfulness and non-stealing are also intrinsic in every moral code of conduct. Greed refers to taking more than one needs, the ideal being moderation in all things. Covetousness refers to desiring something wrongfully, such as fancying someone else's belongings or in other words to let the green eyed monster of envy loose in our lives. Incontinence refers to addictions such as to smoking, drug taking, drinking and sex. The meaning of sexual incontinence is the most difficult to explain, as it can be interpreted in different ways, according to the circumstances. For example, some branches of yoga involve the transmuting of sexual energy into spiritual energy, which, in due course, can flow up the spinal column, affecting the chakras and, in this respect, celibacy is a necessary discipline. On the other hand, the participants of tantric yoga claim to utilise sexual intercourse, with delayed orgasm, as a route to advancement. Many yoga gurus (teachers) will recommend the practice of celibacy by all serious aspirants in all branches of yoga, who would be well advised to live in a monastery or special ashram, in part to avoid the distractions of living in a modern society and being in regular contact with members of the opposite sex and faced with the array of tantalising images in the media. In this context, it's not surprising that many Roman Catholic priests are alleged to fail in their vows of celibacy, which could be a contributory factor to the difficulties being experienced by the Church of Rome in recruiting priests. Sexual continence doesn't necessarily equate to celibacy but to chastity, in appropriate circumstances. For example, sexual relationships are totally acceptable for householder yogis, who live normal married lives. The type of sexual activity, which is discouraged, is the seeking of sensual experiences as a form of entertainment, which can lead to deviant activities and interests and become a major obstacle to the spiritual journey.

The niyamas or observances include purity, contentment, self discipline, contemplation and devotion to God:

Internal and external purity of body and mind is achieved by eating pure foods, including 'living' and vegetarian foods, breathing in fresh air and sunshine, all of which help to purify body and soul. External purity relates to washing the whole body regularly. Hatha yoga, particularly including the 'salutation in the sun', will result in purity of body and mind.

Contentment in all circumstances is about being satisfied with ones lot or in other words to play the cards that one has been dealt in the game of life, knowing that the necessary lessons for self improvement will emerge. The yogi should have the characteristics of simplicity and sincerity and be cheerful, uncomplaining and free from strong desires.

Self discipline/Austerity/Tapas means exercising self control, overcoming bad habits, eradicating destructive emotions, thoughts and desires and improving oneself so that ones energy can be directed into positive progress in achieving the aims of yoga.

Self study or contemplation includes studying key works on Yoga, such as the Upanishads and the Bhagavad Gita so as to understand the steps necessary in the journey to perfection.

Devotion to God, means releasing oneself from egotism and surrendering everything to God.

The last three niyamas or observances are preliminary steps in the practice of Kriya Yoga which literally translates as 'work towards yoga' as defined by Patangali.

The Various Branches of Yoga

There are a large number of methods of yoga, described in a vast array of books on the subject but most authorities agree on four main branches, which are briefly described below:

Bhakti Yoga includes loving and selfless devotion to God, who is often personalised in the form of various avatars and spiritual teachers, such as Jesus, Krishna, Mohammed, Yogananda and Sri Sathya Sai Baba. This is the pathway of the great majority of religious believers, utilising techniques such as reading scriptures, praying, repeating verbal or silent mantras, singing bhajans or hymns and visualising God in many forms. Sometimes practitioners go to live in a monastery or an ashram, being guided by an abbot or guru of great experience, who is able to steer aspirants in the right direction whilst allowing them to discover their own truths.

Karma Yoga is the pathway of selfless duty, the fruits of all one's actions being dedicated to God. This route is particularly suited to people of vigorous temperament, who feel the call of duty and service in the world of human affairs. None of us know our stage of personal spiritual development and that is probably a good thing; otherwise we might too easily fall into the ego trap. Those who are nearing or are already in a final incarnation may suddenly experience enlightenment, such as when cutting the grass or digging the garden, or one might get occasional glimpses or glimmerings prior to full and permanent illumination. This progression is illustrated in Figure 4. It is important to realise that enlightenment is not the end of the journey, but an important staging post, to be reached.

Jnana Yoga is the pathway of intellectual discrimination, which rejects all which is transient, thus Brahman is experienced by elimination of all which is superficial. One becomes dispassionate; tending to be a silent witness or observer of phenomena, particularly during meditation. In other words, experiences tend to become objective rather than subjective. An important characteristic of an aspirant on this pathway is a deep yearning or longing for spiritual liberation.

Raja Yoga Patanjali, who is regarded as the father of yoga, compiled and reformulated the yoga practices, which were already expressed in the Upanishads, which had been written many centuries earlier. In effect he restated yoga philosophy and practice for practitioners of his own time. He outlined eight steps to be followed for ascension into the kingdom of the God within; via Raja Yoga:

Yamas or abstinences - as already described above.

Niyamas or observances - also described above.

These first two steps yield self control and mental calmness.

Asanas - the purpose of these stretching exercises, called hatha yoga, is to prepare for meditation, although they are an excellent way of gaining and retaining a fit and healthy body. Ideally the various positions or postures should be attainable without fatigue or restlessness. A considerable number of books have been written about all aspects of hatha yoga and accordingly, I see no purpose in providing a detailed explanation but recommend *The Salutation in the Sun*, as a marvellous sequence exercise with numerous benefits. It takes only three to ten minutes a day and improves health, strength, efficiency and longevity, which is the right of every human being.

Pranayama is the regulation of the breath leading to integration of mind and body, primarily including complex breathing exercises which are techniques for controlling the life force, calming the heart and breath and removing sensory distractions from the mind. The ultimate aim of pranayama is to arouse the kundalini; which is a powerful spiritual energy, residing at the base of the spine, which on stimulation will rise up the spine awakening the chakras. It is strongly recommended that the majority of these techniques should be practiced under the guidance of a guru or qualified teacher, as they have the potential of unbalancing the whole system, if practiced incorrectly. Notwithstanding this, I particularly recommend the utilisation of the yoga complete breath and alternate nostril breathing, Alternate nostril breathing is a useful method of finishing a meditation, particularly after a deep experience such as one of expanded awareness; as it has a grounding effect, gently bringing back reality, without shocking the system. It is also a very useful way of calming the mind, after a stressful experience.

Pratyahara is drawing the focus of the mind away from outward distraction by observing our breathing. In other words it is the withdrawal of the mind from sensory perceptions into absolute stillness within, to enable the practice of the three remaining steps.

Dharana or Concentration is one pointed focus of the mind on some aspect of God or divine form. For example, one could focus on the heart centre, the third eye or the form of ones guru or spiritual teacher.

Dhyana or Meditation is an unbroken flow of thoughts towards the object of concentration, described by Patanjali as a succession of identical thought waves, which can eventually lead to experiences of expanded awareness and ultimately cosmic consciousness.

Samadhi or Absorption eventually one becomes totally immersed in the object of concentration and ones role changes from being the doer into being the witness. Often in this state, we receive advice from within to stop trying to make something happen and to just become the observer of events.

When the last three steps, of concentration, meditation and absorption are focussed on one subject, they are called samyama. The techniques of making samyama on various subjects were described by Patangali as yoga sutras, which ultimately lead to the aspirant acquiring advanced yogic powers, called siddhis. Many of the miracles of Jesus, and other great spiritual teachers, such as walking on water, multiplication of food and materialisation are in effect siddhis. Aspirants are strongly advised to seek guidance from a spiritual teacher of high repute before practising sutras as they can damage the nervous system and cause immense trauma if the person is ill prepared. For this reason, some authorities advise that the siddhis should be regarded as by-products of the process of spiritual advancement rather than the objective.

14

MEDITATION FOR EVERYDAY LIVING

Yoga, as practised by the ascetic, often necessitating the dedication of ones whole life to seeking union with the creator, is neither practical nor possible for the great majority of people. Also it is inconceivable that they could master such practices as withdrawing the mind from sensory perceptions, one pointed focus of the mind and the ability to create an unbroken flow of thoughts towards the object of concentration. The great majority suffer from, what Sai Baba calls the 'monkey mind', our mind rushing here and there seeking maximum stimulation. Ideally it should be totally under our control but it tends to be in charge, wasting time, energy and effort. Meditation is really about finding ways of training the mind to persevere on the journey towards the God within, which can be visualised as an extremely bright light in our heart centre.

This chapter describes the pathway of meditation and prayer, which is particularly suitable for people living conventional lives in society. The main benefits derived from regular practice are the release of both short and long term stress accumulated in the nervous system, resulting in improved health and performance in all activities and the acceleration of ones spiritual journey. These themes are expanded below.

It reduces the effect of negative stress

Our hunter gatherer ancestors when threatened by dangerous situations such as being attacked by a sabre-toothed tiger, adopted the 'flight or fight' response: in other words, they could stand firm and fight for their lives or run away at great speed. In such a situation, the physiological mechanisms release an abundance of hormones, including adrenalin, into the bloodstream, temporarily changing the functioning of the whole body. The heart beats quicken, blood pressure increases and the lungs take in more oxygen. At the same time, the muscles become tense, fats and sugars are released into the blood to provide more energy and the body retains temperature balance by perspiring, whilst other functions, such as the digestion, temporarily cease to operate. The problem is that our body reacts to danger in exactly the same way but we are often unable to react by fighting or running away and an excess of fats and sugars remain in our bloodstream, our muscles remain tensed, our blood pressure stays high and we feel highly stressed for a relatively long time.[41] The trouble is that this process eventually leads to layers of fat choking the arteries, resulting in strokes and heart problems, and an imbalance of many other bodily systems leading to many types of functional damage and a perpetual feeling of tiredness and depression. In such situations, one has no real alternative but to take on board all this stress. This negative scenario is most destructive for people living a sedentary lifestyle in an urban environment, as they have to contend with high levels of noise and pollution of all kinds.

The good news is that regular meditation, when carried out correctly, and the resulting deep rest, redresses the physiological imbalances created by our inability to either fight or flee. A metaphorical explanation of this stress release is that various thoughts which may occur during a typical day can be visualised as different coloured lines drawn on a blackboard. For example, red lines denote anger, orange lines sexual encounters, yellow lines fear, green lines envy and so on. At the end of the day, one can imagine the blackboard covered with a mass of different coloured chalk lines, all mixed up. The effect of meditating can then be visualised as taking a duster and cleaning the blackboard: the stress, which has accumulated in our nervous system both in the body and mind during the day is dissolved, and we feel a deep sense of peace.

A most comprehensive study of the effects of meditatio, has been carried out on Transcendental Meditation (TM) showing that all functions of the body and mind move towards the relief of stress during meditation, promoting relaxation in many forms and improved performance in all kinds of activities. My own subjective experiences as a TM practitioner confirmed, for example, a reduction of breath and heart rate and dryness in the mouth during meditation, and remarkable improvements in energy levels, co-ordination, reaction times, and the ability to recover rapidly from stressful situations.

The yamas and niyamas occur naturally in ones life

Maharishi Yogi, who first introduced transcendental meditation to the western world in 1953, taught that inner purity and righteous living is an effect of correct meditation rather than a prerequisite.[41] For example, a heavy smoker may well realise some time after learning and regular practice of meditation that he doesn't need to smoke anymore. My own experiences, as a regular meditator over the last thirty years or so, leads me to agree with this assertion. It steadily removes bad habits and improves ones whole attitude to life, the yamas and niyamas, regarded as prerequisites of spiritual advancement in conventional yoga, coming to pass as a natural progression in ones life. Accordingly, one would in due course quite naturally refrain from violence, falsehood, stealing, greed, covetousness and incontinence, in its many forms, in part to avoid accruing karmic debt. Similarly, purity of mind and body, contentment, self discipline are results of regular meditation. Also, because of the immense benefits experienced by regular meditators, they tend to study important spiritual literature and to adopt spiritual approaches to life, seeking and finding the answers within, and ultimately surrendering everything to God. In my experience, the practitioner also needs to address his weaknesses in a conventional manner, in order to gain maximum benefit.

It enhances our spiritual journey

From a spiritual perspective the main purpose of practising meditation is to realise our oneness with the aspect of God, which is located in our heart centre and is called the Atman, in Eastern philosophies. During the process of meditating, we will tend to momentarily dip in and out of this area of love and light; a process which is called transcending. In our earlier attempts, we may be momentarily unaware of this happening but eventually we will actually experience the wonderful stillness, peace, love and light, which are within our being, which will gradually rise into our bodily consciousness, leading to enlightenment. Some people, who are perhaps living one of their final incarnations in this reality, because they have repaid their karmic debt, may have such experiences in their early attempts at meditation. Other people may not. Some people will have psychic experiences, such as the observation of colours, the opening of the third eye, out of body experiences, hearing voices and having visions. Ultimately, some people will begin to have experiences of witnessing, in effect changing from being the doer to being the observer, as described in the previous section on yoga. The main advice to all meditators is not to endeavour to make things happen but to continue your practice in peace and humility and whatever you need will eventually come to pass. The journey cannot be rushed, as we need to assimilate our experiences, learn our lessons, maintain our balance but have faith that our progression is inevitable and when we are ready full spiritual consciousness will return.

Other Indicators of progress

Ultimately, spiritually evolved people in our society will know each others thoughts and their actions will be for the good of all. The philosophy of *'All for one and one for all'* will operate as in Alexander Dumas's wonderful book, *The Three Musketeers*. Already, there is evidence of raising global consciousness as simultaneous events both in the animal kingdom and in human affairs have been observed and explained by Rupert Sheldrake's theory of 'morphic' fields. Sheldrake, in his paper[22], discusses the connection between morphic resonance and Jung's concept of synchronicity. He gives the example of birds of the blue-tit species drowning in milk bottles whilst trying to drink the cream off the top. Many of these birds died simultaneously, without the possibility of communicating with one another in known ways. There are also examples of monkeys on different islands adopting the same habits independently. Many examples of strange coincidences are given by James Redfield in his book, *The Celestine Vision*, in which he refers to work by the Swiss psychologist, Carl Jung.[23] People who are consciously following a spiritual path in their lives often experience coincidences which can be explained in terms of nature supporting right action. Such a coincidence is described by James Redfield concerning Abraham Lincoln, who in his early days yearned to do more with his life than work as a farmer or craftsman. One day he showed kindness to a peddler by buying an old barrel full of junk. On examining the contents, he found a full set of law books, which encouraged and helped him to become a lawyer. This is referred to as synchronicity by James Redfield, in his book as a symptom of spiritual seeking and finding. The rational mind will, of course, suggest other explanations.

Alleged Contra-Indications

Sometimes there are reports of people having negative experiences during or after practicing meditation, such as headaches, muscle twitches, anxiety, depression, de-personalisation and mental breakdown.

As a long term meditator I have been concerned by such allegations; particularly as they are contrary to my own experiences and those of many of my friends who also meditate. My reason for raising this subject, is not to challenge these allegations, but to endeavour to provide possible explanations of such contra-indications.

We are all, in effect, the sum of all the decisions we have made and actions which we have taken, in this and previous incarnations; most of us having a considerable journey ahead to balance our karmic debt to be prepared for ascension into higher realms of conscious experience on our passing from this life. It was explained in part I and illustrated in Figure 1 that by misusing our freedom of choice for numerous lifetimes, we can accumulate considerable karmic debt, which has to be repaid in bearable doses. Intense practice of meditation could conceivably lead to negative experiences as both current and past life stresses could be released too quickly. The experience could be compared with peeling an onion, each layer representing all the negative stress held in our nervous system. As we peel away the layers too quickly, we could be overwhelmed by the consequences. It is not that the meditation is causing distress but that negative stresses, already present, are being released too fast.

Another explanation could be that the people having such negative experiences could be experimenting with other pursuits, which are falsely claimed to enhance spiritual experiences, such as drug abuse, excess alcohol consumption and perverted sexual behaviour, all of which can expose us to infestation by negative entities, creating havoc in our lives in the form of mental problems and illnesses.

Good advice to any meditator, who starts having such negative experiences, is to join a meditation group and consult with a spiritual teacher of high repute and be safely guided forward. Another precaution would be to utilise a technique of psychic protection, such as surrounding oneself with an imaginary bubble of white light, before meditating[8], as described in chapter 5.

Various Techniques of Meditation

To reiterate, the ultimate purpose of meditation is to realise and experience ones connection with the whole of creation, which can be visualised as an infinite field of love and light. The benefits for the individual can vary from experience of deep relaxation to a realisation of oneness with God, which the yogis describe as Samadhi. Regular meditation can induce deep healing of body and mind and enhanced abilities. It is not my intention to provide detailed instructions on the various techniques of meditation, as numerous books have already been written by experienced people on many different ways of proceeding. However, I wish to recommend the TM technique as a wonderful introduction to meditation which provides instruction in both theory and practice.

Great benefits can be derived from people meditating together in groups, either utilising an individual technique, such as TM, or being led through other forms of meditations, such as by visualising light moving through the body or focussing on the chakras. Members of a group can be sitting together in the same room or be a great distant apart imagining the other group members, for example, being surrounded or connected by light. Meditating individually and in groups can have a beneficial effect on local and global society.

There are a number of different theories about the magnified effect of several people meditating together. For example, Benjamin Crème, in his book on *Transmission Meditation*,[24] claims that the effect multiplies in a geometric progression relative to the number of participants. Accordingly three people meditating together creates one triangle, four people will make four triangles, five people-ten triangles and six people-twenty triangles and so on. Similarly, Maharishi Yogi maintained that, when 1% of a population of a city or country regularly meditate, it results in a reduction in negative tendencies; such as crime and accidents. Also, if the square root of 1% of a city or country practises the TM Siddhi programme and especially the yogic flying, it reverses all negative tendencies. These phenomena are described by David Walne in his excellent article on *From Tranquillisers to Tranquillity*, which is presented in chapter 23.

My own experiences in group meditations suggest that when a group of people meditate together, there is a merging of all their energy fields, which can have a healing effect on some people in the group and deplete the energy of others particularly if they have not utilised some form of psychic protection.[8] If one or more people in the group have an experience of expanded awareness, then most people in the group experience increased energy, in one way or another. Also, participants may have varying psychic experiences, such as opening of the chakras, including the third eye and observing various colours and visions. This type of magnified effect is particularly relevant to being in the presence of spiritual masters, who often have a considerably extended and enhanced aura which explains the incredible beneficial effect of being in their presence, even when they are only a distant figure, surrounded by a large number of devotees this experience being called darshan. On this theme, it is interesting to consider that the light of an avatar is universal, as expressed in the following excerpt from logian 24 of *The Gospel of Thomas*[14]:

6. There is a light
7. at the centre of a man of light,
8. and it illumines the whole world.
9. If he does not shine,
10. there is darkness

The Master Omraam Mikhael Aivanhov recommended the following meditation for greater benefit[5e]:

> *'You say that you pray, that you meditate but there are no results. Here is a very simple but very efficient way to link yourself to the Lord. When you want to pray you create an image, that of a multitude of spirits spread throughout the whole world, but who, wherever they are, are in the process of concentrating on the Creator. Through thought you link with these beings so as to pray with them. In this way your voice is no longer isolated in the desert of life and you appeal to Heaven together with thousands of luminous beings. Such a prayer is always heard because of the collectivity, and you benefit too. It is because you act alone that your thought does not reach its goal and it comes back to you. The secret is to unite with all those who are praying, for at every moment somewhere in the world there are beings who pray.'*

Enhanced Healing by Meditation

In my experiences of channelling Reiki, I have found that the healing effect is greatly enhanced if the recipient is in a meditative state. The method, which I have frequently used, is to play a recorded meditation, such as that of the Kundalini Foundation (KF); using the '*Soh-Hum*' mantra, but any meditative tape would probably suffice. Whilst channelling healing in this manner, I rarely touch the recipient, tending to channel from some distance away but sometimes, during the session, utilising a bio-energy technique of sweeping the aura and balancing the chakras. On a number of occasions, the healing effected, utilising this technique has been dramatic. On one occasion, I was asked to give healing to a young man, who was suicidal, after an argument with his girl friend. I taught him a simple meditation, utilising the word 'one' as a silent mantra and as he meditated I visualised a white light moving up through his body and into his head. After his meditation he felt totally relaxed; all his negative stress had dissipated. I asked him what he had experienced during his meditation and to my amazement he explained that a white light had passed from his feet up through his body into his head and he felt at one with everything.

On another occasion a young women who had been savagely attacked by her partner about a year earlier came for healing. Both her shoulders had been dislocated during the attack. She still experienced pain from each shoulder and a deep seated fear of being alone in the presence of men. I played the KF tape and channelled Reiki from a few yards away, finishing off by re-energising and balancing her chakras. All her pain and trauma had dissipated; a healing which was permanent. I heard sometime afterwards that she had later trained in both Reiki and aromatherapy.

The third example happened when two friends called in to see us, the women suffering from a bad back and the man from a deep seated anger resulting from the loss of his children due to a divorce. They were both regular meditators, and so we meditated together; each of us utilising our own technique. During the meditation, I channelled

Reiki energy into both of my friends; observing that they were drawing a deep blue light. They both left but telephoned me later and explained that during the meditation, the women had heard a voice telling her to accept a job as a teacher of a course on colour therapy. At the same time, the man had received a vision of his eldest daughter, sitting in the full lotus position, smiling at him and assuring him that all his children loved him and would always be with him. All his anger had dissolved and he was at peace. On arriving home, the telephone had rung and the current teacher of the colour therapy course asked the women if she would take over as the teacher of the class.

One reason for describing these healing experiences is to ask whether other people have had similar experiences, and to suggest that other Reiki healers should experiment with meditation.

David Walne has especially written an article for this book entitled *From Tranquilisers to Tranquillity*, which is presented in chapter 23. This describes his own experiences in practicing both TM and the TM Siddhi Programme.

PART IV

THE SPIRITUAL EVOLUTION OF SOCIETY

15

OUR COLLECTIVE JOURNEY

Our global society is in a state of perpetual turmoil; seemingly irresolvable conflicts existing between nations, often precipitating wars. Racial and religious tensions abound, sometimes leading to suicide bombings and the slaughter of innocents. The industrialised nations live in relative luxury whilst the majority of the world's population, in the developing countries, live in squalor, poverty and degradation. World resources of fossil fuels are being used as our primary source of power, accelerating global warming, and providing great wealth to a small minority. Apathy abounds as people realise that they have little influence over factors affecting their lives; many of our, so called, democracies being a sham. Many people are becoming disillusioned with these negative characteristics of our global society and are seeking greater meaning and purpose in their lives. This is bringing about a process of healing, which is speeding up as successively more people are either consciously or unconsciously asking for divine guidance to help them play some part in improving society. It is a law of life that when we ask for help for the right reasons then it is received. This process of accelerating positive change will cause a transformation of our society; replacing the current trend towards centralisation with true democracy, as people will become much more confident and self actualising, and will demand positive changes in society.

We human beings are born with a God given faculty of freedom of choice and guidance in making correct decisions by natural and cosmic laws, which although often disregarded can be accessed by prayer and meditation. The particularly relevant laws are those of love, freedom, cause and effect, balance and karma. The 'Law of Love' is related to truth, righteousness and non-violence, which lead typically to peace of mind, peace between nations and ultimately peace on earth. The other laws are very closely related, as when we make incorrect choices an imbalance is created, which has to be corrected, either in our current or in successive incarnations. These laws can be defined as follows:

The Law of Love defined in Christianity as 'do unto others as you would have them do unto you',[25] is love in action or righteousness. Similar statements are made in the teachings of other religions, such as Brahmanism, Buddhism, Confucianism, Hinduism, Islam, Judaism and many others, showing that this is a universal law of life.

The Law of Freedom 'we have the God given right of freedom of choice (or freewill) but we must never use it to restrict the freedom of other people'.

The Law of Cause and Effect 'Action and Reaction are Equal and Opposite' was defined by Sir Isaac Newton in his Third Law of Motion but it is also a law of life.

The Law of Balance the simplest definition is that, 'All natural systems continually move towards a state of equilibrium or perfect balance'.

The Law of Karma states that 'If karmic balance is not achieved in the current life then it has to be balanced in successive lives.'

We can obtain guidance on these laws via our soul, spirit and angel guides, which have always been with us. Other help is sometimes received in the form of synchronistic happenings, messages and visions. As we progress spiritually, this process of prompting and guiding will seem to take place automatically but this is because of our deep yearning to improve our society and help to bring about peace.

In this part of the book some key aspects of our modern global society are considered in the light of its accelerating spiritual evolution. These are democracies, climate change, healing the planet, and a form of education based on universal love. Governments and their administrations tend to disregard the fundamental human right of freedom of choice by applying legislation, which is introduced without proper consultation with their electorates. Society should be 'bottom up' to enable people to influence policies and decisions by making right choices rather than being dominated by their elected representatives and associated bureaucracies, who are creating 'top down' systems, effectively destroying the whole ethos of society by aggravating and frustrating rather than leading and inspiring. The restoration of effective democracies will enable the people of planet earth to make correct decisions by addressing the issue of climate change, which is primarily caused by our living out of harmony with cosmic and natural laws. We can also heal our planet by healing ourselves, as this purifies, strengthens and widens our auras, a process which has a corresponding, cumulative effect on the aura of the planet, enabling it to correct imbalances, with minimum disruption. This whole process of planetary regeneration will be accelerated by the introduction of a form of education based on the application of universal love, enabling enlightened people to gain influence by taking up key positions in society.

16

TRUE DEMOCRACIES

Democracy is defined in *Chambers Dictionary* as *'a form of government in which supreme power is vested in the people collectively and is administered by them or by officers appointed by them'*.[26] In a society based on such principles, common aims and policies would be defined and individuals and groups would co-operate together for their realisation. It is hard to recognise the full application of these principles in systems of government in most countries and no doubt cynics would argue that such ideals are contrary to the self interested nature of mankind. For example, party political systems of government, which are common throughout the world, are very deeply flawed, often failing to provide the majority of the people with sufficient influence over factors affecting their lives. Typically, governments can be elected by a minority. For example, in the UK, the percentage of the electorate that voted for the winning party reduced from 40% to 22% between 1951 and 2005, showing that the government elected in 2005 was not representative of 78% of the electorate. Other disadvantages of this model of government are that candidates must be either very wealthy or represent a political party to have any real chance of being elected; a system which can exclude the majority of the electorate. Also, elections every few years often allow insufficient time for the fruition of new policies. Conversely, due to the rapid pace of change in modern society, manifestos of the political parties can be out of date for most of the term of a government. In this scenario, governments, with few exceptions, such as that of Switzerland, which is extremely successful, seem reluctant to utilise referenda to consult with the electorate. In addition there can be abrupt changes in policy when a new governing party is elected. The most damning criticism of party politics, which is particularly relevant in a spiritually evolving society, is that members of parties are frequently expected to vote against their conscience. Surely, in a true democracy, it would be preferable to allow open voting on all issues and representatives should work together, as a team, taking joint responsibility for policies and outcomes, thus being truly accountable to their electorates in both the short and long term.

Egotism is apparent in all levels of government worldwide and particularly in the European Economic Community. Public servants act as if they are in charge, issuing masses of rules and regulations, which have never been debated with the majority of the people. This philophy of 'we know best' is causing immense frustration, as people have little and reducing influence over major factors affecting their lives. For example if they were consulted during the creation of the rules and regulations, then the advance of surveillance techniques may be acceptable but in the current scenario it is totally unacceptable. We may well ask who decided to apply this system. Who has access to the information? What is its purpose? This whole scenario paints a very gloomy picture of the type of controlling society described by Aldous Huxley, in *Brave New World* and George Orwell in *1984*. Our freedom of choice is being taken away on the pretext of assuring our personal security.

In many countries centralised bureaucracy is expanding rapidly in an uncontrolled manner, frustrating development and demoralising previously vibrant and healthy societies, rendering them ineffective, uneconomic, and impotent. Centralised bureaucracy has become the leader rather than the server. Whereas traditionally good leaders have inspired us with their vision and enthusiasm and carried us forward together to oppose oppression and create better societies, this change is taking place by stealth, like a creeping paralysis, undermining principles based on good will and commonsense.

Many governments have stressed the economic advantages of privatising public services - relatively high capital investment being obtained at minimum cost. From the point of view of the service receivers, the major disadvantages are that the objectives of privatised service providers are so different from the requirements of service receivers. The former surely wish to make the maximum profit for the minimum investment, whereas the latter want the best possible service at the lowest possible cost. Also, it is very difficult to discuss complaints or policy decisions with privatised service providers as they tend to utilise call centres for communication with their customers, in which the operators have very limited knowledge, often reading from a set script. This type of system offers no personal service, as the caller can be passed to a different officer on each call, necessitating an explanation of the whole issue again and again. The motto of most companies used to be that the customer comes first but this is clearly no longer true. Governments claim that privatisation has provided much more efficient services than those previously experienced in nationally managed industries. The contrary viewpoint is that nationalisation, certainly in the UK, was affected by militant unionism and very poor management techniques. If we were setting up a service providing body in this day and age, we would employ experienced professional managers and reward them appropriately for their efforts. The obvious advantage of a nationalised concern is that its operating policies could be democratically derived.

Ideally, the planet's resources, including food, raw materials and technology, should be available to the whole of humanity, when it can reasonably be argued, there would be sufficient sustenance for all. Unfortunately the operation of many large national and global corporations and governments in effect frustrate this utopian philosophy, a minority having control over vital raw materials due to historic, geographic or commercial criteria. For example the wealth of many global corporations, which control the manufacture and distribution of products such as oil, food, weapons, chemicals, pharmaceuticals and services such as banking and insurance, often exceeds that of some of the smaller nations, giving them immense and disproportionate influence, over world affairs because of special relationships with national governments. Also, there have been reports about some administrations, such as the European Economic Community, hoarding or even destroying vast stocks of produce in order to maintain price levels, actions which are difficult to justify in the context of a large proportion of the world's population suffering from starvation. Certainly, there are difficulties in distributing resources to remote communities due to inadequate transport facilities. In addition, it is alleged that some despotic rulers in Third

World countries like those in Africa may hinder distribution purposely for personal gain.

Another disturbing trend is that large supermarkets, although highly efficient and profitable companies, are forcing down prices from their suppliers, including farmers, in order to maximise their profits. On the face of it, their success is well earned as they provide excellent product ranges changing the buying habits of people in all the developed nations. Unfortunately, this success is in effect removing the freedom of choice of their customers, by forcing local suppliers out of business, with the ultimate potential of creating monopolies. It is claimed, in chapter 18, that the maximum benefit, in terms of health and nutrition, can be obtained by eating food which is as near as possible to being freshly collected; an ideal which can rarely be achieved by large supermarkets, which import food from all over the world.

Benjamin Crème of 'Share International' purports that *'economies based on greed and competition can be regarded as forces of evil, being the greatest threat to this planet and are bringing our civilisation to the very verge of destruction'*.[27] We must not become complacent about a situation in which many of the world's population live in squalor and degradation and are suffering from malnutrition caused by pestilence and famine, whilst the most of the populations of the developed world live in relative luxury.

In a spiritually evolving global society, national, continental and global, elected and administrative institutions would still be essential parts of a better future but they would all have to utilise true democratic principles. What is required is not a 'New World Order' resembling a historic feudal kingdom but a global democratic society, based on the principles of liberty, equality and fraternity. As explained in this message channelled by Rita Eide: *'In order for this to be anything but an unrealised utopia, you have to attend to the changing consciousness of the world today.—Understand that if you stop fearing each other by your focus on theft and competition, or fearing lest the way you distribute your finances should become visible, then you may be willing to start anew with a fresh approach to building up a New World Federation of Unity'.*[28]

We have to encourage people to take responsibility for their own and their children's lives rather than to smother them with rules and regulations. In essence, people need to have a sense of governing themselves so that individual and group responsibility can grow. For example, in the European Economic Community there should be a review of Health and Safety legislation and its application to enable us to regain the freedom to make mistakes, take risks and learn from this experience rather than being treated like children in a nanny state. *'There has to be a sense of joy in doing the right thing rather than punitive action for doing the wrong thing'.*[19] There should also be a debate about the application of social and political correctness, which has been introduced without consultation with majorities and is undermining principles of freewill and commonsense. Other improvements which could be considered are that public services should, as far as practically possible, be controlled by directly elected bodies, as exemplified in the USA. Also, we could emulate some countries in which the parliaments work restricted hours to discourage the production of masses of unnecessary regulations. Another useful innovation might be that a proportion of candidates should have appropriate business experience; a seemingly rarity amongst the new breed of career politicians. In addition, the role of employed public administrators, at all levels in society, should revert to that of public servant instead of public master. All legislation, which has been derived from non democratic sources, should be progressively repealed and reviewed. An example of European legislation, which should be reviewed, is the 'Human Rights Act', which, in its application, has resulted in chaos.

Governments and their associated bureaucracies created this problem and will inevitably endeavour to retain their power base and personal security, but these positive changes are already taking place and will continue inexorably. In any case, highly motivated activists could help to precipitate positive changes in many different ways; such as by organising petitions, marches, civil disobedience; as very successfully practiced by Mahatma Ghandi and the suffragettes. Another possible action is the utilisation of the internet to create democratic networking; enabling debating, voting and lobbying on line. Such a system has already been created, specifically to enable communities throughout Scotland to have greater influence over factors affecting their lives[29], but it could be adopted by any group which wishes to network. The vision statement of the Scottish group called *Scottish Communities Together*, which I founded in 2004, is copied below:

> *Our vision is about enabling citizens to have a timely and effective influence over the factors which affect people's lives.*
>
> *Scottish Communities Together (SCT) is established*

specifically to advance education, citizenship and community development.

'—By 2012, SCT will be providing citizens and communities across Scotland with effective means to influence factors affecting their lives.

All community councils in Scotland will have the opportunity to use their own interactive websites which will:

Enable members of their community to debate issues, which citizens consider to be important.

Enable local community councils to interact with other community councils in Scotland, deciding lists of key issues in priority order and then debating them and lobbying the relevant authorities for appropriate changes in policy.

Enable the authorities, whether local councils, service agencies or the Scottish, UK or European Parliaments and their administrations, to listen and respond to informed community views which can influence timely decisions.

'Scottish Communities Together' will be supporting democracy that inspires community engagement: the people speak and decisions are made. There will be no bar to access influence through the local democratic process.

As a result, Scotland will be regarded as an exemplar of community-led internet democracy'.

17

ARE WE RESPONSIBLE FOR CLIMATE CHANGE?

Major debates are taking place about climate change, which might ultimately endanger the world. One explanation is that global warming and cooling are natural phenomena, which take place at regular short and long term intervals; for example approximately every 50,000 years with the next occurrence being overdue. Accordingly we must learn to adapt to changing circumstances over which we have no control. Another theory is that the earth's ecosystem is designed to maintain equilibrium in its own way, accordingly, there is no need for us to address the issue as nature will maintain balance, without our help. This seems logical, but could it equate to massive earth changes, such as more earthquakes, tsunamis and volcanic eruptions? Other mechanisms which the planet can utilise to maintain balance are expansion or contraction of vegetation, cloud cover and the polar ice caps relative to the proportion of greenhouse gases in the atmosphere, but do they all equate to climate change? Scientists have now accepted that the earth maintains equilibrium by regulating physical, biological and chemical factors. This natural balancing system of the planet was named the 'Gaia Theory' in 1972. It is now generally agreed that global warming is accelerating due to the excessive use of fossil fuels, during and since the Industrial Revolution and we need to urgently address this issue to avoid a major calamity. This viewpoint is supported by our current observations of climate extremes, such as record rain fall, high winds, hot summers and the rapid melting of polar ice caps.

A further explanation is that our way of life conflicts with natural laws, which in the course of endless evolution destroy anything, which is out of harmony with them.[13a] The particular laws associated with global warming are related to the essence of Jesus' teachings as expressed in the Beatitudes and The Lords Prayer, which were discussed in chapter 11. When we break the law of love we place emphasis on our separation, resulting in wars, terrorism and predatory competition forcing local suppliers out of business and creating monopolies. Similarly, in disregarding the laws of cause and effect and karma, we tend to become selfish, materialistic and egotistical, states of mind epitomised by the continuing use of fossil fuels, driven by vested interest, the indiscriminate destruction of the rainforests. There is also a tendency of focussing on the accumulation of wealth and possessions, a state of mind epitomised by 'I am what I have', encouraged by the advertising industry. Similarly people can become obsessed with their personal appearance; a trend utilised by the advertising, fashion and other industries encouraging us to purchase in excess and throw away serviceable items. Other contributory factors are the utilisation of non-bio-degradable packaging by manufacturers of all kinds of goods and designed and built-in obsolescence of manufactured products, which creates continuous demand and excessive waste. These issues are being debated by 'The Intergovernmental Panel on Climate Change', governments and in the media, many nations making genuine efforts to reduce their carbon footprints but unilateral action is essential to reverse these negative trends.

The law of balance is particularly relevant to the problem of climate change, which is in part the effect of our living planet endeavouring to maintain equilibrium despite the excesses of the human race. It is demonstrated when a block of ice is placed in a warm room it melts, and the resulting water eventually reaches room temperature. Those who are working in harmony with this spiritual law will only take what they need from nature to survive and be reasonably comfortable. It is exemplified by nature staying in balance with the seasons; growing in the spring and summer and closing down in the autumn and winter, this cyclic pattern being beautifully expressed in the following poem, which is a mini philosophy of life:

> *Gladness after sorrow,*
> *Sunshine after rain,*
> *Harvest after seedtime,*
> *Comfort after pain*
> *Blossoms after pruning*
> *Victory after strife*
> *As the way of nature*
> *So the way of life.*
> Anon

Another aspect of imbalance in our society, is the distribution of wealth between the developed an un-developed nations; the former having in excess of 80% of the wealth and the latter less than 20% ratios.

When we break this law, our lives are out of balance with nature, typically resulting in the drive by developed and developing nations for continuous economic growth, which is contrary to the cyclic patterns of nature. This is particularly worrying as we observe the Eastern nations, such as China and India, following in our footsteps with their own industrial revolutions, typified by the indiscriminate use of resources and the pollution of the waterways and oceans by inadequate sewerage systems, killing off plankton, which is fundamentally essential to the maintenance of the planet's eco-system. This is especially relevant to urban communities, which create relatively large volumes of sewage and waste. Conversely, similar materials, in less volume, can be absorbed in rural environments, without upsetting the eco-system.

Another recent innovation is the replacement of well tried agricultural practices, such as crop rotation, by forced growth, utilising man made fertilisers, which are destroying the top soil and resulting in food lacking in mineral salts, which are essential to health. This malpractice is a short term expediency, which will inevitably result in the karmic consequence of fertile land being changed into deserts. The planet's energy field and centres are also being damaged by uneducated design of buildings and mining practice, a subject discussed in chapter 24 by David Cowan, in an article entitled *Ley Lines, Ill Health and Spirit Lines*, which he wrote for this book.[30a]

Global warming and climate change, which threaten the survival of our civilisation, are the karmic consequences of living out of harmony with these natural laws. As we evolve spiritually, our attitudes and actions will tend to modify. Our perception of separation will change into an experience of oneness and togetherness, leading to peace and co-operation. Selfishness and materialism will typically transform into the sharing of resources, much greater focus on finding alternative forms of energy and products being designed and built to last. Self interest and egotism, focussing on possession, wealth and appearance will ultimately evolve into expanded awareness and spiritual enlightenment. Excessive consumption of resources will give rise to moderation; people only taking what they need. Also, in the realisation that survival is more important than economic growth, well tried, traditional farming practices, such as crop rotation will be re-introduced. Thus the balance of nature will ultimately be restored ensuring the future of our civilisation.

Many of these issues could conceivably be addressed by encouraging more people to adopt a rural lifestyle, particularly if major population reduction occurs due to global warming, as predicted by Professor James Lovelock[31]. The trend towards urbanisation commenced in the Industrial Revolution, as people who had previously been employed on the land moved into close proximity with the factories. Whereas during feudal times the majority of people worked and lived in rural areas, during the industrial age the proportions changed; the majority then and now living in urban areas. Other factors which have tended to reduce rural populations are the centralisation of food production, as small farms have been replaced by much larger, more efficient operations, utilising far more sophisticated equipment and less labour.

Circumstances are changing; the decline in industry in many countries results in high unemployment in large towns and cities and the development of a dependency culture, which is detrimental to the unemployed and unfair to tax payers. Also in an urban environment, there are shortages of fresh air, fresh food and sunshine with difficulty in experiencing peace, harmony and happiness, so accordingly urban life can lead to both physical and mental ill health. A rural lifestyle has the potential of enabling people and communities to re-gain influence over many aspects of their lives, reversing the tendency for centralisation of policy and decision making, which is demoralising society. For example, rural communities could be encouraged and helped to set up their own power supply for individual houses and whole communities, utilising wind and water power and other forms of renewable energy, making them independent of the large privatised utilities. They could also grow food, rich in mineral salts and life energy, utilising crop rotation and/or hydroponics, providing local employment and reducing the need for food products to be transported long distances to central warehouses of large super-markets. This food could be distributed locally utilising re-usable containers. Food which still had to be sourced from elsewhere could be purchased in bulk, stored and distributed locally by farm and village shops. Communities could, as appropriate, manage local sewerage plants, very considerably reducing pollution of waterways, as the relatively low volume of pollutants could be treated without endangering the local eco-structure. They could also take control of their own water supply, utilising modern technology, asking for help and advice from a central service, only as necessary. Similarly, they could carry out maintenance of local facilities such as toilets, park lands and cemeteries, having the equipment and labour to cut grass and clear snow and recycle waste materials by applying the principles of permaculture, thus making it illogical to transport waste materials to large towns, when it could conceivably be organised locally, providing employment and reducing fuel consumption. It would also be beneficial to organise pastimes locally, in some ways reverting to the type of community life which was common before and just after the Second World War. This would help in the building of community spirit and team work and reduce dependency on ready made entertainment, such as TV, which has so many disadvantages.

Fundamental to this concept of a bottom up society is the need for communities to be represented by a new type of local council with elected members, which employs its own staff. Conceivably, groups of relatively small communities could operate under one umbrella body, which must be both morally and financially independent of the existing top down structure of councils and parliaments so that it can't be obliged to apply policies or measurements derived from a centralised bureaucracy, which waste time and effort and cause great frustration. Ideally it would need to have authority over all community issues, including service provision. An over-riding policy would be that all services will be provided as locally as possible, but it would comply with appropriate national policies and laws. Its finances could conceivable be provided by means of local taxation; central taxation being reduced proportionately. There would be no party politics, all debating and voting of elected representatives being derived from inner guidance. As previously suggested, national or even global networks of highly motivated rural communities could utilise the internet to very effectively lobby against many of the negative factors already discussed. The whole point is that a highly motivated self actualising society can best be organised by the people for the people. It can't be formed by decentralisation or devolution but by evolution from the bottom upwards. To encourage people to adopt a rural lifestyle, bold legislation will be necessary to allow communities to acquire all land both within and around their boundaries, to facilitate the re-creation of an agricultural society.

Colin Roxburgh expands on this theme of community futures in chapter 25, which was especially written for this book.

18

HEALING THE PLANET BY HEALING OURSELVES

Our planet is a living being, with a life energy field both within and around its physical body, its chakras being power points, which are connected by a network of ley lines and its energy field projecting out across the universe and meeting energy fields of other celestial bodies. This explains how the planets influence one another and their inhabitants, which incidentally is the basis of astrology, as opposed to astronomical phenomena.[5b] Unfortunately the life-energy field of our planet is being diminished by our life style, which is one of the causes of global warming, as explained in the last chapter. According to the *'Cosmic Law of Macrocosm and Microcosm'*, the whole is equivalent to the sum of the parts and therefore as we brighten and widen our individual auras by correct thoughts and actions, there will be a corresponding effect on the aura of the planet. The only person that we can really change is our self and as successively more people endeavour to improve themselves and take responsibility for their own health and happiness, there will be a corresponding effect on the well-being of society, which will be improved from the bottom upwards. However, in our society many people rely on their doctors for their state of health, rather than accepting personal responsibility.

Medical science has developed many wonderful treatments, which have greatly improved both the quality of life and the longevity of their patients. Advances in organ replacement and joints, quick diagnostic techniques, are now utilised by doctors for analysing blood and urine content. CAT scans, can provide a step by step picture down the spine or across the brain, pinpointing defects and enabling their repair. Numerous wonder drugs, such as penicillin and other antibiotics have been developed to help in the treatment of all kinds of conditions, such as tropical diseases, including smallpox, polio and malaria. However, orthodox medicine is based solely on healing the physical body (and mind), which can be discerned by our five senses. The thinking, in most developed countries, is that illnesses occur either due to inherited genetic defects or for reasons that could have been avoided by choosing a healthy lifestyle. For example, the fall in the number of deaths before the age of 65 from stroke, coronary heart disease and certain types of cancer can largely be attributed to a fall in the number of smokers and a better understanding of what makes a healthy diet.[32]

A contrary view is that illnesses occur because of mistakes that we have made either in previous lives or in our current life. Life is a school and we are students who have incarnated of our own freewill to learn lessons and face challenges to fulfil our life's purpose. If we are born with defects or disabilities, we should try to recognise that we chose this path for good reasons. If we suffer from illnesses or even have accidents, they can be regarded as lessons in life and we should endeavour to establish their purpose, because when we have truly learnt a particular lesson, we can move on to new lessons, challenges and experiences. If we fail to learn such a lesson, then similar experiences will keep recurring in this life or others until the lesson is learnt. Life is like a game of cards in which we should endeavour to play the hand that we have been dealt to the best of our ability. We are not victims-we are not having negative experiences due to bad luck; we made our own past and this affects our present and our future.

Many complementary therapists believe that the life energy field is the blueprint for the continual regeneration of cells and therefore defects in our aura will reproduce themselves in our body and mind. Conversely, if we can find out how to enhance and balance our energy field and its chakras, and those of others, we can considerably increase the opportunity for effective healing, enabling the physical body to heal itself. The majority of complementary therapies, some of which are described in Part V, are based on aspects of this thinking. For example, a bio-energy therapist locates blockages in the energy field, draws them out and balances the aura and a colour therapist utilises colours to strengthen and brighten the aura. Similarly, a Reiki healer channels universal life force energy into various parts of the body to re-energise various organs and injured areas with life energy. Our life energy field is also greatly affected by the type of food, drink and medicines that we consume. A very important characteristic of herbal remedies is that in their most potent form, they have retained the life force energy in suspension, because they are either freshly gathered or processed into drops, oils or ointments soon after collection. For example, it is claimed that the life energy of dew drops from leaves and petals are retained in the Bach Flower remedies and similarly that aromatherapy oils retain life force energy.

We would all like to be perfectly healthy and not have to consult with doctors or have to be treated in a hospital but we may or may not accept responsibility for our own health; regarding some illnesses as hereditary and others to be bad luck. We may also tend to seek the magic pill or miraculous treatment for our condition, rather than accepting personal responsibility and altering our lifestyle. This is one of the reasons for the success of the pharmaceutical industry which has developed in the last hundred years, and since the Second World War into a number of corporations, which have immense influence over health care throughout the global society. They invest a great deal of money in medical and scientific research to produce new products but many of their allopathic drugs result in unpleasant side effects, described as contra-indications. For example, phenacetin, a pain killer, which was included in over eighty compounds and marketed during the twentieth century, was banned after causing kidney and bladder disease. It was also linked with a potentially fatal children's disease, Reyes Syndrome, leading to all preparations containing the drug being withdrawn in 1986 for children under 12.[33] Similarly, it is alleged that aspirin has been responsible for over 7000 hospital admissions each year in Great Britain alone because of problems with stomach and intestinal bleeding leading to anaemia. In her book, *Death by Modern Medicine*, Carolyn Dean claims that 7 to 8 million people suffered death by medicine between 1990 and 2000; some of these being prescribed Vioxx, and Celebrex, and others committing suicide after taking Prozac.[34] A prime objective of pharmaceutical companies must be to maximise profits and increase their market share, which seems reasonable, but these reports on contra-indications lead to a serious ethical consideration of whether sufficient trials were completed before products were marketed. Another worrying issue is that medical practitioners have tended to become channels for the marketing pharmaceutical products, whereas there could conceivably be more effective holistic forms of treatment. One way in which sales are stimulated is by convincing people that some minor conditions such as constipation and indigestion require medical treatment, whereas they could be resolved by changes in diet. Similarly, many drugs address symptoms of illness, rather than their root causes. For example, the medical professions' treatment for backache is to provide painkillers, which hide the pain but do not cure the condition, a situation which can be risky, as the body has created the pain as a warning about excess exercise - rest perhaps being necessary. Similarly, various painkillers are used to alleviate the effects of headaches perhaps caused by over-consumption of alcohol and other drugs whereas the most effective treatment could be fresh air, exercise and drinking water, to clean out the system.

The medical establishment denies the effectiveness of many forms of complementary therapies, typified by their criticism in the media of treatments such as homoeopathy and acupuncture, sometimes writing off cures as either temporary remission or placebo effects. These views may be genuine, or, conversely such treatments may be regarded as serious competition, the general public being drawn to alternatives due to their loss of faith in orthodox medicines. In the fullness of time, many of the claims of complementary therapists will be accepted even by science, and this will result in a paradigm shift in medical theory and practice.

The medical establishment, including pharmaceutical companies, don't seem to have any understanding or appreciation of the existence of a light energy field, both inside and around the physical body, which are now scientifically demonstrable, and accordingly all their drugs are focussed on treating physical (and mental) illnesses and injuries, along with conditions caused by stress overload. Often when new herbal remedies are found or rediscovered, pharmaceutical chemists try to isolate their active molecules, possibly to guarantee supplies but also so that they can corner the market and increase profitability. They argue that patients could receive overdoses by taking herbal remedies and that the appropriate doses of their medicines can be controlled by their doctor's instructions 'take two pills, three times a day'. However, this procedure doesn't allow for variations in weight, build and metabolic rate of patients and is therefore flawed. Also, drugs which have been synthesised in this manner possess no life force energy, which is the most significant characteristic of many herbal remedies. An important consideration is that the molecules, which are isolated and synthesised, whilst minute, are still part of the material reality, which can be observed by our five senses utilising magnification devices. As we evolve spiritually, we will realise that many natural herbal remedies possess unique life energy field characteristics, which are their true essence and disappear soon after collection, rendering them relatively ineffective. It is also relevant to mention that humankind and other life forms were not designed to enable them to effectively metabolise chemicals.

It can be reasonably argued that the success of pharmaceutical companies is partially dependent on the continuation of illnesses rather than absolute cures; because if they managed to cure all illnesses, they would be redundant. In this context, we can understand why they deny the effectiveness of many new complementary treatments, which come to light, particularly if they are cheap and effective in treating a variety of common illnesses. For example, Dr F Batmanghelidj, known as 'Dr Batman', a British educated physician, made a revolutionary discovery, whilst a political prisoner under sentence of death in a crowded Tehran prison. He gave a man suffering from severe abdominal pain, associated with peptic ulcer disease, two glasses of water and within minutes, his ulcer pain became less severe and disappeared completely after eight minutes. He went on to treat over three thousand stress-induced peptic ulcer cases with just tap water. Over many years, he treated numerous ailments, such as heart disease, asthma, sleep disorders, diabetes and obesity with water and appropriate doses of sea salt.[35] The reason for telling this story is to claim that such a cure would be an anathema to pharmaceutical companies, as they would lose control of the situation; masses of potential drug users turning to water and salt. Certainly, one could wonder whether Dr Batman's claims have been investigated by the medical establishment, if they are true, they could bring about a major breakthrough in treatment of diseases, at virtually no cost.

Another most controversial aspect of this scientific research is the use of defenceless animals for trials on new drugs and treatments. The karmic consequences of ignoring one's inner guidance or conscience by continuing with this type of torture must be most severe. It doesn't really matter whether one is an employee or an employer, one must refuse to carry out these despicable experiments, as they are contrary to the cosmic Law of Love. We are the custodians of all life on earth and it is therefore our role to treat all God's creatures with love and kindness.

History provides an interesting perspective of health and healing; natural therapies and herbal remedies have been utilised for over 10,000 years in various cultures, such as Indian, Egyptian, and Greek and by the Essene brotherhood of Jesus. The following fragment from *The Essene Gospel of Peace*.[13b] supports this theme; '*And in this manner did the Brothers teach the Holy Law to them who would hear it, and it is said they did marvellous things, and healed the sick and afflicted with diverse grasses and wondrous uses of sun and water*'. Natural healing practices were used for thousands of years, the situation was changed by two main developments. Firstly, in the middle ages over zealous Christians, persecuted and even killed off those who practised, what we now call complementary therapists, branding them as witches, and a great deal of knowledge was lost. Secondly, science from the eighteenth century onwards, led to the evolution of modern medicine and its professional institutions, with the requirement of professional qualifications for its practitioners, thus excluding and marginalising those who practiced natural healing.

Notwithstanding the fact that most complementary therapies and alternative remedies have been used for a very long time, many having been rediscovered only recently, the orthodox medical establishment, which has been in existence for a relatively short time, tends to ignore or ridicule them, which is unfortunate as much knowledge and experience is being under-utilised. Instead, medical scientists should work with complementary therapists (and spiritual masters) to investigate healing therapies and endeavour to co-operate in finding the truth, for example by studying life energy fields, finding reliable ways of viewing these light energy patterns and colours and comparing these observation and descriptions by psychics. Also, the effects of various types of healing and the consumption of 'living' foods should be investigated.

In our lives, our ultimate aim must surely be to experience exceptional health, rather than suffering from degenerative diseases, such as arthritis and diabetes, which are primarily associated with lifestyles in developed countries. In this context, it is beneficial to study the lifestyles of various ancient civilisations, which are renowned for their health, strength and longevity. Edmund Bordeaux Szekely (EBS), who has reported that the members of the Essene brotherhood lived for an exceptionally long time, extracted appropriate information from the writings of the historian Josephus, Philo and other authors, about the lifestyle of the Essenes.[13c] He reported that they never ate meat, consuming vegetables and fruit in moderation and taking no other drink but rainwater or the juice of fruits, living chiefly on the fruits of trees and bushes, and on seeds and vegetables. Also, they ate in solemn silence, thanking God in prayer before and after meals. Their chief collective occupations were agriculture and arboriculture, in which they had great skill. Their morning baths were followed by special breathing and gymnastic exercises. They never let themselves be overcome by anger, hatred vengeance or ill-will, being champions of faith, truth and honesty. In addition, they had profound knowledge of the art of healing and were acquainted with the medicinal herbs and plants, which they prepare as medicine for man and beasts. They were opposed, without exception, to life in big cities; always living in the country and by lakes or rivers. Generally these people lived to an extraordinarily old age. According to Josephus their life and principles were also practised by Pythagoreans and Stoics.

Another good example reported is the Hunza people, who are indigenous to the Hunza Valley, which is 2438 metres above sea level and is situated in northern Pakistan, in the Himalayas. It is claimed that the Hunza have a life expectancy of 90 years, some living in excess of 120 years. They maintain good health throughout their lives, with no occurrence of cancer or hereditary illnesses and with no known cases of obesity. Hunzas of all ages, including elders, work seven days a week, their diet being based on unprocessed food, many fruits, vegetables, whole grains such as buckwheat and millet, mulberry, figs, almonds, walnuts and apricots.

The Book of Living Foods by Edmond Bordeaux Szekely[13e] reports that all the great civilisations of the past, at the height of their power, were strongly rooted in agricultural societies whose citizens ate the simplest of natural foods. Typically, the health and longevity of the citizens of Greece and Rome began to deteriorate only when exotic imported foods started to be popular. In its early days of splendour the staples of the Greek diet were figs and milk, while the fantastic stamina of the Roman warrior was attributed to whole-wheat bread and onions. The main food of the Mongols, led by Genghis Khan, who conquered all of Asia and most of Europe, was sour milk. There is nothing magical in any of these foods; they simply ate what was readily available in its crude natural state. The Romans, Greeks and Mongols were not nutritional experts. They only ate what nature provided, thereby ensuring the maximum vitamin, mineral and enzyme content. Of course, the advent of large cities with their population generally isolated from a natural source of fresh foods makes it more difficult to eat as simply and naturally as they did, however it is possible for each and every person, regardless of age or physical disposition, to choose and prepare simple, natural foods, minimising their consumption of processed foods. It was Hippocrates, the father of modern medicine, who said, 'Common sense is the rarest of commodities'. In the field of nutrition, common sense is reflected in the sane, scientific use of natural foods, prepared in a simple and wholesome way.

So let's now consider the main points of all these examples of good practice, which have ensured a long and healthy life, and reflect on whether they could be applied in our society. We are, to a large extent, responsible for our own health and as successively more people realise and accept this fact and take appropriate action, it will have a corresponding effect on society. We are light beings and our health depends on our receiving light energy in what we consume and from our environment. Accordingly, we need to eat food, which is freshly collected and as raw as possible and we need to spend as much time as possible in the fresh air and sunshine, preferably by living in the countryside. We should reduce our consumption of processed food as far as reasonably possible. Food should be prepared with the minimum of cooking, because cooking kills 'living food'. Different methods of cooking vary in their effect, but microwaves kill food instantly. Similarly, freezing completely removes life force energy from food and drink. We should take very regular exercise, recent advice for those with a sedentary lifestyle is that there should be a minimum of 30 minutes of aerobic exercise, at least three days every week. Aerobic exercise is such that the operation of the lungs and heart is pushed to a maximum level, which can be sustained for about 30 minutes, depending on the physical condition of the individual. This could be achieved by walking up-hill, jogging, cycling, swimming. It is important that such exercise is stimulating and enjoyable, not becoming boring or seen as a chore. Manual work should be carried out in the fresh air, in a happy and carefree atmosphere (not forced labour, as in the Industrial Revolution). We must be most careful to ensure the necessary intake of mineral salts, vitamins and enzymes to maintain health. This is particularly relevant to the consumption of fruit and vegetables, which may look wholesome but their growth has been forced by the application of fertilisers and also they have been protected by pesticides. Organic fruit and vegetables can be difficult to find and so we must investigate their source and cultivation methods. The only way in which we can guarantee that food is wholesome is by growing it ourselves.

There are a number of benefits claimed by supporters of a vegetarian diet. Vegetarian food is more likely to contain all necessary nutritious elements such as mineral salts, enzymes and vitamins. Also, if consumed soon after harvesting, it will be 'living food', exhibiting a powerful aura, an essential constituent for good health. Statistics produced by The Vegetarian Society (UK) Ltd, in Figure 9, shows the

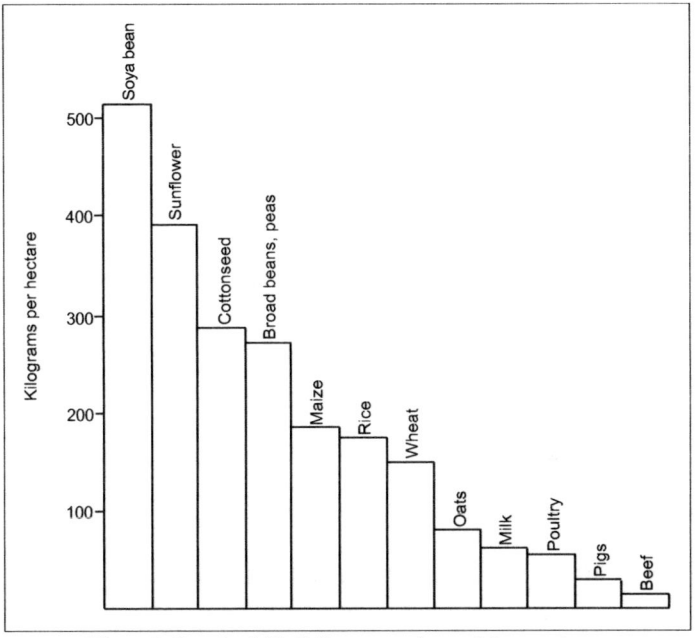

*Figure 9. Protein yields [kilogram per hectare] from various crops.
Source: The Vegetarian Society [UK] Ltd.*

protein yield per hectare from various crops. Effectively, vegetable products have to be consumed by animals in order to produce meat, which is a highly wasteful way of utilising land.

Practising Christians should consider the following words of Jesus about killing and eating meat, [13b] *'Thou shalt not kill, for life is given to all by God, and that which God has given, let no man take away. For I tell you truly, from one Mother proceeds all that lives upon the earth. Therefore, he who kills, kills his brother. And from him will the Earthly Mother turn away, and will pluck from him her quickening breasts. And he will be shunned by her angels, and Satan will have his dwelling in his body. And the flesh of slain beasts in his body will become his tomb. For I tell you truly, he who kills, kills himself, and who so eats the flesh of slain beasts, eats of the body of death. For in his blood every drop of their blood turns to poison; in his breath their breath to stink; in his flesh their flesh to boils; in his bones, their bones to chalk, in his bowels their bowels to decay; in his eyes their eyes to scales; in his ears their ears to waxy issue. And their death will become his death. For only in the service of your Heavenly Father are your debts of seven years forgiven in seven days. But Satan forgives you nothing and you must pay him for all. 'Eye for eye, tooth for tooth, hand for hand, foot for foot; burning for burning; wound for wound; life for life; death for death. For the wages of sin is death. Kill not, neither eat the flesh of your innocent prey, lest you become the slaves of Satan'.* Jesus goes on to suggest a vegetarian diet, including herb-bearing seeds, the fruit of trees and the milk from animals.

Perhaps the Church Fathers, at the time of the Roman Emperor Constantine, decided that a vegetarian diet was not a saleable product in the meat-eating Roman Empire. Similarly, it seems probable that they concocted a version of Christianity, which could be acceptable to the Roman people by adopting the birth date of Mythras of 25th December and the concept of the virgin birth, which was attributed to Isis. Mythranism and the worship of the Egyptian God, Isis, were popular religions in Rome, at that time.

Some people, for example Eskimos, used to have no choice but to eat meat and fish but their lifespan was relatively short. If you must eat meat, then consider very carefully how and where the animal was reared. For example, did it live a natural and happy life? Was it fed growth hormones and antibiotics, which could be passed on through the food chain? Think very carefully about these issues because it is quite obvious that the main criteria of the large supermarkets is profit; the health of their customers being a very secondary consideration. It is often said that 'we are what we eat' and there is some truth in this but really we are much more than that. It is more relevant to think that we are the cumulative product of all the decisions we have made and actions we have taken, in this and previous lives, and the decision on what food to eat and to provide to our children is important in this context. Killing animals and eating their flesh creates negative karma, which will have to be repaid in this or future lives. If these animals were cruelly treated in life and death, then these negative vibrations will be passed on to the consumer.

A very good practice is to bless food, either by prayer or utilising a healing technique, such as Reiki, which can re-energise food. Similarly, if we pause before our meal and think of the animal which gave its life for us then consciously give it thanks for providing us with food.

A number of articles on complementary healing, which have been especially written for this book are presented in part V.

19

EDUCATION BASED ON UNIVERSAL LOVE

Our society is deeply perplexed by many negative tendencies and in particular those affecting impressionable young people, such as substance abuse, vandalism, theft, violence and bullying. One reason for this is a breakdown in family and community life, particularly influenced by TV, videos, computer games and the like, which can damage mental and physical health if over used. In the past children played outside with other children much more often than they do now, for example in the parks. We found ways of providing them with creative pastimes but it's now so much easier to utilise these ready made forms of entertainment with most parents both at work. Neither does unemployment always generate an emotional state conducive to interacting positively with children. Another reason is peer pressure, combined with the rebellious nature of youth which may lead to experimentation with drugs, regardless of the numerous stories of destroyed lives. Money is required to buy drugs, leading to crime. Drug abuse is often about low self-esteem. That is why the SSEHV (Sathya Sai Education in Human Values) programme, which is described in this chapter, cures problems at the root cause by raising self esteem and helping young people make better value choices. Other reasons for this trend are changing norms and expectations in our multi-cultural and multi-racial society and a lack of self respect resulting from a sense of helplessness due to neither parents nor their children having sufficient influence over factors affecting their lives. A further most important cause is misguided legislation aimed at improving the situation but having the reverse effect by undermining personal responsibility. Surely, we need to encourage people to take responsibility for their own behaviour and that of their young children, but how can we bring this about?

Present day education tends to emphasise academic achievement above good character or, 'filling the head with information, emptying it out onto the examination paper and coming away empty headed'.

Children up to about the age of seven are genetically programmed to accept what they are told by parents and teachers as there is insufficient time for them to learn by trial and error.[18] It is therefore essential that we teach them true values at the earliest possible age, to provide a firm foundation for their later education. To help bring this about a teaching programme based on five human values, including universal love, has been written. It is based on a philosophy of Sathya Sai Baba, who is India's foremost educationalist and social reformer, and whose entire life has been devoted to helping society. This SSEHV programme is designed to bring back fundamental, basic principles into homes and schools, and is being implemented with much success in many countries around the world.[36] As the children, whose education is based on this system mature they tend to become self actualising, taking the lead in society which inevitably changes for the better. People are encouraged to seek guidance from within, to be prompted by their conscience and to follow their hearts. To quote Sathya Sai,

'If human values take root in the educational system, the emerging individuals will have the following attributes: they will want peace and justice in the world that acknowledges the rule of law and in which no individual or nation will live in fear; freedom and self reliance to be available to all; the dignity and work of every person to be recognised and safeguarded; all people to be given an opportunity to achieve their best in life; and they will seek equality before the law and the equality of opportunity for all'.

SSEHV is a self-development programme designed for children and young people everywhere. The programme has a multi-cultural and multi-faith approach and has been developed and culturally adapted for use by all countries in the world. It is designed to help the young to be in touch with their own feelings and nurture awareness of the qualities within themselves which form good character and behaviour, not at dictating the actions of individuals, but rather to offer them a secure base from which they may arrive at their own informed decisions. The objective is to develop human values in young people so that they can live life to their fullest potential and share and contribute to the general welfare of the local and global community

Children are shown, by various methods that love in writing and speech is the truth, love in action is right conduct and non-violence or non-violation of oneself, of others, or society, of all forms of life. The effect of love is peace – peace of mind, peace in the home, peace between nations and peace on earth. The entire programme is based on these five human values of love, truth, right conduct, non-violence and peace. These are taught in schools, preschools, after-school clubs, etc. through the five components of silent sitting, story telling, group singing, role-play and theme for the week.

Silent Sitting (SS): these are guided visualisation exercises used at the start of a lesson when the children sit quietly for a few moments; typically beginning with less than two minutes and gradually increasing the time - depending upon the age of the children - up to four or five minutes. These types of relaxation exercises are now becoming more popular in schools and SS fits in with exercises such as 'Brain Gym'. The substantial benefits derived have been demonstrated by the research carried out at the Universities of Fehr in Cologne, Germany, Shaw & Kolb in Texas, USA and the Chulalongkorn in Thailand. These include improved reaction times and memory[37]. An experiment was carried out at Abrams University of California, in which three groups of students were tested on their ability to remember. The first group had not learnt to control the mind by SS, the second group had practised SS for a period of one year and the third had practised SS for two years. The experiment showed that the first group was able to remember 40% of information, the second group 60% and the third group 70%. It has also been demonstrated that silent sitting calms the minds of children making them quieter in the classroom, and, also more receptive to learning.

Story Telling: children love stories and will listen intently if they are told with feeling and meaning. Each story contains one or more of the values, and always ends on a happy note, where the 'goodie' is always the hero or heroine. Stories should be chosen which teach about life, the child's identity and their place in society. For example, the following story, called 'The Slippery Slope', addresses the human value of 'peace, the theme being that kindness brings peace

THE SPIRITUAL EVOLUTION OF SOCIETY

of mind, related values being faithfulness, gratitude, self-acceptance, harmony and understanding[38]:

'Thomas and Dafydd were friends and were in the same class together. When Dafydd had his ninth birthday, he invited most of the class to his party. Thomas was having a great time dancing with his girlfriend Sian, but Dafydd was jealous. Halfway through the party Dafydd played a trick on Thomas, he put a huge spider down his back! (That poor spider!) Now Thomas had already told Dafydd how scared of spiders he was, so it was really unkind of Dafydd to do this to him. He was so frightened that he cried, shouted and danced around looking really daft but he couldn't help it. He was so scared that his heart felt as if it would jump out of his body! Thomas was glad when the party finished and he could go home. On Monday he had to face the whole class and, worst of all, Sian. He felt so embarrassed that he felt sick. He had to keep swallowing to keep down the really nervous feeling that he had. Dafydd laughed at him and called him 'Chicken'. He made his arms flap up and down like the wings of a chicken and he made clucking noises. Thomas was starting to feel very upset, until he caught sight of Sian who smiled at him. That somehow made him feel much better about himself.

About a week later Sian and Thomas were walking up the 'Slippery Slope' together. This was a steep part of the mountain just behind Thomas's house. His mum would watch them from her kitchen window sliding down on plastic bags. It was brilliant! It was great except for the fact that there was a big drop at the bottom. If you were clever you could steer either left or right to avoid it. But if you weren't very good at it you would go right over the edge straight into the brambles - OUCH!!!

As Thomas and Sian walked past the brambles and trees they heard someone crying, a sad whimpering cry. They peered into the brambles and saw a round white face covered in dirt, tears and scratches staring back at them. Guess who it was? It was Dafydd! Now I think if I had been Thomas and Sian, I might have laughed at him or even been tempted to leave him there with his bottom stuck in the bushes. But Thomas stretched down to help him. Sian pulled the brambles away from Dafydd's face while Thomas pulled until Dafydd was standing on the slope. He looked down at his feet, because he was ashamed of how spiteful he had been. Do you know, Thomas never told anyone about Dafydd crying or how he helped him? And now the first two boys to run into the yard together at break-time are always Dafydd and Thomas. Dafydd is very lucky to have a friend like Thomas to whom he had been unkind but who, even so, could be a good friend to him in return.

Questions

1 How did you feel when you heard this story?

2 Why do you think Dafydd was unkind to Thomas?

3 Have you ever been embarrassed about something you have done?

4 Do you think Thomas was right to help Dafydd even though Dafydd had been very unkind to him?

5 Why didn't Thomas tell anyone that Dafydd had been crying?

6 What lesson did Dafydd learn?'

Group Singing - this is a way of involving the children by helping them to relax, enjoy music and possibly discover that they can sing. Each song contains a value, relating to the story told, or a related value.

Role Playing - this helps to build confidence in children, helps them to work as a group, have good fun and is also a means of involving the values in action. Children like to act and the 'sillier' the game the more likely they are to remember.

Theme of the Week - this is when one value is upheld for the entire week and emphasis is placed on that value. The use of posters around the classroom as reminders is useful. This exercise can be very valuable for children, and is a good way of learning the values. Examples of the meaning of each value, which can be drawn out of the children during discussions, are listed below[36]:

Love - affection, care, compassion, consideration, devotion, empathy, forgiveness, friendship, generosity, kindness, patience, sacrifice, selflessness, service, sharing, sympathy, thoughtfulness, tolerance.

Truth - accuracy, fairness, fearlessness, honesty, integrity, justice, purity, self-analysis, self awareness, sincerity, enquiry, trust, word and deed.

Right Conduct - self-help skills, such as care of possessions, diet, hygiene, modesty, posture, self reliance, tidy appearance, social skills, such as good behaviour, manners and relationships, helpfulness, not wasting and ethical skills, such as, courage, dependability, duty, efficiency, ingenuity, initiative, perseverance, punctuality, resourcefulness, respect for all, responsibility and a code of conduct.

Non-violence includes psychological skills- benevolence, concern for others, consideration, co-operation, forbearance, forgiveness, happiness, loyalty, morality, social skills- appreciation of other cultures and religions, brotherhood and sisterhood, care of the environment, citizenship, equality, harmlessness, respect for property and social justice.

Peace includes attention, calm concentration, contentment, dignity, discipline, equanimity, faithfulness, gratitude, happiness, harmony, humility, inner-silence, optimism, patience, reflection, self-acceptance/control/discipline/esteem/respect, sense control, surrender, understanding and virtue.

The programme is available to all schools in every country, is non-denominational, and is free of charge. All teachers and interested persons can be instructed in the method of implementing these values by fully trained persons who give of their time on a voluntary basis. In the UK there are a number of manuals available, suitable for children of various ages. This programme does not interfere with the school curriculum, and can in fact make teaching easier for teachers. Its aim is not only to educate children for a career in living, but to build a good character for life.

Application of the Programme

There are a number of ways in which the programme can be taught in schools. For example, the 'Direct Method' is a series of separate lessons in 'Personal, Social and Health Education or Citizenship'. Here the lessons can be linked to other curriculum areas, such as religious education, English, story times and assemblies.

Values can be integrated into curriculum subjects, for example when a teacher is teaching young children arithmetic, any negative aspect can be expressed in a positive manner; for instance, the teacher might say *'A farmer had twelve sheep and someone came along and stole five of them, how many did he have left?'*.

Alternatively, this can be explained as *'A farmer had twelve sheep; his neighbour had none so he gave him five of his sheep. How many did he have left?'.* The value being explained by this story is 'love', with a related value of 'sharing'.

The main emphasis in teaching values is by example and experiment rather than by academic studies, which is very challenging and certainly is not an easy option for the teacher. Everyday events occurring in the classroom can be used directly to illustrate the values; for example, by discussing the differing types of conduct within a group and realising the effect that one person has on another. The programme is most effective when training is given, not only to teachers, but to the entire staff of a school so that the child is surrounded by value conscious adults; the whole school is involved in the programme, which becomes the whole ethos of the school. The ultimate method of achieving this ideal is by setting up special 'Sathya Sai Schools', one such school is in the UK in Leicester, but there are numerous similar schools throughout the world.

An article, especially written for this book by Lesley-Ann Patrick, who is the founder and headmistress of a school in St Andrews, Scotland, which utilises SSEHV is presented in chapter 30.

PART V

COMPLEMENTARY ARTICLES

20

INTRODUCTION

The aim of this book is to provide a simple but comprehensive guide for people wishing to embark on their own spiritual journey towards enlightenment. This is undoubtedly a most ambitious undertaking, which I believe can be facilitated by including this selection of articles written by colleagues involved in complementary therapies and other similar pursuits. I feel that this approach is preferable to basing it solely on my own knowledge and experience. For example, I am a Reiki healer but have not practiced regularly for some years, whereas Linda McCartney has started her own centre and is a current practioner. The articles are presented in order of my references to them throughout the book,

When I started to compose this introduction, I was trying vainly to find a common theme between all the articles. Later, having slept on it, I realised that the elusive theme was meditation, and in particular Transcendental Meditation (TM), which I learnt in 1975 and have practised regularly ever since. People, who meditate routinely, generally observe that life starts to flow in a positive way; in effect providing them with nature support, although the rich pattern of life is more easily understood from a historic perspective. Events that seem to be negative, at the time, may turn out to be positive, in retrospect.

My career was in the metallurgical and engineering industry and, as I progressed from being a metallurgist

JOURNEY TO PERFECTION

through various supervisory and management positions, in a number of companies, it became very stressful; particularly due to conflicts between management and militant unions. In 1975, after seeing an advert in a local paper, I decided to learn Transcendental Meditation (TM), although at the time it seemed to be very expensive; costing the equivalent of a weeks wages. This was a major turning point in my life, as TM provided me with a simple technique to deal with the problems associated with stress and also increased my energy, reaction times and in fact enhanced my performance in all my mental and physical activities. The TM teacher had explained that meditation often has a life changing effect and this certainly was so for me because soon afterwards an opportunity arose for me to realise a long term dream of starting my own company but it was in Dundee, 400 miles away. In the early months, I was commuting; only returning to our home in Worcestershire every two to three weeks and missing my family dreadfully, however the regular meditation helped me to cope. On one occasion, at the end of a meditation I had a very strange experience in which there was a loud noise, like an express train going through a tunnel, cascades of colour and light, my body gyrated like a cobra being charmed and waves of energy moved up my spine. I had no idea what was happening but the whole event was most exhilarating. My TM teacher later explained that this was an effect of the awakening of the kundalini; a female spiritual energy, located at the base of the spine, which, when appropriately stimulated, moves up through the energy centres eventually joining with male energy located in the head. I was recently introduced to a TM teacher, called David Walne, who has also practiced the TM Siddhi Technique and has kindly agreed to write an article for me, which is presented in chapter 23.

My life and career was disrupted again in 1982, when I parted from my fellow shareholders in our Dundee Company and my wife and I decided to buy a family hotel in a small village called Tyndrum located in the Central Highlands of Scotland. We were unfamiliar with hotels, except as guests, but had a great deal of business experience. We built up the hotel business over almost 20 years and, ignoring the advice of local business owners, decided not to close down in the off season, in fact remaining open continuously from 4th June 1982 to 31st October 2001, when we sold the business, with the intention of retiring. Our decision to stay open led to the employment of permanent staff, which eventually created a demand for low cost affordable housing. Other businesses also decided to stay open. Amongst other factors, this led to my interest in community regeneration and my being co-opted on to the local community council. Not long afterwards, in 1991, we formed the Strathfillan Community Council, to represent the two small villages of Crianlarich, Tyndrum, and surrounding area, and utilised a technique called 'Management by Objectives', which I had experienced during my career. The community council was so successful that in 1995, we were invited to take part in a community regeneration project, in partnership with Stirling Council, Scottish Homes and some consultants. In 1997 we started a company limited by guarantee, of charitable status, with great help, particularly from Colin Roxburgh, one of the consultants, who later founded 'STAR' (Small Town and Rural Development

Group). Colin has written an article for my book in chapter 25, which describes his philosophy and involvement in community regeneration. The Strathfillan Community Development Trust (SCDT) was remarkably successful and became the pioneer for the regeneration of communities in the whole Stirling and Loch Lomond and Trossachs National Park areas. Our efforts and achievements were rewarded in 2004 by our obtaining the runner-up prize in a ceremony at the House of Lords from BURA (British Urban Regeneration Association). We were quite amused when we were told that the first prize had been won by Liverpool City. During the same year we received a couple of 'Calor Gas Awards' in a ceremony attended by Prince Charles in Edinburgh. I believe that strong independent community bodies will have a key role in the evolution of true democracy and therefore the BURA report is shown in the Appendix to demonstrate what can be achieved by earnest endeavour.

In 1991, I was introduced to Mary Latimer by the proprietors of a shop, who were both practitioners of TM. During my ensuing shopping trip around the town Mary and I met, quite by chance, on three more occasions, which is an example of synchronicity, as described in chapter 14. Mary offered to write an article for my book on colour which is presented in chapter 22. Soon afterwards, we joined a group of 23 people on a trip to the ashram of Sri Sathya Sai Baba, in southern India who is regarded by his followers as an avatar (God incarnate). The meetings of this group took place at 'Culdees', the home of Anu Anand, who has written chapter 21. In the mid 1990's some of us got involved with a teaching method, founded by Sathya

Sai, called 'Sathya Sai Education in Human Values'(SSEHV) which was described in chapter 19, our intention being to open a Sathya Sai School. Lesley-Ann Patrick, who lived at Culdees for a while, left to form her own Sathya Sai School in St Andrews, which is described by Lesley, in chapter 30. Chris Hughes, who was a member of the SSEHV group has been a close friend ever since and volunteered to write an article, which is presented in chapter 27.

During the early 1990s, I decided to try giving hands-on healing but realised that not only was I discharging my energy but I was temporarily experiencing the symptoms of the receiver. Mary suggested that I should learn Reiki, as the universal healing energy is channelled through the healer but should not deplete the healer's own energy. Accordingly, over the next few years I learnt Reiki, eventually obtaining my Masters Degree in 1996 and taking refresher courses in 1997 and 2002. It is impossible to foretell whether a healing session will result in a cure; sometimes nothing seems to happen and on other occasions significant healing is observed. Most healers are well aware when healing is taking place as sometimes there is significant energy flow and observation of heat and cold in their hands (and sometimes even up the arms). I have experienced a number of minor miracles, such as in my healing session with Linda McCartney, which she describes in chapter 29. Linda went on to learn Reiki and teach a number of people in Tyndrum, including Moira Robertson, who has written an article on aromatherapy massage, presented in chapter 26 and Heather Clement, who later learnt kinesiology. I invited her to write an article but instead she introduced me to Diane Piette, whose article is presented in chapter 28.

In the early 1990s, Mary introduced me to David Cowan, who was the vice-president of the Scottish Dowsers' Association. At my invitation, David visited Tyndrum and observed that the village was affected by negative earth energies emanating from historic lead mine workings on a nearby hill. He demonstrated, using dowsing rods, that sinusoidal energy waves created negative spirals, when going to earth, probably being attracted by underground faults. He explained that these spirals could drain the life force energy of people who spent a great deal of time sitting or sleeping in them, an effect which would eventually lead to serious illnesses, which were inherent in their genetic make-up. For example, it could accelerate the onset of cancer in a person with that genetic weakness. David found a number of such spirals in our home but demonstrated how the energy waves could be diverted around the house. This protection technique and many more of David's experiences are described in chapter 24.

21

A LOOK AT LIFE

Anu Anand

Anu Anand trained as a medical doctor and was a general practitioner in Scotland from 1972 until 2002. He always had a great interest in natural medicine, has carried out research at Strathclyde University in Scotland and has world patents on medicines for both cancer and psoriasis, which are currently undergoing further development. He was greatly disturbed by the way in which the pharmaceutical industry has been operating, in that despite the vast worldwide expenditure on their medicines, illness is increasing. He was also concerned by the evidence of increasing corruption and self interest amongst the leadership of many countries and believed that they should be accountable for their actions to some kind of globally constituted body, similar to the United Nations. [Anu Anand passed away on 21st July 2008 and will be sadly missed.]

Shall we ever find the answers? We have been searching for millennia – our thinkers, philosophers, physicists, cosmologists and scientists have been trying for so long to solve the big riddle of whom, what and how we are here on the surface of this beautiful planet. The mystery is very deep and would it not be so much better to enjoy it rather than keep struggling to understand it? Life is the only thing we have got, either you are living or you are not living. What else is there – tell me plainly? Don't impress me with your great or small acquisitions of world's materials, houses, villas. SUVs and bank balances and so on, which are no use, once your life factory gets shut down. The most valuable thing is "life"; to be lived enjoyed, respected by us and all other humans, flora, fauna and all varieties of life. Albert Schweitzer, the great lambarene physician, philosopher and musicologist coined the phrase "reverence for life". I would like to even go further and call it a celebration of life.

Our beautiful planet is hopelessly divided, with ever changing borders, leaders and governments which bungle, blunder, plunder and continue making war against each other. The human races' beliefs in parochial causes, religions and oppressions and suppression of the others cause strife, war, death and destruction on our earth every day and continue unabated. We should learn from our yesterdays and our mistakes, but we really don't; controlling, suppressing, and exploiting the weaker ones appearing to be out generic modus operandi.

Do we love ourselves and do we value and treasure and enjoy the big gift of life? If we really adore this gift then why is there so much misery, depression, disease and hatred? If we start to adore this gift we should also remember to adore it in all others, all humans and all other life forms. Everyone should respect all others as they have the same gift of life. A radical change of attitude is needed and has to be inculcated at all levels, ages and all times. How can we bring it about? The big brothers; CNN, BBC and the mega-corporations and universities are not teaching it. Jesus expressed it as love thy neighbour and who is the neighbour? I say everything and everyone – this kind of transformation is essential before the human race can take the next leap. It would make our planet so much more beautiful, colourful and happy.

I believe we are on a work permit here: we are put somewhere and we always want to do something, and that something has to be done before the life factory shuts one day unknown and unannounced. We can do whatever we wish, provided we do not declare it difficult and impossible. We have all the faculties and powers inherent and stored in us and we can utilize and bring them out to accomplish our desire – our objective and our goal. Little in life is achieved easily – the workers are tested, tried and tortured even and the test is to determine their tenacity, depth of desire to do and dare and staying on course – whatever the difficulties. Giving up on the way is so easy and so common. But carrying on regardless is the only way to reach the goal and achieve the target. If you love yourself – you also love your faculties and thus you can utilize them to achieve your objective, your desire and remit. Stress, restlessness, anxiety and anticipation only help to pollute the outcome of your effort. The great philosophy enunciated by Lord Krishna – *'do the work with your entire devotion and joy and do not look for the results of one form or another'*. He says, even forget the results, they will come anyway – stress-less and thus less disease and suffering. Our anticipating a particularly shaped kind of result produces sickness in us and then gradually we start to be afflicted by all manner of illnesses and infirmities.

We should be happy with our lot, as otherwise we will be stressed and sick doing what we are forcing ourselves to do. This is the place to practise love of everyone and everything. Imagine the change when we decide to love and respect everyone and glorify life and our planet. Our birthright is freedom from oppression, control and being led by others, and we should endeavour to realise this in our lives. After all we are not here forever and during our limited sojourn we have to accomplish whatever we feel is important. Everything and everyone has a purpose – there is no one and nothing that is useless and not beautiful. Life is totally beautiful, deeply shrouded in mystery and completely unknowable. Have we understood really the great mystery at all? I will say 'no': we have understood little despite our efforts which continue at all levels. For example, have we understood the structure and workings of an atom – a living animal, human or a plant cell? The mystery remains, although libraries of the world are full of books about them. In an atomic space, there are nuclei particles in orbit all in a constant state of very high speed revolutions of millions of miles in a second. The atom is so very small that we can only observe it at great magnification. How can this happen? My little mind stops at this: tens of different types of fundamental particles all moving at great speed without any food. More fundamental particles are being discovered and the big enigma only remains. In a living cell the ultra-structure, the chemicals – the organization – are so complex – sophisticated and deeply perceived that we yet do not exactly know how it really functions. Our scientific research, our philosophical insights have not provided any real answers.

We are denizens of our beautiful planet and of course the whole universe, which is ever evolving and expanding and would take many billion light years to traverse. The feeling that I am a part of everything is extremely powerful and transformative and the changeover is completely radical and fundamental, and can become a basis of our new now. All we have are the 'now' and 'life', which we should treasure and we will see the makeover – a different larger 'we' emerging – it is all inherent in our attitude, comprehension and understanding. The tomorrow will then be much fuller, purposeful, promising and above all happy and beautiful and we can shed our misery, unhappiness, sickness and suffering and bring smiles all around. Just look at the grasses, flowers, plants and trees: silently they do their work and sustain us, and the sun comes out at the exact nanosecond and gives us all necessary light, heat, life and energy. Clearly it is a created universe and even life – yes life evolves but it has been created by a higher designer, which in the USA, was recently defined as 'Intelligent Design'. Surely once created, the whole thing keeps evolving – don't tell me the molecules of earth, air and water came together myriad years ago to form the mega-phenomenon of life. The design is so deep, mysterious and super-structured that our minds and our instruments have provided few answers and the mystery remains. Instead of trying to understand it, let us love it, revere, adore and treasure it and be a means to a lasting happy celebration. With this attitude alone we can reform and cool this burning, warring and hatred infested planet. Everything, including all forms of life, is made of atoms. If you look on the inside of an atom – whichever-it is almost totally empty – these myriads of empty spaces constitute us, our planet, our universe and everything else – the solidity and weight of things depending on multiple energy particles moving at inordinate speeds in microspace. In fact the whole universe has been created from empty space and energy; Einstein's big E being all that there is. How has it all been so cleverly assembled? Imagine consulting an architect and asking him to make a big building out of 'nothing' – he will in the next minute throw me out of his office. But this is exactly what the great creator has done, made us and the planet and the whole universe out of nothing. Big Bang or Small Bang – whatever - we have been placed here to respect, honour, and love, adore and glorify it through our allotted work – work permit, faculties and immense possibilities. We have to relearn the ultimate principle of love and by deliberation, slowly, shed other qualities that afflict our lives and emerge as a new 'me' and 'you' thus bringing about a new tomorrow, a new age and a golden age on our wonderful planet.

22

THE GIFT OF COLOUR

Mary Latimer

Mary Latimer studied Iridology with the British School of Iridology in London and Cambridge where she became a member of their register. She was also a member of the International Association of Colour Therapy. She practised both of these disciplines for several years before retiring to further her interest in spiritual matters; especially in her own spiritual growth. She has a keen interest in Eastern philosophy and has travelled to the East on many occasions, with much having been learned, although she believes that all guidance and wisdom comes from within. Mary is the author of The Essence of Living, *which received the review:* 'An excellent book, written from the heart, explaining our spiritual nature and evolution. It is an ideal source of information for anyone who is a seeker of Spiritual truth'.

The importance of colour, as a medium for helping the body to heal itself, is becoming recognised by more and more people as it is being realised that we must take more responsibility for our own well-being, as we witness the limitations of our National Health Service which just is not meeting the needs of the people. This situation in itself may not necessarily be a negative one, and might indeed be instrumental in helping mankind to wake up to the fact that is is now time to seek other avenues whereby the body can respond to the more gentle healing therapies which are being presented at this time and which have the ability to treat the entire body holistically. This is achieved by bringing alignment to the whole person, rather than treating the specific symptom which, yes, may be relieved through the use of pharmaceutical drugs, but unless the energy field which surrounds the body is realigned the symptom will very often return. It is not being suggested that prescription drugs should never be used, but that rather they be taken in an emergency situation, and not for minor ailments for which patients often expect their doctor to prescribe.

The use of colour has been known to be effective in the prevention of illness, and also in the treatment of many adverse conditions which occur within the finely tuned system which is commonly called the body. It is not known how far back in the history of the planet that colour has been used as a therapy, but when the great continent of Atlantis was part of the planet, which reputedly sank beneath the Atlantic sea west of Gibraltar, the Atlanteans were using crystals as a medium through which the seven rays of the sun would shine, giving a concentration of each ray, which gave great power to these colours, and in their ability to heal. Unfortunately, this great power was misused when the negative human aspects of greed, self-importance, power etc. became their way of living, which eventually caused the demise of this once great civilisation.

At the time of the Cave Man, or Paeolithic man, when survival was paramount, very drab colours, such as ochres, dark yellows and browns, which were a reflection of the brutish nature, were prevalent. In other words they were only operating from the magnetic colours of the earth, which are connected to survival, procreation and self-centredness, which was the state of evolution at that period in history. The Egyptians, at a later date, brought colour back to the fore again. They worshipped the sun, and erected temples for the sole purpose of healing through colour, where people would go and sit and receive the healing rays to restore the balance of energy which could be misaligned, thus creating an imbalance within their structure. These temples would also be used to relieve the tension within the people, which could prevent the onset of illness.

In the Middle Ages, Paracelsus, a Swiss physician and alchemist was also a pioneer of the colour rays for the purpose of healing. He was well ahead of his time, though his work was ridiculed throughout Europe; his manuscripts being destroyed and his valuable research work lost to mankind forever. It is interesting to note however that he is now regarded as one of the great healers of his time. In more recent times Sir Isaac Newton, the English Physicist and Mathematician was responsible for bringing the importance of colour and light to modern society, and is noted for his astronomical telescope in which light is reflected from a large concave mirror on to a plane mirror, and through a hole in the side of the telescope could see all the colours of the spectrum through the white light. This all served to fire the imagination of the people of his generation, much of which is a forerunner of today's knowledge of the science of light. So it can be seen that healing with colour has not just been discovered in the twentieth century, but has yet again been rediscovered through a rise and fall situation over a long period of time.

Interestingly, crystals were used by the Atlanteans as a

healing medium a very long time ago and that, that same medium is also being used at the present time.

The body contains all the seven colours which are directly linked to the endocrine system, or glandular system with each colour responsible, to a large degree, for the health of that particular gland. The stronger and purer the colour, the healthier the gland will be, and conversely the weaker the colour, the less energy will be being produced by that particular gland.

There are many ways in which the body can replenish the diminished colour apart from being treated by a therapist. The food which we eat and drink has a direct effect upon the system, with the colour from the food being absorbed by the body. The colours which we see through our eyes also have a large effect on the system, especially on the pituitary and pineal glands which are located on the forehead and the top of the head respectively, and are responsible for how we perceive situations ; whether we see them as positive or negative. The sunlight, which contains all the colours of the spectrum, is especially good for balancing the glandular system, and in particular the solar plexus which is the seat of the emotions, and which responds to sunlight in a very positive way. Its ruling colour is yellow. A very effective way of alleviating mild depression, anxiety and worry is by using the very powerful tool which we all possess, of imagination. By imagining the golden colour of sunlight entering the body through the opening at the top of the head, and bringing it slowly and gently down the body to the feet, suffusing every part of the body with this colour. When it reaches the feet area imagine that all negativity is leaving the body and being absorbed by Mother Earth, where it will be transmuted from a negative energy into a positive one. This exercise is very powerful, and if used with sincerity will reap rich rewards from a health point of view, and can be repeated as often as necessary without any ill effects.

The seven colours of the spectrum are connected to the seven main chakras, or energy wheels, within the body, with each chakra connecting to its respective gland, and when functioning properly should be rotating in a clockwise fashion from the base of the spine to the top of the head.

Each colour has its complementary colour, and should a colour be too strong for the person being treated, then the complementary one would be used in conjunction with it. For instance, the colour red might be too stimulating for a person who is hyperactive, has high blood pressure, or even too grounded, in which case the air colour of blue would be used with it in order to temper the effect. This is blending the Earth colours with the Air colours and so bringing in the correct balance. At the base of the spine there is the root chakra, which connects to the Adrenal glands with its colour being RED. This is sometimes known as the area of 'Fight or Flight' because it causes adrenalin to flow when in a dangerous situation, and where extra energy- flow is needed. Red is the colour of energy and is connected to the magnetic field of the earth, which helps to keep us grounded, or to keep our feet on the ground when need be. This is especially so when someone has an idea which could be beneficial in some way and which, if not earthed, could just fly into obscurity and be lost.

ORANGE is the colour which is connected to the Gonads, or reproductive system, and is also an earth colour which vibrates at a slightly higher level than red, with the chakra, or wheel turning more quickly. It is, like the red, associated with the adrenal glands.

It is the colour of purity of thought, and has the ability to transmute sexual energy of desire into a creative nature by blending with its complementary colour of indigo: in other words by bringing a spiritual aspect to a person's thinking. This is particularly helpful to persons who have chosen the path of celibacy. Orange is the colour of joy and people who are attracted to this colour, either in their décor, or in the clothes they wear are usually people with a great zest for living; this is often demonstrated by people who enjoy being on the stage as entertainers, or by artists who get inspiration in their chosen work.

YELLOW is the last of the earth colours and is associated with the glands of the lymphatic system, and is located in the solar plexus area which is the seat of the emotions. It is the colour of brightness and joy and has the ability to disperse negative thoughts which accumulate in the solar plexus, and which may have been stored there for a long time, causing the person to have feelings of inferiority, apprehension and many other negative emotions. This is why, when a person is upset when hearing bad news, has an interview, or any other situation which they perceive as negative the affects are felt in the stomach area, or solar plexus, which can make them feel nauseous, or even be physically sick. With the help of a therapist these stored-up feelings can be gradually released by meditating on the yellow ray and replacing negative situations with positive ones. It must be remembered however that it is usually through these very seemingly negative situations that we learn most, and that the person must be ready to release them and move forward. The colour yellow is a mental stimulant, associated with wisdom and knowledge so is a good colour to have around children in the classroom, as it promotes clear thinking, together with a positive energy. It is the colour of the sun so is a good colour to use in the winter months when the sun is low. It is particularly beneficial to the many people who suffer with Seasonal Affective Disorder (SAD) and can be introduced in many ways, with some of the most effective being to have a vase of yellow flowers in the room (daffodils are especially good) brightly coloured cushions, bright lights and even wearing yellow on their person. Much research is being done with this condition which is a fairly common one, but the use of colour is a good alternative to medication, and will not disturb the delicate balance within the seat of the emotions. It is very often the simple and inexpensive things which are the most effective! Yellow is the last of the earth colours, and vibrates at a higher rate than that of the other two as it ascends the spinal column and connects with the green colour. The complementary colour to yellow is violet.

GREEN is the colour which separates the earth colours from the air ones, and is connected to the thymus gland and the heart centre. This is one of the most valuable of all the colours, especially in nature as it allows the flowers to be seen in their true glory by acting as a foil whereby these colours are not lost to the eye. It is a generous giver in the garden and does not seek to detract from the beauty of the flowers, but rather to enhance their glory. When observing the green which abounds in nature one can hardly imagine what it would be like to be without this colour. The green fields, hedges, trees etc. are all backgrounds which create space and provide rest to the eye of the beholder. Pale green is a therapeutic colour to have in hospitals and mental institutions where it provides relaxation for the senses and promotes healing. It also gives a relaxed atmosphere within the home, and gives a feeling of space, as well as being restful. It is the colour which is associated with abundance in life, hence it is known as the colour of expansion, providing freedom in thought and action through helping people to break through the self imposed limitation of their thinking and allowing them to move forward and expand their lives. Green is a giving colour, and when one is depleted of energy it is beneficial to walk bare-footed on the green grass, especially in the morning when the dew is still on the ground. If this is physically not possible, then it can be done mentally by visualizing this as an exercise where much benefit will be gained. This exercise is a good start to the day when practised in the early morning because it clears the mind and allows for creative, expansive thinking throughout the day, especially within a working condition. Another exercise which is beneficial is to stand with the back against a tree with the right hand on the trunk of the tree and the left one on the solar plexus. This action has the effect of balancing the emotions and giving peace to the mind, with the tree having absorbed the stress which most people carry around on their shoulders and elsewhere. It is important, after having completed this exercise, to give thanks to the tree, remembering that it too is a living, vibrating entity. Green does not have a complementary colour.

BLUE is the start of the air colours, or spiritual ones, and is connected to the thyroid gland which is located in the throat. This colour emits peace and tranquillity and gives one a sense of beauty as it is linked to music and the arts, and is also associated with the soul's journey, and for its purpose in reincarnating into the world at this time. The throat chakra is in the area of communication and is more active with people who do public speaking, or singing, and moves at a faster rate because that area is open, and not blocked. It is also larger and brighter in size than average due to it being a very active centre. If someone is going to give a public address and feels nervous, or lacking in confidence it can be helpful to either visualize the colour turquoise around the throat, or wear something which contains that colour. Blue is a good colour to use when practicing meditation as it has the ability to still the mind, and calm the nervous system, both of which can be difficult to keep under control, especially for those who are beginners. It is also good to use with group meditation, by asking each person to visualize the colour blue surrounding their body and then being absorbed by the senses and at the same time to mentally say "peace, peace, peace" very slowly. This practice has the effect of unifying the group and creating an atmosphere conducive to deep meditation. A particular shade of blue will be chosen by each individual; whether it is pale blue, turquoise, azure or any of the many hues of this colour. Whichever one is chosen will be the right one for that person.

Blue is considered to be the most beneficial colour in the field of healing due to its relaxing effect upon the nervous system; with most inharmonious conditions within the mind and body being due to stress-related circumstances, which are very often the cause of illness, in its many forms, and because of the calming effect which it has on the nervous system encourages the body to heal itself. The complementary colour to blue is red.

INDIGO is the second air colour and is located in the third eye centre between the eyebrows, and is connected to the pituitary gland. This chakra, or energy wheel, is sometimes referred to as 'The All Seeing Eye' especially in eastern philosophy where it is the practice to focus the attention on this centre when meditating. Indigo is associated with clairvoyance, desire for knowledge, truth and spirituality. It is the colour which heals the etheric body which surrounds and shields the physical body, and can also help to alleviate pain and discomfort when visualized on the offending area. The brow chakra is the one which separates the left and right sides of the brain, but yet unifies at the same time: the right side of the brain being the intuitive one, or feminine, and the left being the practical or masculine one. When these two halves are working in unison it makes for balanced thoughts and actions. When there is instability in this centre it can cause conditions which affect the nervous system, creating anxiety, irritability, lethargy and many problems associated with the nervous system. It can also be responsible for severe to moderate headaches, due in part to the disturbance of the sinus area, or to the onset of migraine. These conditions will disappear when the centre has been stabilised through the regular practice of meditation. When one sees visions of a clairvoyant nature it is within this centre where they are seen, with colour in varying degrees usually seen first. The complementary colour is orange which adds energy and joy to this colour thus preventing depression which can, like the blue colour, be too intense, where one can forget the joy of living, and to bring balance again to the earth and air colours.

VIOLET is the last of the colours and is associated with the pineal gland which is located at the top of the head, and is sometimes referred to as "The Thousand Petalled Lotus". This is the most spiritual of all the colours, and is related to self-respect, dignity and service to humanity without thought for self-gain or recognition. This is the centre where all humans will eventually reach, and to which all should aspire. When this colour is seen in the aura of a person it denotes self-sacrifice with deep spirituality. Mother Theresa was one such person who was seen to have this colour in her aura. Violet is an inspirational colour, which affects artists and musicians greatly when working in an environment where this colour is present. It connects the person with their higher creative self, where much work of a spiritual nature can be produced, and which will be a great source of inspiration to a many people. The complementary colour is yellow which is associated with wisdom, knowledge and learning, and when these two colours work in unison it makes for a very special person who will be able to combine learning with spirituality. This can be found in some physicists and spiritual masters who in the past have played a large part in the evolution of mankind, and no doubt in society today there will be those amongst us who will also be contributing to the betterment of the world, and be instrumental in effecting change. The chakra, or energy wheel, in this centre spins at a very fast rate, and the more evolved the person the faster it spins, and will take the person beyond the physical state to a more heightened state of awareness. When one has reached a high level of spiritual awareness the seven chakras can be seen as one column of light, with each single chakra merging with the other, and rotating at great speed where one is not discernible as a single unit, but rather the seven merging together and creating one single, vibrating column of energy.

This is sometimes referred to as enlightenment, or the awakening and arising of the kundalini energy which is stored at the base of the spine. In the teachings of eastern mystics this is deemed to be a necessary step in ones spiritual growth, whereby the heavy earth-energy is transmuted as it travels up the spine through the chakras until it reaches the crown centre where it is purified, and where the person attains a greater sense of freedom, but at the same time realises the responsibility that freedom always brings with it. Kundalini is spoken about more freely in eastern countries than in western ones, but there is a growing interest being shown in the west also, where more information is being made available.

These, then, are the attributes of the most magnificent of colours with which we have been endowed, and it is up to each one of us to use them wisely and generously and in so doing will greatly assist the body in its on-going fight to keep healthy throughout its earthly sojourn.

23

FROM TRANQUILLISERS TO TRANQUILITY

David Walne

> *David Walne awoke one night, after a period of great stress in his life, and realised that all down his right side was dead, and his speech was very slow. He thought he'd had a stroke, but the doctor assured him that he was suffering from nervous exhaustion and prescribed tranquillisers, which presumably he would need to take for the rest of his life. Fortunately a friend told him about Transcendental Meditation (TM for short) as a way of coping with stress and anxiety, a technique which he learnt in 1978. He was so impressed with the effect that TM had on his life that a year later he learnt the TM Siddhis and during the next twenty years ran the Morecambe and Lancaster TM. Centre encouraging numerous people to learn. In 1999 he joined several hundred other practitioners in setting up the 'Maharishi European Sidhaland' in Skelmersdale, which is focussed on improving the quality of life in the UK by reducing stress in society. His main aim in life now is to improve his relationship with God.*

My journey to higher states of consciousness....

Apparently, one's development through life can be evaluated in approximate steps of seven years: the nervous system having developed by the age of seven, puberty by the age of fourteen, physical maturity by the age of twenty one and in an ideal world, spiritual enlightenment by the age of (seven x seven) or forty nine years. On this basis, something significant should be happening at the age of twenty eight years, and it certainly happened to me, because at the age of twenty eight I learnt transcendental meditation, which has had a most wonderful effect on my life.

I was very close to my mother but after her sudden death from lung cancer, I was prevented from mourning her loss due to pressure of work. At this same time, one of my daughters was suffering from insomnia and so it was no surprise, when one night I got up to attend to her that I realised that all down my right side was dead, and my speech was very slow. I thought I'd had a stroke, but the doctor assured me that I was suffering from nervous exhaustion and prescribed tranquillisers, which presumably I would need to take for the rest of my life. During that same period, when I felt highly stressed I simply reached for my vallium, to release the pressure; perhaps another life long necessity.

Fortunately a friend told me about Transcendental Meditation (TM for short) as a way of coping with stress and anxiety. I thought it must be better than valium so I would give it try. The day came for me to learn, and I got so worked up about it, thinking that I would not be able to do it and that it wouldn't work for me. I was told that I would be given a sound, called a mantra, and because this would be in tune with my body's vibration, I would be able to relax and get rid of the stress. So off I went, but my hay fever flared- up and my eyes started running nearly as fast as I was sneezing, so I thought I would never be able to do it, however when I did arrive, although I was in a bit of a state, the teacher assured me that I would be alright. I paid the fee which I think it was £100. This seemed good value as the course was one to two hours per day over 4 consecutive days, with a further meeting 10 days later to make sure that everything was going fine. The teacher first went through a short procedure; a traditional thanksgiving, which helps him to remember that it is not his technique and to enable him to remain objective.

As soon as I commenced using my mantra, I started to relax and to feel very settled, and so I was on my way to my first meditation which was very good. Apparently most people find the first one is good. I remember coming out of my room and jumping in the air with delight, with a feeling that a large weight had been lifted from my shoulders. The following meetings were very helpful and enjoyable as we were taught a lot more about the technique and how to react to interruptions, such as the telephone ringing during meditation. Also, it was explained that thoughts arising during meditation should not be regarded as an interruption, and pushed out as in some techniques, but as part of the process as TM is easy and effortless. Maharishi says that the purity of meditation has been lost and in its pure form should not involve any effort.

By the end of the fourth day I was feeling much happier, more relaxed, was sleeping better and had more energy. In my experiences of attending many courses, over the years, I can report that as many as 80% of participants feel some benefit by the end of the fourth day. I remember one lady who, after the death of her husband, was only able to sleep for four to five hours nightly. After her first day of practising TM in her home at 5.30 pm, she felt very tired, went off to bed and didn't wake up until 9.00 o'clock in the morning; the stress which was causing the sleeplessness having been completely dissolved.

I found after starting TM that I would feel very tired around 7.00 pm and would go to bed, where I would sleep throughout the night. This pattern lasted for two weeks; allowing me to catch up with sleep deprivation, resulting in me feeling less anxious and much happier.

I observed numerous other benefits over the ensuing months:

My squash improved - for the first time ever I topped my league and my group, and continued to do so every following month for thirteen months, until I ended up in league one, and then got into the team. Research on the physiological effects of TM has shown one of the many benefits is improvement in mind/body co-ordination.

My interest in other spiritual matters increased, including religion, even though TM is not a religion.

My work was affected- after having nearly got the sack before practicing TM. I was finding all manner of improvements, for example, I was eventually promoted to sales manager.

My health improved very quickly, for example, only four weeks after learning TM, I no longer needed tranquillisers. It probably saved my life as my previously high blood pressure started reducing.

After 2 years I noticed that my heart centre was expanding and started to feel much more love for my wife which unfortunately came too late as she left me for someone else. This was a most stressful time both for me and my two daughters but TM helped me to cope.

There were times when I would not want to practice my meditation as my mind would suddenly become overcome with thoughts. I realise now that these thoughts were not like 'everyday' thoughts, but a symptom of more stress being released by my nervous system.

I was so pleased with the vast improvement in my life that a year after learning TM, I decided to learn the 'TM Siddhi' programme, including the 'Yogic Flying'. Maharishi says that, in addition to the three normal states of consciousness of waking, dreaming and deep sleep, we can experience a fourth state of `Transcendental Consciousness', which enables even greater stress release and leads eventually to "Cosmic Consciousness", in which our awareness is unbounded.

There are many other benefits derived from practicing this advanced technique:

More incidences of clear premonitions: for example, you've just been thinking of someone, the telephone rings and it's that same person. Such incidents are regarded as coincidences but as we develop spiritually they seem to happen more frequently.

As the process of spiritual refinement continues, we may experience progressively higher states of consciousness, in which our relationship with the creator is enhanced, such as 'God Consciousness'.

Our heart centre begins to open giving rise to a greater capacity for universal love and a compassion for all living creatures. A further refinement of this is the experience of the seventh state of 'Unity Consciousness' or full enlightenment, in which our awareness becomes fully developed and we experience oneness with the universe.

Anyone wanting more information about these higher states of consciousness should read Maharishi's books; *The Science of Being* and his revolutionary interpretation of the *Bhagavad Gita*.

Maharishi has introduced these more advanced techniques or Siddhi's, described by the sage Patangali, the father of yoga, to accelerate the journey into unity consciousness.

I found learning these Siddhi's to be a thoroughly enjoyable experience, although I did have to take out a bank loan to pay for the course. The 'Flying Sutra' or siddhi is given in a two weeks residential course.

Although, 'flying' in a group is very enjoyable, the benefit to society is more important, research showing that when the square root of 1% of the population practice this technique, as a group, it brings about a reversal of negative trends in society, such as crime rates.

There are three stages of yogic flying:

- A feeling of energy moving up and down the spine.
- A desire to fly into the air and then to be able to hop.
- Levitation.

The majority of practitioners have only experienced the second stage, which may not impress the observer, as some effort is involved. All I can say is that if I sit cross-legged on the floor and try with all my might to pull myself up from the floor, I would maybe achieve a ½ inch bounce after great effort - whereas, during the flying, with a tiny amount of effort, I am able to lift into the air, perhaps as high as 6 inches and for a hop of 2 foot long. Some other practitioners are able to lift up to about 3 feet into the air, with relatively little effort. So I know that something is happening, and research shows the brain wave coherence to dramatically improve on lift up, the most important point being that it is practiced for both individual and collective benefit and not to impress observers. One way of explaining the benefits of practicing this technique is to compare a non-meditator, a meditator and a practioner of the TM siddhi technique: A non meditator would be moving at walking pace, a meditator would use a Rolls Royce and a siddhi practitioner would be like flying by Concorde.

My progress was now much quicker and I became more successful at work, achieving 'star dinners' and winning trips to Rome and Majorca etc. I achieved a great life - with big houses , new cars, three holidays a year - so felt quite fulfilled - Maharishi says that it's only by fulfilling our desires that we can experience enlightenment, and that if we still have desires , they must be fulfilled first.

Maharishi warns against becoming too involved in any esoteric practices as he says '*It's like going along a road or path to a castle and wandering off to look at interesting items such as - mediumship, clairvoyance and the like; getting totally involved in other things and forgetting the path to the castle*'. Instead he says it's much better to keep focused on capturing the castle (i.e. gaining enlightenment) then you can have access to all these 'gems'.

So 18 - 20 years after learning TM and the Siddhis, I started to go into a phase of purification, in which much stress was released – This was like defrosting a fridge, initially you chip away at the ice, but then near the end big chunks start falling away. Some of my observations during this time are described below:

I found it difficult to concentrate on anything and just wanted to go swimming or walking in the countryside. This phase lasted for about 18 months.

One day whilst walking in the countryside I had a glimpse of 'Unity Consciousness': I looked up at the tree and felt a wave of 'Bliss' (happiness somehow doesn't really give it credit) come over me; it was lovely to have that glimpse, albeit very brief. At the same time I started noticing my awareness growing. Typically, if I was eating with no appetite, my meal would be interrupted by the telephone ringing, whereas, if I was eating with an appetite for the food, the meal was never interrupted, in this manner.

I started noticing all manner of ways in which `nature` was advising me, and I knew this was early signs of cosmic consciousness (CC) I also experienced a state of CC, called 'witnessing', for example while lying in bed, my mind would be thinking away as usual when I would hear a noise which I would not recognise, and then I would realise that it was my body sleeping.

I also felt my relationship with God becoming a reality rather than some mind-making exercise. I know that God is with me all the time and that my love for my wife, my beloved Christ, my beloved Maharishi and his teacher Guru Dev and God are increasing.

Maharishi has really blessed us by bringing out knowledge of the Vedas (pure knowledge). For example, by applying the teachings of 'Staphatya Veda', we obtain maximum nature support in all tasks which we undertake, such as in building a house, we are protected from harm.

Maharish is also promoting Ayurveda, which is a study of the operation of the human body; 'ayur' meaning 'knowledge' and 'veda' meaning 'life'. This form of traditional medicine, which has been developed in India, during the last 4000 years, includes eight main branches or limbs and includes paediatrics, gynaecology, obstetrics, ophthalmology, geriatrics, study of the ear nose and throat, surgery and general medicine.[39] Each type of medicine is addressed in terms of the three doshas or signals: called VATA, equating to 'wind' or movement, PITA, equating to 'fire' or heat and thus digestion and KARPHA, equating to 'earth' and 'water' and creating mucus; thus, for example, the common cold is regarded as excess 'karpha'. Another way of understanding the three doshas is as the first sprouting of the manifest field of consciousness into the manifest world of matter: each has a potential for being in balance or equilibrium......if in balance then we are happy and healthy....a trained doctor can tell, by putting three fingers on the pulse, which, if any of the doshas are out of balance and then what to do to gently bring back into balance ... this is done long before an illness has manifested, in order to prevent illness. If, however, illness is already present then this knowledge will help any traditional medicine or healing to have a swifter and more potent effect. For example, after I had my leg broken at age of 19 the front of the leg or calf was completely 'dead' i.e. nerves so badly damaged there was no feeling at all.....this is how it stayed till at the age of 43, when I started bringing my vata dosha, which controls the nervous system, among many other areas, back into balance just by cutting out certain foods and introducing others. Six months later I noticed feeling coming back into the front of my leg and gradually I got full feeling back——quite remarkable. Another effect was the curing of my insomnia; enabling me to get off to sleep like a child in under four minutes A consultation with an ayurvedic doctor does cost money but is worth every penny, many times over.[40]

During the purification process, which is an effect of taking part in the siddhi programme, my weight started dropping, reducing from 10.5 stone to 8 stone. The doctor said my thyroid was out of balance and that I would have to be on thyroxin for the rest of my life. I thought this was ridiculous and went to see the Maharishi's Ayruvedic doctor in the clinic in Skelmersdale. He checked my pulse and said it was just an imbalance of the Vata dosha and that I would only have to change my diet and a few other things. I followed his instructions, and very gradually my Vata dosha regained balance, my thyroid started working correctly and my weight returned.

Another area of knowledge to be revived, by Mararishi, in its purity, is 'Jyotish', the ability to prophesy, which is the Vedic equivalent of Western astrology. This is very accurate procedure, in which an expert practitioner of 'Maharishi Jyotish' can calculate one's time of birth, when provided with several important dates in ones life. They then work out within 2 minutes, one's exact birth time, which is amazing. One branch of 'Jyotish' is called 'yagya', which is a ceremony carried out by Indian pundits to prevent negative affect of planets, and to deflect karma, which is created by the cosmic law of cause and effect: For example, when we do good to someone then good comes back to us, and similarly if we do bad to someone, we will eventually be repaid: 'As you sow so shall you reap'. One of my acquaintants fell out of the third story window onto his head. The doctors were sure that he wouldn't live, or, at the very best would be in a vegetative state! Yagyas were done for him and he has now, four years later, made a full recovery.

Another fascinating practice is the use of Jyotish Gems; which will protect the wearer from the effects of negative energy, or karma. These can be selected by reference to ones birth details, and have to be very pure; with few inclusions, for the experience of maximum benefit. Also, they should ideally be worn so that they are touching the skin. It is interesting that Paramahansa Yogananda describes, in his book *Autobiography of a Yogi*,[6b] being given an amulet by his spiritual master, which contained appropriate gems for his protection. It has been said that TM deflects 50% of ones karma, gems 25% and yagyas the remaining 25%. Apparently, the most suitable gems for protection against the effects of negative energy are yellow sapphire, emerald, coral, pearl and diamond.

To summarise, the purpose of ayurveda is to purify and balance our bodies and the purpose of Staphatya Veda is to ensure that our houses give us the maximum benefit, and protect us from the negative effects experienced in ordinary houses. Transcendental Meditation and the TM Siddhi programme and Yogic flying, accelerate our spiritual evolution. Maharishi has said that prior to the introduction of TM and in particular the TM siddhi technique, Yogananda's Kria Yoga was the most powerful meditation technique. We are advised to choose one technique and persevere with it, rather than being impatient and experimenting with numerous techniques.

Research has shown that if as little as 1% of a population of a city, or country regularly meditate, it results in the reduction of crimes, divorces, accidents, and other negative trends. Similarly as previously stated, research has shown that if the square root of 1% of the population of a city or country, practice the TM Siddhi programme, and especially yogic flying, it reverses all negative tendencies: This is very exciting for the world and this effect has now been labelled 'The Maharishi Effect'.

(Nostradamus, the seer, said in one of his quadrants *'he from the east, he who talks of immortality, he alone has the answer'*.)

Maharishi claims that practicing these advanced techniques is the only solution to the world problems, including terrorism. When the square root of 1% of a population of a country practice these techniques then that country ultimately becomes invincible.

Maharishi was very concerned this year (2006) about the negativity increasing in the world, and so asked that meditation be carried out, especially extra 'Flying' in different parts of the world and especially in 'Fairfield' USA where they have nearly 2000 participants. This very quickly resulted in the reduction of hostilities round the world. However, we desperately need more people who care about the world to take up the flag, as it were, and learn meditation, to completely remove negativity.

I regard myself as being greatly blessed by being a participant in the wonderful TM Siddhi programme, which is providing me with the following benefits:

- Giving me the opportunity of easily experiencing a higher state of consciousness.
- With Jyotish to take care of karma.

- Ayurveda to take care of the body.
- Staphatya Veda to take care of my house.
- And Maharishi Yogi to take care of the world.

I believe that we practitioners are most fortunate to be enabled to not only help ourselves by utilising these techniques as a route to enlightenment but in so doing, we are helping to create peace on earth. Apparently the very exciting news from the TM Siddhi course in Fairfield in USA is that people are experiencing all the states of higher consciousness, including cosmic consciousness and someone has reported an experience, explained by Maharishi as a refinement of unity consciousness, in which the person experienced with his eyes closed, 360 degree vision of everything in his surroundings and also is able to see into the far distance.

I have now had most of my desires fulfilled: I am remarried to a wonderful, ex-beauty queen and planning to have a family. There is so much love in my life, which is expanding beyond my family to Maharishi and the whole of creation. My life is now fulfilled, knowing and taking right action, my awareness becoming more and more unbounded and my realisation that there is no such thing as coincidence; as what is needed will manifest itself in my life. I now confidently look forward to experiencing God Consciousness, and ultimately Unity Consciousness -Maharishi has said that marriage in Unity Consciousness is very special indeed.

Maharishi has stated that the phase transition that we were going through is now completed: for the last 2000 years, we have been living in the 'Kali Yuga', which might be regarded as the winter of our souls ..... when the art of transcending was lost and the world consciousness sank to its lowest level. Just as God sent the Christ to shed light, 2000 years ago, Maharishi has been attempting to enlighten the world and precipitate the age of enlightenment; known as the 'Sat Yuga', when people will, with the practice of transcending, realise their full potential, and we will at last see world peace and an end to the suffering. Maharishi claimed that the phase transition, from Kali Yuga to Sat Yuga, was completed by December 2006 with the help of meditators everywhere. This period will hopefully last for 1000's of years until, with the space of time, slowly the purity of meditation will be lost and once again humanity will return to the 'winter' and consciousness will drop......this is why Maharishi goes to great lengths to keep the purity of the teaching, so that it can last a long time.

Maharishi explains that given time, once again people will think meditation has to involve effort........Maharishi came to dispel this incorrect myth and explained that true meditation should be effortless, and that this is the true meaning of Christ's words, only with the innocence of a child can you enter the kingdom of God (within).

Jai Guru Dev (Maharishi will never accept praise or thanks for himself, but always gives thanks to his teacher ...Guru Dev...Jai means thanks to). So I give thanks to my beloved Christ, Maharishi and Jai Guru Dev.

This article was written prior to Maharishi Yogi's death on 5 February 2008.

24

LEY LINES, ILL-HEALTH AND SPIRIT LINES

David R. Cowan

David Cowan spent his childhood in Glasgow, before relocating to Crieff, Perthshire, where he entered the printing trade, working in various printing shops for some 35 years. In 1975 he watched the BBC programme Tomorrow's World *which highlighted the use of divining rods to follow the energy emitted from a 'black box', a device which, the designer hoped, would allow aircraft and ships to navigate a very precise course. Intrigued, he investigated the strange world of dowsing, (using it to locate and follow the waves of energy from standing stones and circles), which he discovered was a very simple and natural ability which most of us have. It took him eight years and well over 3,000 miles of tough walking over Highland Perthshire to map out the ley lines (energy leys) in that area, before turning his attention to Geopathic Stress which seems to be involved in ill-health. More recently he has investigated the very strange world of 'spirit lines', energies from burial grounds which also seem to be involved in ill-health. He is presently investigating the puzzling round towers of Ireland and Scotland. He is convinced that the ancient art of dowsing (rhabdomancy) is the key to understanding the secrets of our megalithic building stone-age ancestors, many forms of ill-health and paranormal activity which scientists appear to be unable to under-*

stand. David has had two books published; the first book, Safe as Houses?[30b] *deals with geopathic stress and ill-health. His second book,* Ley Lines and Earth Energies[30c] *co-authored by Chris Arnold, explains, for the first time, the effect of standing stones and circles of Scotland, and also paranormal phenomena, like ghosts, poltergeists and demonic attack, ball lightning, one legged devils and the like.*

Dowsing Rods

Many people associate dowsing with the 'V shaped hazel twig. In fact, there are over two hundred different types of dowsing instruments, each with its own advantages and disadvantages. For detecting earth energies, in my opinion, the best dowsing implements are angle rods, two lengths of wire, about 21 ins (53 cms) long, with 6ins (15 cms) bent over at right angles to form a handle. A little experience will show the length which will best suit the individual. Made from heavy fence wire or very often from metal coat hangers, they are extremely sensitive, even in the hands of a complete beginner. For working outside, the rods should, ideally, be made of the heavier fence wire or welding rod since heavier rods are much less influenced by rough terrain and wind. Some people find it an advantage to use handles of some description; others prefer to feel the bare rods turning in their hands. For handles, ball point pen cases are perfectly good, or 1 inch (2.5 cm) diameter dowelling rod or broom handle, bored down its length to take the short end of the instrument or even several cotton reels glued together. The bare ends of the rods may be made safe by covering them with fibre wall plugs or taping them over with cellotape or electrician's tape, so that they don't penetrate the body. In all cases it is essential that the rods move freely in their holders. Don't be misled by the simplicity of this instrument or any other dowsing implements, as the amount of information that can be obtained from them is quite phenomenal. In order to work correctly, angle rods (like any other dowsing tools) need to be in a state of balance. Try holding the rods perfectly level in front of you, in a comfortable position, just above waist height, pointing away from your body. Now gently raise the tips, so that the rods are slightly above the horizontal and you will quickly find that they go out of control and swing back towards you. They are at their most sensitive position when the rod tips are just a few degrees below the horizontal. A sketch of a simple set of dowsing rods is shown in Figure 10, below.

Now try to locate the energy emitted from an electrical appliance in your home - a television, computer terminal or microwave oven, for instance. Give your hands a brisk rub until they are nice and warm, and then give the divining

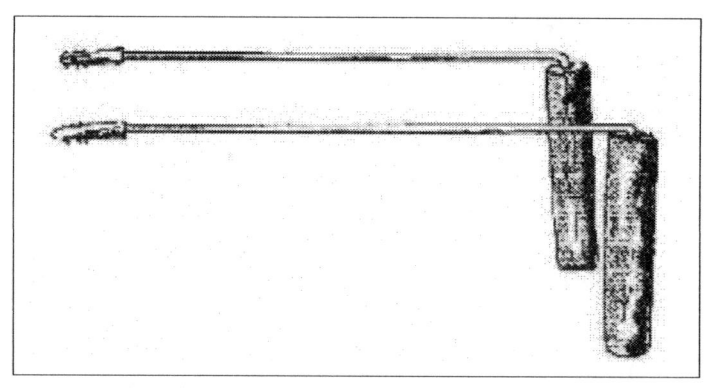

Figure 10. A simple and very efficient pair of divining rods made from fence wire.

rods a rub as well. Holding the rods in front of you, tips slightly down, walk across the face of your chosen appliance, saying to yourself *'find the energy emitted from this object'*. You will observe that they will turn either away or towards the unit. Follow the tips of the rods carefully as they turn at right angles away or towards the appliance, noticing that they are weaving slightly from side to side - this is the wave that you are tuning into, and the wave will be emitted from the appliance for a metre or so before looping back. Once you gain some skill in picking up the waves you can practise on other installations, like microwave towers or electrical sub-stations, then progress to more subjective objects, like the aura; electro-magnetic field around each person, or the energy above an underground stream. With practice you will find that it is much easier using only one divining rod, since you are picking up individual waves, but always remember to protect yourself by visualising a white or purple orb of light around your body, or whatever means of protecting yourself feels comfortable.

One of the most interesting uses of divining rods is to locate the waves emitted from standing stones and circles which our remote ancestors constructed. These are often called ley lines, or more correctly energy lines and occur in various patterns, such as straight or sinuous streams of waves crossing at ancient sites as shown in the research by Hamish Miller and described in his book *The Sun and the Serpent*. Also, roughly circular circuits of waves bounded by straight energy leys can be observed as in my own book *Ley Lines and Earth Energies*.[30c]

Common beliefs of people involved in researching this subject are that there is connection between earth energies and ill-health and that the human spirit survives after death of the physical body.

Ley Lines

We have read how the wife of the Roman Emperor Justinian was implicated in our present refusal to believe in the survival of the human spirit. Science also has a large part to play in this, of course, but we have only to investigate the admittedly arcane knowledge of our ancestors several thousand years ago to discover that they had knowledge about spirits, which we now class as 'paranormal' phenomena. The heritage they left us is of a megalithic system of standing stones and circles which can - even millennia later, yield much useful information, albeit obtained by the use of divining rods, an ancient craft, very unscientific, but then, our remote ancestors were not in the least interested in repeatable science as we know it today. The sensitive shaman could find these perfectly natural energies and instruct the builders to erect the standing stones, dolmens and circles in a highly sophisticated series of circuits, or energy leys, if you like, many of these with the intention of focusing energy through their dead in their burial-grounds.

To understand standing stones and circles and also the seemingly unrelated problems of paranormal activity and ill-health, it is necessary to research cup-marks or petroglyphs, as shown in Figures 11 and 12. These are saucer-shaped depressions carved, or more correctly, percussed, into some standing stones, free-standing boulders and earth-fast rocks sometimes surrounded with one or more spirals, often with a line carved through the spiral into the central cup. Figure 11 shows the side view of the cup-marked stone at Connachan Farm, Sma' Glen, near Crieff, with Foulford Inn in the background. Figure 12 shows the plan view of cup-marked stone at Connachan Farm. This has approximately 60 cup-marks on its surface. Notice the prominent dumb-bell shaped petroglyph.

These phenomena have mystified scholars and scientists for generations, which is not surprising as the only way to understand them is to use the ancient technique of dowsing (rhabdomancy) to follow the energies they emit. This may sound extraordinary, but my recent discovery should make even the most hardened sceptic think again - all the cup-marked stones around my area of Crieff, Perthshire, Scotland, near the Highland Boundary Fault, have been carefully situated above geological faults and dykes - this is the source of their energy, and our ancestors during the Stone Age used them as a basis to form a quite extraordinary net-

Figure 11. The cup-marked stone at Connachan Farm with Foulford Inn in the background.

COMPLEMENTARY ARTICLES

Figure 12 (above). The cup-marked stone at Foulford Inn.

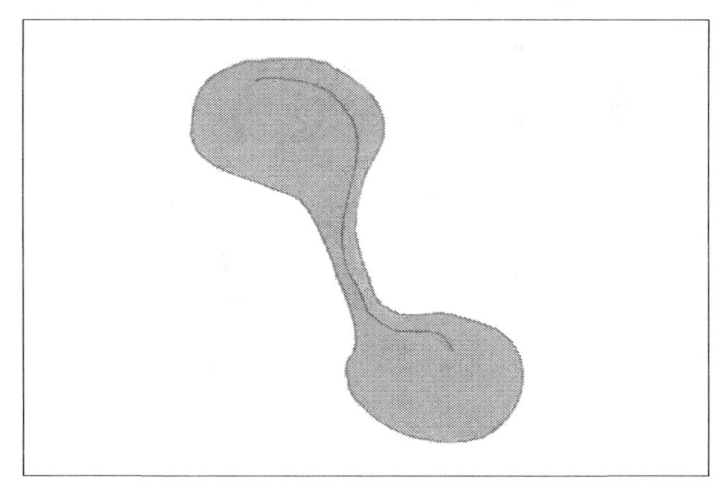

Figure 13 (below). The dumbbell shaped petroglyph.

work of energy leys. One large prostate boulder situated in the Sma' Glen, near Crieff (Figures 11 and 12), is on such a powerful fault, and has around 60 cup-marks pecked into its surface. Two petroglyphs joined by an 'S' are the most prominent feature of this stone, as shown in Figure 13. In particular, observe the worn incised mark, which depicts another shell of energy inside. I spent many years following the waves emitted from this stone across much of Perthshire to make the first map of the ley system. The waves emitted from this boulder are 23 ft in wavelength and 3 ft amplitude, have a cycle time of almost 2 minutes, and extend vertically above the surface of the Earth, as shown in Figure 14. This type of Earth Energy wave moves slowly backward and forward; an effect which can be simulated by tying a rope to a post and waving it from left to right. These are not straight leys but are almost circular - mirroring the petroglyphs themselves - and they have several strange qualities. The most important is that they tend to contour hills, but can be attracted to lochs (lakes) built on the ridges of hills in the appropriate places to pull the energy up and over. Another important discovery is that this form of ley (cup-mark energy ley) seeks any cavity in its neighbourhood, a characteristic which the stone-age geo-

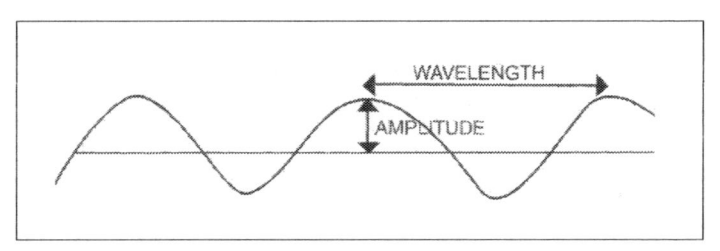

Figure 14. Plan view of a sinusoidal wave.

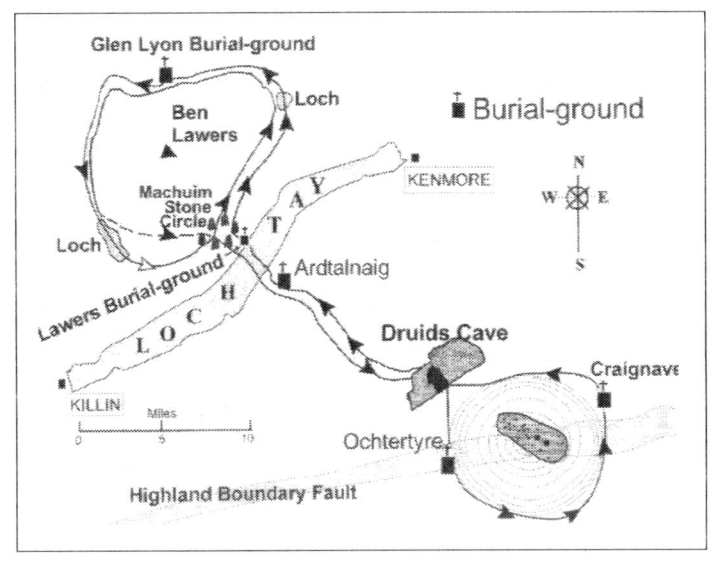

Figure 15. Ancient burial grounds.

mancers used to their advantage.

From the cup-marked stone at Foulford Inn, shown at the bottom right of Figure 15, a wave spirals out anti-clockwise, further and further from the stone, attracted to the huge cavity of the man-made Druid's Cave at Glen Almond, which is 15 feet high, comprised of six boulders, as shown in Figure 16. The energy line carries on northwards to the exact centre of Loch Tay, then further north to the Machuim stone circle which warps the cup-mark ley in two circuits around Ben Lawers with Glen Lyon at its most northerly point. Returning to Machuim it now flows south, back to the Druid's Cave, which it enters through interstices provided at the rear, then back to the Foulford Inn stone in a pattern which mirrors the dumb-bell shaped petroglyph. There are other circuits both inside and outside this, each warped by

Figure 16. The Druid's Cave at Glen Almond.

six-stone circles, but for the purpose of this article I will stay with the basic building block of the dumb-bell ley: its periphery is the most powerful part of the circuit, as the waves, spiralling out from the cup-marked stone are closer together at this point, the 'working edge,' and it is on this outer part of the ley that their ancient burial-grounds were built, in all probability where geological faults also intersect the outer part of the ley - this is still to be investigated, but like cup-marked stones, all of the ancient burial-grounds around my home town of Crieff are carefully placed above such faults, and it appears that the builders used every conceivable means of focusing natural earth energies of various types through their dead. Their belief in the afterlife and the survival of the human spirit was very strong, as was their conviction that the spirits of the dead could harm the living; a similar belief system to that of ancient Chinese Feng-Shui.

Earth Energies and Ill-Health

During my research into the ley system I was asked to investigate the poor health of a woman, living in Ayr. This led me into yet another fascinating facet of this research. Over the last thirty years, I have observed that almost every person suffering from a wide variety of illnesses has a range of 'black' lines, similar to energy leys, passing through their beds. Using divining rods I can easily locate these and determine whether they are healthy or unhealthy. It's a tantalising thought that some illnesses may be related to these 'paranormal' energies, which could explain why difficulty is being experienced in finding their root cause.

The range of various types of earth energies in a bed of a person suffering from post viral fatigue syndrome are shown in Figure 17. A beam of energy from a fault vertically beneath this bed travels down the person's body and

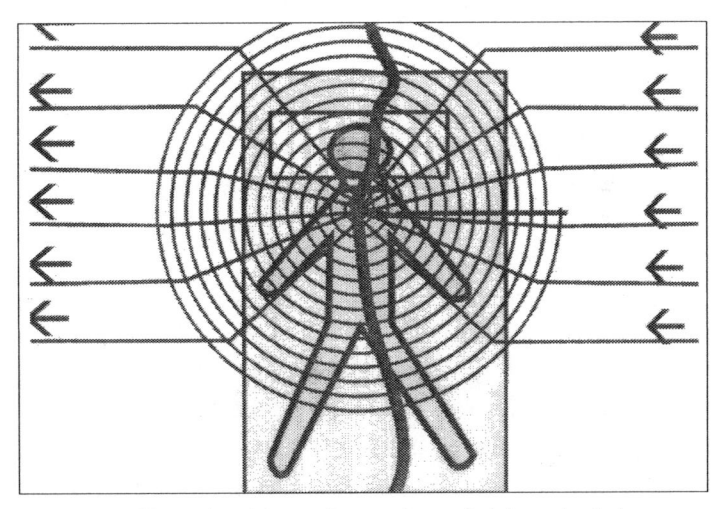

Figure 17. A beam of energy from a fault beneath a bed.

generates overlapping spirals, which in turn attract an unhealthy ley line from right of illustration. Any person with such a network of natural earth energies in his bed will wake up feeling drained and tired even after a night's sleep. This will lead, sooner or later, to ill-health. This sequence is described below:

1. A beam, about 5 inches wide is emitted vertically from a fissure in the geological sub-strata through the bed, and wanders around apparently at random. In this case it passes down the length of the victim's body, the worst possible scenario.

2. Along the length of this beam overlapping spirals (only one shown) are initiated, one will be centred in the bed at the site of the illness of the person occupying the bed.

3. Hartmann and Curry Grid patterns, a few yards apart, (not shown for clarity) focus into the spiral.

4. 'Black' ley lines, a stream of vertical waves, perhaps as close as a few millimetres apart, focus into the centre of the spiral. (A ley stream may be perfectly harmless originally, but will turn unhealthy after passing through polluted matter - a rubbish tip, sewage farm, dirty canal or river, for instance. 'Black' energy can be found utilising dowsing rods painted black to focus the mind of the dowser that he is looking for unhealthy energies - white for healthy energies).

Open-cast coal mines are one particularly bad source of unhealthy earth energies, quite possibly causing one of my clients in Fife to suffer from the most unpleasant condition of necrotising fasciitis (the flesh-eating bug).The ancient Chinese were aware of these energies from quarries and open-cast mines, as they referred to digging quarries as 'breaking the dragon's bones'.

One of the worst places I have experienced is in Tyndrum, Perthshire, where the seams of a lead mine spew out massive quantities of black energy. In this small village I investigated a house where one family member was losing her eyesight and observed a black line running across her pillow. Following the line back to source I found that, in the course of passing across the garden it had tuned into a sewage inspection pit, presumably increasing its potency as it travelled across the heads of the occupants in bed. This was no emission from an underground stream or fissure, but spirit lines, an even stranger anomaly which I had only recently discovered.

Spirit Lines

I investigated a shop in which a poltergeist had been present for forty years. Spray cans, which the owner had replaced on the shelves late at night, would be found in disarray in the morning, clothes below the shelf were also scattered around, and the heavy door occasionally opened and closed on its own. The owner and staff have seen the figure of a man on the close circuit TV (unfortunately this does not have a tape recording facility) walking around the shop when it was securely closed. Other incidents were a loud cough behind the owner when he was alone at night in the locked shop and loud noises from the vacant upstairs flat. When I surveyed the shop I observed a beam of energy coming through the window and curving round to the left-hand wall, forming a black spiral where the spray cans and clothing were disturbed. The owner told me there was a door and a flight of stairs behind the wall at that point, but I ignored this at the time. Spirit lines have very close waves, about 1 mm or less apart. The illustration in Figure 18 shows one as a 'beam' rising vertically from the ground.

A few weeks later, Archie Lawrie, a Scottish psychical researcher, read the story and took a medium called Francesca, to the shop. He did not explain the circumstances; leaving her to reach her own conclusions. After walking around the shop she stopped at the counter, where I had found the black beam, and also where the owner heard the loud cough, and said she could visualize a small man coming through the shop window (it was originally the entrance to a courtyard) and walk round to the left, through a door and up a flight of steps. She gave some more highly relevant information which stunned both the shop owner and his wife, but it was the fact that she stopped on the black line which interested me most - we were both approaching the problem from different angles: she stood in the black beam and could psychically 'see', whereas I found the beam with my divining rod. Later that night, I traced this beam from the window, around the shop into the ancient Parish burial ground immediately behind the premises, to find that it spiralled into one of the ancient graves. It seemed that I was following the energy back to source. In fact, that thousand year old burial-ground was emitting countless beams, each one spiralling up and wandering around apparently at random away from

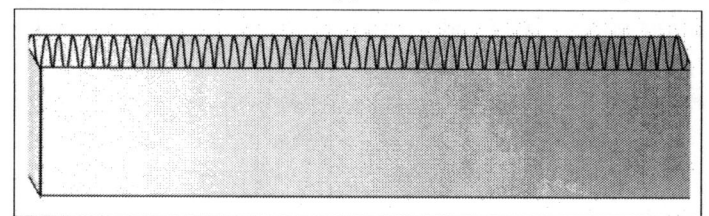

Figure 18. Spirit lines.

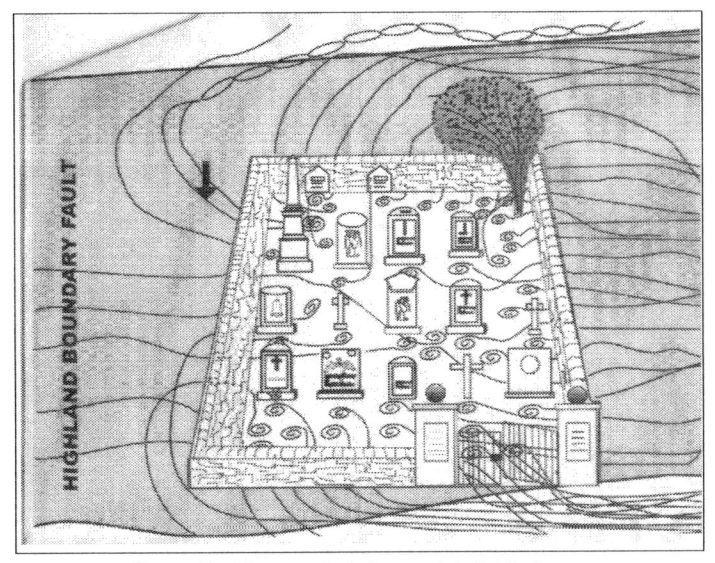

Figure 19. Energy spirals from each individual grave.

the graveyard, while the spirit line I was investigating was on an endless cycle from the grave to the flat and back again. Puzzled, I walked to the nearby Ochtertyre burial-ground, on the Highland Boundary Fault itself, and found exactly the same phenomenon. Here, in open farmland, I could easily find the spirals above the graves and follow the beams. The majority travelled to Crieff, the nearest town, where most of the occupants of the cemetery had lived, but a few, belonging to members of the Murray family, travelled in the opposite direction, to the huge country mansion that family owned at one time. Curiously, the spirit lines from the graves seemed to return to where the owners used to live - or possibly died. Figure 19 shows energy spiralling up from each individual grave, most travelling to Crieff (right of illustration). The beams are about 5" wide, are vertical, and the waves forming the beams are very close together. They tend to escape through the open gate or breaks in the wall, prefer to keep their distance from each other, and seem to cross over other spirit lines with some difficulty. The spirals are of two polarities, the black one spiral up clockwise in the plan view, and its counterpart, the 'white' one anti-clockwise. These two beams keep apart for some few hundred yards, but when they eventually coincide, they modulate, exhibiting wave motion of a few metres (top left, arrowed).

I investigated another graveyard at Monzievaird, a few miles away, on the same fault line. Here, by chance, one grave gave not only the name of the deceased, but very unusually, the name of her house as well, which was only a few miles down the road. Carefully I followed this spirit line, across some fields until it settled down, following the road just a metre away from the wall, until it approached the village in which she had lived. Since energy of any sort always seeks the easiest route, this beam would not pass through the wall until it came close to her little cottage, where it penetrated a wooden door, presumably into the back of the cottage itself.

Leukaemia

Another co-incidence occurred a few weeks later when a lady asked me to investigate her farmhouse to establish the cause of her ill-health. I observed not only the vertical beam from the fissure beneath her bed, but a spirit line as well: this squeezed between the glass window and the stonework on the left hand side, as both are seen as obstacles to this type of energy, and passed down the centre of her bed, as shown in Figure 20. The hollow metal pipe on the right-hand side of the window stops another spirit line.

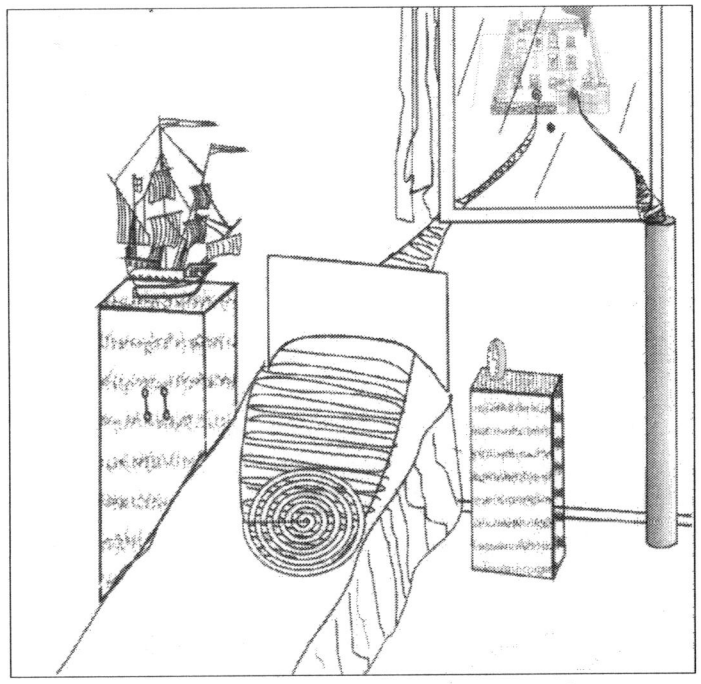

Figure 20. A spirit line spirals up from a graveyard.

Returning a few days later to try and eliminate this strange energy, I took a 3 ft long 1" wide brass tube with me and put it in the centre of her bed, just where her spine would be. The 5" wide spirit line focused into the tube and widened out at the other end. Quietly she told me that she had leukaemia. Since leucocytes are formed in the spine and major bones of the body could it be that this unusual energy causes or at least exacerbates the problem?

During the many years, in which I have been researching this phenomenon, I have come to the conclusion that geopathic stress, as well as life-style and hereditary conditions, is a significant factor in ill-health. It seems to be a contributory factor in such diseases as post viral fatigue syndrome, cancer, motor neurone disease, necrotising fasciitis (the flesh-eating bug) amongst many others. Frequently, I have observed that people with a hereditary disease seem to have these spirit lines focused at the site of their disease, almost as if the spirit lines were tuning into a weakness. Also, I have observed that even when I moved the beds of such clients into another room, free of any such energy, spirit lines soon found the person and vamparises their energies again. Another observation is that the negative energy remains in the bed even after the owner has left; a characteristic, which led me into discovering these weird energies. One possible explanation is that we imprint our aura into any place which we frequent, our beds, most importantly, and it is this electro-magnetic field which attracts the spirit lines.

Methods of Eliminating Unhealthy Earth Energies

Spirals of wire:

A spiral of unhealthy (black) earth energy, which is formed above a subterranean fissure, a river or a stream, can be diverted. This is achieved by placing a spiral of fence wire or similar (either clockwise or anti-clockwise about 6 inches wide) in the exact centre of the black line as it approaches a bed: the correct position of such a wire spiral can only be located using a dowsing rod.

Cup-marked Stone:

This can divert an entire ley line around a house or building.

To follow are step-by-step instructions on how to make your own cup-marked stone. It is easier if the selected stone is carefully kept in the same position throughout the exercise.

1. Find a stone with a diameter of about 1ft (30 cms) or more. It must be of a size which you can pick up without too much difficulty, but sufficiently heavy that it will not be disturbed easily when in place. You will need a type of rock that is not too hard. The rocks I have used contain some quartz, which may help to create the effect we want.

2. With a heavy hammer and cold chisel, make a depression about 2.5 cms deep and 5 cms across. Use goggles when cutting the stone, and gloves, as stone chips can easily damage eyes and hands.

3. Accurately chalk a line from the centre of the cup-shaped depression towards the Sun and hammer this until you have carved a deep groove. It is best to wait until the Sun is fairly low in the sky, and not overhead, unless you wish to experiment - accuracy here is essential.

4. Chalk a ring, about 5 ins. (13cms) diameter, around the depression, and carve this out as well.

5. Check, if possible, with your dowsing rod, that the waves are, in fact, flowing in the direction marked.

6. Carve your initials prominently on the stone, to avoid the possibility of the local amateur archaeologist removing it to the much safer premises of the museum.

7. The energy waves from the stone will have become 'fixed' after a few hammer blows, and, after completion, the stone can be turned in any direction, the Sun now having no effect. It can now be bedded down in an area of the garden where it will not be disturbed, within one metre of your house, with the line from the centre of the cup pointing directly forward to the wall of the house, as

shown in Figure 21. In other words, the line from the stone which was originally pointing to the Sun, now points to the wall of the house, forming a 'T'. Any side of the house will do, although I prefer the sunny south side. The stone should be preferably at the middle of the house rather than near a corner. If this has been done correctly, energy waves projected from the stone should travel towards the building, split into two, then follow the walls in both directions, forming a complete 'shield ring' around it. Any size of house or building can be protected by this simple and inexpensive device, even an entire street, providing all the buildings are connected and have no alleyways for the energy to return to the stone. Any incoming unhealthy waves (but not spirit lines) will be diverted around the building, down the streets or lanes at either side. You can check this with your dowsing rod for unhealthy energies, although anyone without this ability can protect their own house perfectly easily by simply following the instructions.

Check any unhealthy spiral that entered the dwelling before the cup-marked stone was placed, to make sure that it

Figure 21. Placing a cup-marked stone in its correct position, outside the wall of a house.

has changed polarity. This can be verified if the incoming *healthy* energy now passes through glass windows and mirrors into the centre of that same spiral.

I have found that over a period, the pool of energy created by the stone tends to contract back towards the stone a little. It may eventually fall short of the building itself, if it is placed too far away, therefore set the stone as close to the building as possible as a wise precaution.

If the exercise does not work, it may be that the stone is directly above an underground stream which may be causing your problem. The energy wave above the stream serves as a carrier wave, sending the energy from the cup-marked stone downstream and negating the exercise. Shift the stone to another part of the house, if necessary, until any incoming unhealthy waves are diverted around the house.

Another problem is when the energy waves from the stone are not projected towards the wall at 90°, and, instead of splitting and running around the house, are diverted to one side or another for only a few metres. If this happens, try turning the stone just a few degrees at a time until any unpleasant effect in the house is removed.

There should now be no incoming unhealthy waves except from spirit lines, which this type of device will not shield, or from a line directly above any water vein. Even this line can be diverted by inserting a metal stake, or better still, a wider sheet of metal in the upstream side of the underground stream in the garden.

Crystals under pressure:

This is a simple and inexpensive way of eliminating 'spirit lines'.

Buy four small, naturally grown, quartz crystals, with facetted sides and a point or point at the end/s. These only work when under pressure, so take a small 'joiners' 'G' clamp and tighten it on the sides of each crystal, as shown in Figure 22.

Putting a quartz crystal under pressure in this manner can effectively stop spirit lines from entering the bed space. The crystal must lie flat on the floor beneath the bed.

The crystal will now transmit a beam of energy along its length for about 2 metres in each direction. Place four of these, one at the middle below each side of the bed, and top and bottom, in a place where they won't be disturbed. Each must be placed so that the emitted energy travels down the length of the crystal; along that side of the bed it protects forming a 'box'. Any spirit line which is attracted to the bed will bounce off the protecting beams, as shown in Figure 23.

Metal Tubes:

It is also possible to place a steel or iron tube about 5

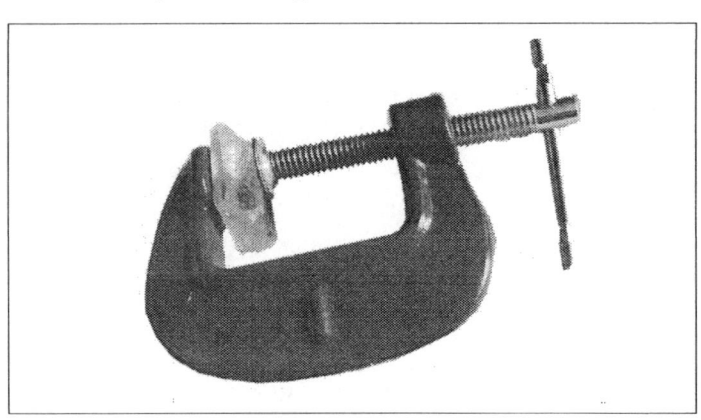

Figure 22. Putting a quartz crystal under pressure.

Figure 23. Quartz crystals used to protect a bed from negative energy.

inches (12 cms) in diameter and two feet or more in length just where the spirit line enters the bedroom, usually between the glass window and the stone framework of the building, although this is rather clumsy, and in any case these spirit lines can come through the sides of the fireplace (again, a weak point) and also through the doors of the house, almost as if the spirit was returning to its own home, or worse, its own bed (see Figure 20).

An Explanation of a Small Cup-Marked Boulder

During my research into energy leys I decided to investigate another of the smaller cup-marked stones which I had discovered. This was located high in the hills to the north of Crieff. Pecked into the face of an earth-fast boulder there were nine cup-marks, one surrounded with a ring.

Unaware that this stone, like all the other ancient stones with petroglyphs was located over a geological fault, I picked up the emitted energy from it - eighteen waves, two for each cup-mark - and followed the stream of energy across country, over two waterfalls which I belatedly discovered were also on faults, walking on some ten kilometres to the Loch Turret falls, on the Highland Boundary Fault itself. Here the stream of waves turned up the river, round the present reservoir, then further up into the hills, still hugging the banks of the river. Instinctively I realized that the energy I was following was 'healthy' as it would be picking up the negatively charged ions from the tumbling water.

Several days passed as I continued with this quest, walking up the main feeder river, wondering if I was wasting my time, until the river quietened down near the foot of Ben Chonzie. Suddenly, and quite without warning, my divining rod turned at right angles away from the river. Sensing something important, I slowed down, carefully following my divining rod, and then realized that I was heading directly towards the foundations of an ancient homestead or shieling. To my surprise I found that the wave of energy looped in through the remains of the door and out the wall at the other side, returning to the bank of the river and back down. Why only half of the building, I wondered? Instinctively I tried to find the other half, which I did quite easily, following this particular wave back to the stream running nearby and crossing it, returning down the other bank, back to the cup-marked stone.

Sitting on the bank of the stream cooling my painful feet I wondered why our intuitive ancestors would surround their dwellings with this esoteric energy. As it happened, I had only recently discovered that I could use a divining rod painted black which allowed me to pick up unhealthy energies only, so I tried to find these in the vicinity of the shieling. There were quite a number, but when I followed them I discovered that they were all warped around the shieling.

The immense amount of tough walking I have done in eight years, with thirty two years of research in total, including ten years writing about my discoveries, without any income, are now almost forgotten memories. It has been a quite fascinating life, but for me the most important aspect of it has been to make me realize that the spirit world does exist, our essence not being extinguished after death.

25

COMMUNITY FUTURES

Colin Roxburgh

Colin Roxburgh works in community development and was one of the pioneers of the community and social enterprise movement in the early 1980s.

Over the last 10 years he has worked mainly in rural Scotland assisting communities to consider their future and organise so that they can be partners in their own development. He is a partner and senior consultant in the Small Town and Rural Development Group. Colin is the joint author of Community Futures *published by Loch Lomond and Trossachs National Park.*

Community Futures is a programme designed to support communities in planning and shaping their own future. It has been designed in the belief that Communities matter

Communities want to be proactive and shape change rather than just react to change that happens to them.

Communities can be players and partners in their own development

Communities can be enterprising – they can plan, organise and make things happen

Community Futures embodies the belief that it is worth while helping to empower communities – and that on the contrary if we don't then what we have is disempowered communities. Importantly we believe that this is detrimental not just to the communities as a whole but to the individuals that live in them. In other words there is a link between the well-being of individuals and the well-being of communities.

Before diving into a more detailed explanation of the Community Futures process we want to dwell a wee bit further on this connection between individual and community well-being.

This connection of our well-being to our attachment to community was famously denied by the conceit of Thatcher and Thatcherism – which linked us uniquely with the market place as a fulfiller of all our needs. In many ways it was also neglected and denied by extreme forms of socialism and communism that saw the state as taking care of all individuals needs.

However there is now an increasing body of evidence coming to light that links individual happiness, mental well-being and even longevity to a sense of belonging to community. The importance of social capital – the quality of our connection to others – is now being recognised as worthy of investment. This growing interest stems from the knowledge and documented fact that as we have got wealthier in the Western world we have not become happier – in fact there is evidence that we have become less happy than we were in previous times. The market place and increased wealth has not catered for our deeper needs, spiritual desires and humanity. Instead research is revealing that the main factors contributing to our happiness are indeed connection to community, our ability to be effective in our lives, believing in something bigger than ourselves - religious belief, and our perceived sense of security. Research has for example shown the value in getting people who did not belong to any social grouping to join something – a community group, a voluntary organisation even a football fan club. They live longer.

So creating ways in which people can participate in their own community can have real significance in terms of their individual well-being and happiness. Developing policies and practice that enables this participation should now increasingly be at the top of the list of any enlightened country or government concerned for its citizen's welfare.

These policies and programmes need to ensure that being part of a community is an *effective* way of being involved in society. It is not sufficient for our well-being to be involved in powerless impotent communities and organisations – and for our participation to be seen as tokenism by others. If we participate in disempowered organisations and disempowered communities we ourselves become disempowered – we certainly don't become happier or spiritually rewarded!

Participation and sense of belonging to community and something greater than ourselves must be linked to effectiveness.

Communities must have effective ways of encouraging citizen participation. Participation needs to be effective in shaping outcomes, and the communities need to have recognition from public agencies as potentially effective partners in their own development.

Participation needs to be linked to a community's ability to shape change and to positively contribute towards its sustainable social, economic, environmental, and cultural future.

Community Futures is a programme that tries to honour and support the need to belong to, be part of and contribute to an effective community.

In practical terms Community Futures aims to provide an effective way of communities planning and shaping their own future. It assists communities to prepare their own Action Plans which describe:

- The vision for the future of the community
- The community's current situation
- The main issues that need tackled and the priorities for action.

The planning process encourages full participation from the community but is not belaboured. Most communities take around 6 months to produce their own Community Futures Plan.

The Community Futures process creates opportunities to involve all in the community through:

- Community surveys
- Listening to the views of different stakeholders
- Compiling a profile of the community
- Collective discussion at Community Futures workshops and events

The process is a way of not only engaging people in talking and thinking about their community, but also of inviting them to stay involved in organising to take action and in making things happen. Community Futures creates an arena for people to step into and make a contribution to their community and to their own well-being.

To honour this commitment it is also important that we create a context for this involvement and community animation. Community Futures is therefore not just about the work in each community but about creating a climate particularly within the public sector that is supportive of this type of community endeavour and involvement.

We have been fortunate over the last 10 years to have established such a climate in the new Loch Lomond & the Trossachs National Park. Strathfillan was one of the first communities in Scotland to empower itself through preparing its own Action Plan through a process of citizen participation. This extended and led to the organisation of the community as a corporate entity through the creation of the Strathfillan Community Development Trust. This in turn has enabled the community to become a partner in its own development. The community have brought into being affordable housing, community forests, local path networks, and community play areas with the support of a range of public and charitable sector partners.

Following on from the inspiration of Strathfillan a Community Futures Programme was established that has assisted all 24 communities in the National Park to prepare plans for their future and like Strathfillan over 20 of them have gone on to establish Community Development Trusts. This collective empowerment of a number of communities throughout one area is unique in Scotland and the UK. It has been supported by the National Park Authority who recognised the need to listen to its communities and to build its own plans, programmes and services from the bottom up. It is this context that has ultimately given the communities the confidence to take time to plan and involve their citizens in thinking about and helping to shape the community's future. They realise that external agencies are there not just to provide services but to listen to what communities have to say and to support them in becoming partners in their own development and in that of the National Park.

Over the last 6 years communities have made a hundred and one things happen – play areas, youth projects, residential care for the elderly, community parks, path networks, community newsletters, heritage projects, tourism projects etc. They all, in one way or another, help to create stronger communities. They build in numerous ways social capital and networking in and between communities. There is now a strong National Park family of communities and involved individuals.

While much of the work carries with it the stress and frustration that is associated with any attempts to make things happen it is also probably safe to say that it contributes to the well-being of us all within the Park community – and allows us to express more and gain more than could ever be achieved from thinking purely of our own individual economic wealth. We are richer for it.

For more information about Community Futures and Community Development Trusts contact Colin Roxburgh, STAR Development Group, email: colin.rox@cali.co.uk

For more information about the work of Strathfillan Community Development Trust, email: strathfillancdt@btconnect.com

26

AROMATHERAPY MASSAGE

Moira Robertson

> *Moira Robertson trained in Glasgow in 1996 at the Scottish School of Herbal Medicine and achieved a Diploma in Anatomy, Physiology and Massage from I.T.E.C. [International Therapies Examination Council]. This course introduced her to essential oils and the following year she studied aromatherapy, achieving Diplomas in Aromatherapy from I.T.E.C and the Scottish School of Herbal Medicine. In 1999 she became a Reiki practitioner and has progressed to Reiki Master. Moira lives in the Highlands of Scotland and has been an active community worker since 1994 and believes wholeheartedly in community empowerment. She believes that love for our fellow man will eventually bring peace to the world and be spread by complementary therapies which take into account mind, body and spirit.*

My name is Moira Robertson and I first got involved with massage in about 1990. I had previously trained as an Enrolled Nurse when I was 36 but due to family circumstances had not been involved with it for several years. I was working in the tourist industry and when the place closed down for the winter, I went to London to work as a live-in carer for an agency. One of my clients was in her late forties and had MS. She was in a wheelchair and liked her feet massaged during her morning bath, and her back and legs massaged afterwards. She told me that I was a natural and should not waste this talent.

When I returned to Scotland, I looked for an evening class on massage and eventually found one and attended the six-week course. This showed me that I could do massage, and so I enrolled in a Diploma course run over a year at weekends by The Scottish School of Herbal Medicine. I followed this up with a course in Aromatherapy at the same school.

I believe that massage and aromatherapy go together – oil is used in all massages and adding essential oils to it means that the treatment goes on working after the massage.

First a little bit about massage and its history. There are five senses, sight, hearing, taste, touch and smell, and society rates them in this order. We have become sight-orientated; which is not surprising when we write down language and music, produce paintings and television is in almost every home. Hearing – our ears are blasted with noise all the time - in most homes television or radio is on even if no one is listening. Then there is traffic noise, mobile phones etc.

Touch and smell play only a small part in our lives and this creates an imbalance. For many people the only touch they feel is violent, many single people never feel touch. Smells are often unpleasant, such as sewage, industrial waste etc. We have grown away from touch, as Desmond Morris says- *'unhappily and almost without noticing it, we have gradually become less and less touchful, more and more distant, and physical untouchability has been accompanied by emotional remoteness. It is as if the modern urbanite has put on a suit of emotional armour and, with a velvet hand inside an iron glove, is beginning to feel trapped and alienated from the feelings of even his nearest companions.'*

Massage is touching – everyone needs it. Babies would die without it – remember the dreadful sights in Rumanian children's homes of children lying in cots without any stimulation. Touch has always been used in healing – a mother rubs a sore spot better. It is necessary in all walks of life – social, sexual and sense awareness. Without touch we would be emotionally sterile. Massage can help physically; it increases blood and lymphatic flow, stimulates repair and eliminates waste products and toxins, thus producing healing. It is great for muscle tension, from which we all suffer. Life today is stressful, it is lived at a fast pace and thus opportunities for releasing tension are often absent. The muscles hold this tension and become painful. Massage can give lasting relaxation on both a physical and mental level.

The beginnings of massage lie in the oldest cultures of both the East and West. Man has always rubbed a sore or aching part to relieve it. Hippocrates believed that all physicians should be trained in massage. Julius Caesar was massaged daily to relieve neuralgia. Ancient Chinese, Indian and Egyptian manuscripts contain many references to the benefits of massage, how it can help heal injuries and cure diseases. Massage went out of favour in the Middle Ages, but returned to favour in the 16th century; several European monarchies using physicians who practised massage. In the 19th century Per Hennk Ling, a Swede, on return from a trip to China, introduced to Europe what is today known as 'Swedish Massage'.

Massage is touching, which has today become acceptable only in restricted circumstance, Lack of touch can lead to stress and all the diseases associated with it, both psychological and physical; asthma, eczema, psoriasis, ulcers, phobias, 'nervous breakdowns', stiff necks, back-ache, anorexia, bulimia and many more. To touch someone is to give them a sense of worth, of being accepted, of being loved. Massage also relaxes or stimulates the nervous system, relaxes muscles and drains away waste products. It gives a feeling of well-being that cannot be achieved by drugs. The therapeutic benefits of massage are today recognised as being of enormous value in dealing with the continuous onslaught of problems we face in everyday life – whether in the form of tight knotted shoulders from being hunched over a desk, tension headaches because of the fast pace of life today, aching legs often experienced by pregnant women, or the painful arthritic joints, encountered increasingly in old age – massage can and does help.

There are two basic types of massage – relaxing and stimulation and four basic movements:

1 EFFLEURAGE; a French word meaning 'skimming the surface' may be very light or relatively firm and is generally used at the beginning and the end of a massage, and also to connect various movements one with another

2 KNEADING; just what it sounds like, and works deeply on large muscles and fleshy areas, relaxing muscles and draining waste products.

3 PRESSURES; just what it sounds like, and penetrates below the superficial muscles and reaches to where most inner tensions lie.

4 TAPOTEMENT; percussion, used to stimulate fleshy areas. Methods include pummelling, cupping and hacking.

Massage is best received in a quiet, warm room and it is enhanced by adding essential oils to the carrier oil.

Now for a brief history on Aromatherapy.

Ancient man, as far back as the Neolithic age, has used plants to aid digestion and to heal. The Arabs, in particular the Egyptians, learnt much about plants and their healing properties by, for example utilising the preserving properties of some of the oils to good effect in embalming. When they distilled the oils, they also collected the perfumed water, which they used to perfume the air and their bodies. The Greeks and Romans carried on this knowledge and advanced it. All three of these civilizations used herbs and aromatic plants as medicine, incense and perfume. In India, herbs have been used as cures since 3000 BC right through to this day; in the form of the Ayurveda System of Medicine, which incorporates spiritual thought into treatment of ills. An early example of a distillation apparatus was found in Pakistan, and believed to date from 3000BC. In China, acupuncture and herbal medicine have been in existence since 3000BC again right up to the present day. This treats the person holistically, incorporating emotional, spiritual and physical well-being.

The healing properties of plants have been utilised continuously in the Middle East but the knowledge was suppressed or lost during the Dark Ages in Europe and reintroduced by the Crusaders on their return from the Arab world. Scientist of the day investigated the properties of plants, which were used in preserving, dispelling odours, perfumes and antiseptics; for example in protecting people against the plague, many ordinary people knowing how to use the local plants.

During the First World War the chemical industry grew very rich and powerful making bombs. After the war, between 1920 -1930 the perfume industry flourished, for example, in France, Gallefosse found that if you used the whole plant instead of isolating a particular property, then it was more effective in healing. During the Second World War the chemical industry was again called on to make bombs but after the war, they switched their interest to fertilisers and drugs. The National Health Service in the UK had been set up to give free treatment to all, but the rich and powerful drug industry dictated a policy preventing doctors from prescribing herbal treatments. This situation has improved; herbal treatments having been gradually reintroduced in France, Dr. Valnet began treating specific ailments with oils. Madame Maury applied this technique to create blends for an individual's health problems and in the 1968 Medical Act herbalists were permitted to prescribe herbs and oils.

In the last 20 years, Aromatherapy has been seen by the public as a safe treatment and is becoming ever more popular, especially with the growing knowledge of the side effects of pharmaceutical drugs. The ancient civilizations knew that smell had an effect on the body, mind and spirit. Aromatic woods were burnt to drive out evil spirits and to cleanse areas. An Egyptian perfume, kyphi, was said to lull you to sleep, allay anxieties and to brighten your dreams. In Ancient Greece, they used aromatic oils as anti- depressants, aphrodisiacs and to make you drowsy. Odours were also known to make you more susceptible to a religious experience by creating a heightened emotional state.

There is a connection between the sense of smell and the brain and nervous system. Odours have an immediate access to the brain via the olfactory epithelium, situated in the upper part of the nose. None of the other senses are connected so directly. The receptor nerve endings are in direct contact with the outside world and the brain extends down into the nose. Essential oils go along this route, as well as into the skin and circulatory system. Most other remedies and drugs use only the circulatory system. There is a brain/blood barrier: the walls of the tiny capillaries are very selective about what they let through and this excludes most drugs. Aromatherapy by-passes this barrier and goes straight to the brain. The essential oil doesn't go any further than the nose, but it does trigger off nerve impulses which have far reaching consequences. Depending on which essential oils are smelled, the reaction will be somewhere else in the body. Some essential oils can stimulate the brain and aid concentration [Rosemary] or refresh the brain [Grapefruit]. Others relax muscles [Marjoram] or aid digestion [Peppermint].

The limbic system circles the brain stem and includes the olfactory bulb. This system has to do with emotions and memories. Thus odours can also effect the emotions. If a particular smell brings back a pleasant memory [not necessarily consciously] then you get a feeling of well-being. An unpleasant memory/smell association will make you feel angry or depressed. Smelling a fragrant flower makes you feel good, smelling an essential oil can also make you feel good.

Fragrance researches have discovered that odours can influence moods, evoke emotions, combat stress and reduce high blood pressure. Aromatherapy makes people feel better by aiding relaxation, increasing confidence, energy levels and ability to cope with stress. Many people burn vaporisers to alter their mood or kill bacteria or viruses in the air. Many religions use incense to alter the atmosphere to create a desired mood. Primitive people also used odours to enhance the performance of their 'magic- man' or witch doctor. Bergamot and most of the citrus oils are uplifting. Chamomile is calming, whilst lavender is balancing. Clary Sage can make you feel euphoric. The tree oils such as Sandalwood bring you down to earth. Thus essential oils can have a holistic effect on mind and body; aromatherapy massage being an excellent treatment for the stressful lives we live, with no negative side effects.

27

BIO-ENERGY THERAPY

Chris Hughes

Chris Hughes has a business background, having been the proprietor of a number of small businesses. Partly due to this background, he is convinced that all happenings must have a logical explanation. One of his early observations was that many people suffer from physical and/or mental limitations. He was no exception, as at an early age he developed arthritis, which he treated by learning yoga and meditation, and from this evolved his interest in complementary therapies. He took a course in Hypnotherapy at St Anne's Hospital in London and became a Reiki healer. He has travelled extensively in his search for spiritual direction having sat at the feet of many spiritual teachers, most recently being influenced by Eckhart Tolle and Sir David Hawkins. He is not prone to making spontaneous decisions and thus it was with some surprise that he found himself enrolled on a course in Bio-Energy Therapy, which is the subject of this article.

Some years ago I found myself signed-up for a diploma course on Bio-energy and sitting awaiting our teacher Michael D'Alton to explain the principals of this healing modality. I am not in the habit of making spontaneous decisions so I had really surprised myself in going for this training without researching it beforehand, but in retrospect, it was one of the best things I ever did. I was greatly relieved at Michael's opening statement: *'There is nothing in this world but energy, atoms in movement'*. I understood this but didn't realise its full significance. Coming from the business community I was at that time of the mind that there had to be a logical explanation for everything, including healing and though open-minded I was a bit sceptical.

I continued on to qualify as a practitioner and learnt that healing should begin by clearing energy field blockages, enabling the body to heal itself.

Our immune system is truly amazing; protecting the body from illness and enabling healing to take place, by providing whatever is necessary to affect a repair. No physician can heal a cut or a broken leg, they may well assist but truly the body itself is the great healer. If there is no or slow recovery you can be sure that there is a blockage preventing the immune system from getting to the root of the problem. The body does what it is designed to do; its natural inclination being to bring the body to balance, thus good health.

Scientists have now proven that the whole cosmos is an electromagnetic field. It is everywhere; within you within me within blades of grass, birds and all of creation. This omnipresent energy field has been called by many names by different belief systems; such as God, Presence and Life. For me this brings home the magnificence of a Creator that is beyond our understanding; dwelling within and without everyone and everything: the totality of all. I am in awe.

The Mechanism of Bio-energy Treatments

Independent research by Dr Robert Becker and Dr John Zimmerman during the 1980's investigated what happens whilst people practice therapies like Reiki. They found that not only do the brain wave patterns of practitioner and receiver become synchronised in the alpha state, characteristic of deep relaxation and meditation, but they pulse in unison with the earth's magnetic field, known as the Schuman Resonance. During these moments, the bio-magnetic field of the practitioner's hands is at least 1000 times greater than normal, and not as a result of internal body current. Toni Bunnell (1997) suggests that the linking of energy fields between practitioner and earth allows the practitioner to draw on the 'infinite energy source' or 'universal energy field' via the Schuman Resonance. Prof Paul Davies and Dr John Gribben in *The Matter Myth* (1991), discuss the quantum physics view of a 'living universe' in which everything is connected in a 'living web of interdependence'. All of this supports the subjective experience of 'oneness' and 'expanded consciousness' related by those who regularly receive or self-treat with Reiki.

Zimmerman (1990) in the USA and Seto (1992) in Japan further investigated the large pulsating bio-magnetic field that is emitted from the hands of energy practitioners whilst they work. They discovered that the pulses are in the same frequencies as brain waves, and sweep up and down from 0.3 - 30 Hz, focusing mostly in 7 - 8 Hz, alpha state. Independent medical research has shown that this range of frequencies will stimulate healing in the body, with specific frequencies being suitable for different tissues. For example, 2 Hz encourages nerve regeneration, 7 Hz bone growth, 10Hz ligament mending, and 15 Hz capillary formation. Physiotherapy equipment based on these principles has been designed to aid soft tissue regeneration, and ultra sound technology is commonly used to clear clogged arteries and disintegrate kidney stones. Also, it has been known for many years that placing an electrical coil around a fracture that refuses to mend will stimulate bone growth and repair.

Becker explains that 'brain waves' are not confined to the brain, but travel throughout the body via the perineural system, the sheaths of connective tissue surrounding all nerves. During a treatment, these waves begin as relatively weak pulses in the thalamus of the practitioner's brain, and gather cumulative strength as they flow to the peripheral nerves of the body, including the hands. The same effect is mirrored in the person receiving treatment, and Becker suggests that it is this system, more than any other, that regulates injury repair and system rebalance.

The Healing Technique

Bio-energy therapy promotes good health because the practitioner's hands are like electro magnets, which locate and then remove energy blockages within the client. By good health I mean in the holistic sense i.e. mental, physical, emotional and spiritual. It is simple enough in operation but developing the skill required takes time and dedication. Meditation is a key element of the ongoing learning process and helps to still the mind and reduce ego, so that healing takes place without the interference of the practitioner. The healer should be aware that he is a channel for the healing energy and not its source and should not regard himself as the healer. The moment that he thinks that he is personally doing it, the healing ceases. All thoughts are energetic; thought waves have a vibration, a frequency, so thoughts can be helpful or damaging.

The Bio-energy treatment commences after the practitioner has handed over the end result to a power greater than himself. It is not necessary for the client to provide a comprehensive medical history though this can be helpful.

Techniques vary as practitioners possess different skills, but my preference is to firstly carry out a body scan, with the client standing. I pass my hands through the main energy centres (chakras) of and around the physical body. As my pass my hand over I will feel something similar to static electricity and that conveys to me that all is well. If I get no feedback it is an indication that there is a blockage at that point and I will work on that part in particular till I sense the energy is normal. I may find my hands experiencing intense pain; an indication of a serious condition. I am not carrying out a diagnosis, that being the responsibility of a qualified medical practitioner: it is enough for me to work in an appropriate fashion and observe the reaction in my hands. After the initial scan I work on the blockage by moving my hands in anti- clockwork fashion around the chakras sensing a release of stagnant energy which just seems to bounce against my hands. I am using a mixture of energy coming up from the earth and a lighter energy from the cosmos. While most of the work is conducted without touching the body, if I feel it helpful I will ask permission from the client to put my hands on the relevant part; this seems particularly effective on back problems.

Through intention and the focus of that intent, the energy behind it removes the blockage, often giving relief, and sometimes with total healing taking place fairly rapidly.

There is an order, call it Cosmic Law if you will, to everything: try stopping breathing for a few minutes and see who is in charge of that bodily function. This reminds me of a true story. Anne (my partner) and I were at a business meeting and afterwards she directed me to a lady who had a sore back. (I don't normally intrude on a person's pain without being asked.) However I asked the lady if I could put my hands on her back, with her permission I did so. I could feel the movement of healing energy removing a blockage under my hands within a few moments. I asked the lady how sore her back was and was astounded by her reply. 'I don't have a sore back' she said. I thought I had the wrong person. Thankfully she explained that up till that moment her back had been extremely sore and that her hobby was horse riding but she had not been able to get on a horse for many months. Next day she was happy to report that she was in the saddle again pain free.

My oldest son Stephen had a cycling accident, he does mountain biking as a hobby, (having had an argument with a tree). He was told that it would be weeks before his shoulder and arm would be working properly and pain free. He asked me to see what I could do (Family are always the most sceptical.) and within minutes the pain was greatly reduced and mobility improved; several days later all was back to normal.

One client who was clinically depressed and who had spent years on several prescribed drugs was greatly helped, and four sessions later a completely different self- assured lady stood in front of me.

One lady, called Mirjam, was suffering from chronic asthma and tennis elbow, and she was so impressed with the cure that she herself qualified with the Bi-Aura Foundation to become a Bio-energy practitioner

There are many such stories. I have never had a client who did not have at least healing of some significance and many had permanent full recovery.

The thoughts of the client are very important as they affect the ability to maintain good health. Healing can be sabotaged by negative thoughts.

The most important thought/prayer is one of gratitude, not for the practitioner's benefit, but for that of ones own healing. The power of prayer or positive thought if you prefer it is amazing. There is always something to have gratitude for and that feeling of gratitude sets up an attractor field, a magnet if you like, that attracts more of the same. All is just atoms in movement. Thought is very powerful in manifesting that which you consistently think of with emotion. E-motion is energy in movement. Emotion /energy bring about change.

There is one other great benefit which is experienced, albeit fairly rarely, of a healing experience triggering a spiritual awakening, Bio-energy therapy being typical, in this respect. Most people who conduct energy healing whatever the modality will have had clients who have experienced states of bliss during and after the process sometimes, with profound changes taking place in their attitude to life. Such happenings are thought to occur by Divine Grace, rather than the ability of the healer.

In conclusion I would advise anyone to have an open mind and to be receptive to all of life's changes and challenges.

28

KINESIOLOGY – THREE IN ONE CONCEPTS

Diane Piette

> *Diane Piette is from Switzerland and lived in Glasgow for eight years. Whilst there, she suffered serious health problems – half of her body became completely numb, and she spent several weeks in hospital undergoing tests, where she was told she was perfectly healthy and there was nothing wrong with her physical body. She then discovered 'Three in One Concepts Kinesiology' and the power of emotions. It helped her where allopathic medicine couldn't and she recovered within four months. After this revelatory experience, she trained professionally for three years and qualified at Harmony Kinesiology College in Glasgow. She has since opened her own clinic at Dronfield near Sheffield where she practices Kinesiology.*

Kinesiology is a holistic therapy using precise muscle testing to identify imbalances throughout the body. A muscle test is the application of slow, gentle and light pressure to a muscle in its contracted or extended position. This process will help decode symptoms which are early warning signals from our physical body and release blockages to assist self-healing. There are many different branches of kinesiology working on a broad spectrum of different aspects and applications of holistic healing, but they all have the same core therapeutic which is the testing of different muscles to identify stressors in order to release them using Western techniques as well as Traditional Chinese Medicine.

The beauty of kinesiology is that we can actually communicate directly with the body and get some precise biofeedback, so it is important to choose the right technique to help with the healing. This entails actually asking the body what it needs to get better instead of imposing any treatment which might not be appropriate and would therefore slow down the recovery to full health.

After reading about different branches of kinesiology, I decided to study the fascinating *'Three in One Concepts'* created by Gordon Stokes and Daniel Whiteside. This is a specialised area of kinesiology working to defuse the stress and fear resulting from learning difficulties, past traumas and negative experiences. These blockages create imbalances in the subtle energy system and stop us from achieving our goals, what we really want in life, and the best for each of us. Three in One Concepts helps us change these negative images into more positive ones and gives us back the CHOICE to get better.

In order to identify the cause – or negative emotional pattern – behind physical symptoms such as Irritable Bowel Syndrome, chronic pain, allergies, skin disorder, asthma and emotional symptoms such as phobias, learning difficulties, Attention Deficiency and Hyperactivity Disorder, ME, anxiety, depression, 'Three in One Concepts' uses a chart called 'The Behavioural Barometer'. This details an impressive range of emotions which the body will recognize through muscle testing to help identify and understand the negative pattern underlying the issue or any form of misperception about past events.

Most symptoms and illnesses are a conscious or unconscious interpretation made regarding a situation or a person. They don't appear randomly on the body. The area affected will give us a good clue about the mechanisms. For example, the front of the body represents present time: any pain or problem on the front relating directly to a present situation. The back represents the past. A burning throat represents something we said and regret or something we should say but can't let out. Headaches represent the pressure we put on ourselves. The heart is related to the love we give and receive. A deaf ear relates to that which we don't want to hear anymore. Neck problems relate to people or situations, which are a pain in the neck in our lives. Each part or organ in the body has a related emotion or meaning, which needs to be studied to help us to understand and resolve the issue behind the symptoms.

Because physical imbalances are the result of past traumas or negative experiences, working on these symptoms in present time will not prevent the stressor from reappearing in identical future situations. Therefore, with 'Three in One Concepts', we can go back in time using a process called 'age recession' and identify the cause of the problem itself. For example, when someone has a phobia about flying, no matter how much work they do on themselves, like breathing exercises or visualisation, this fear will keep on occurring every time they fly. Or dealing with dyslexia in present time and ignoring that the cause of it lies in the past will mean a very slow and laborious process to full learning potential. Urgent action is necessary in treating children with learning difficulties or the system will marginalise them by placing them in special classes, which provide no opportunities to return to the normal program. Using age recession combined with the barometer will indicate the specific time where it all started. The stressor will then be defused with gentle non-invasive techniques, utilising acupressure, sounds, colours, chakras, meridian therapy, flower essences, emotional energy balancing, visualisation to mention just a few. Clients will ultimately be able to deal with problem situations without the same stress reaction.

> *Once we relieve the pain, most often the physical symptoms ease off, and then vanish. When the past defuses from the present, positive changes DO take place.*

Gordon Stokes

As an example, I once treated someone who had a phobia about closed spaces when in cars. She would become very panicky if the traffic were to slow down in a tunnel or experience sweat, difficult breathing and very fast heart beat in the car bay of a ferry, waiting for the doors to open. During the session, we identified the event which was triggering all these symptoms. Fifteen years ago, she had got stuck in a tunnel for an hour because of a car accident. The other drivers didn't switch off their engine for a very long time and rapidly the air turned foggy with exhaust fumes. She could remember the rising panic and the urge to get out of the car and run. Luckily the other passengers of the car managed to stop her. After using the protocol for phobias which includes some meridian tapping, we managed to change the image of the memory itself. All that work was done during the age recession. After defusing the stress caused by that event, the person never experienced panic attacks ever again. This example shows how traumatic experiences create energy blockages and will be programmed to reappear in similar or even less dramatic circumstances. But some of them are more subtle and less straight forward. When traumas appear during childhood, the can have terrible consequences throughout one's life. In the case of abuse, mentally, emotionally or physically, emotions such as guilt, fear, anger or resentment will become buried deep inside as the child will not know how to deal with them. Her energy will be disturbed at the deepest level of the unconscious, the cellular memory. This is like a foot print in the soul and the whole system will be disturbed. After a few years or even decades of energy imbalances, physical or mental symptoms will appear. IBS, MS, depression, skin disorder, numbness are a direct result of suppressed emotions. Conventional medicine can only attempt to help in treating the symptoms without giving a chance to the soul to heal and there are good chances that the symptoms will recur. Traumas and negative experiences do not only happen in childhood. We face them daily in losing a parent or a friend, moving home, car accident, and pressure at work, impossible deadlines etc. They all affect us on an emotional level. With '3 in 1 Concepts', we deal with all these emotions on the conscious level, the subconscious level and the body – Cellular Memory – level to help rebalance the energy.

And where do learning difficulties come from? What if you had a parent at home who repeatedly called you 'stupid' or said that you will never achieve anything in life! Or during the first years of school, what if the teacher 'didn't like you' and was showing it by picking on you, but you had to go back everyday in the classroom to learn how to write and read? Under stress our mental capacities and performances diminish. Some blind spots will appear creating more stress. The pressure increases from parents and teachers and we start imagining that maybe we are not good enough, that we will never solve this math problem that this book is way too long etc. By thinking this way, we start creating a Negative Self-Image which creates even more stress and ... dyslexia appears. How children perform at school is a direct result of the Self-Image they've created, what they believe to be true about themselves. The 3 in 1 Concepts program for learning difficulties focuses on changing the Negative Self-Image by identifying the person or the experience causing it. With positive change comes the realisation that more is possible. We go about changing our situation by changing the way we FEEL about it.

'Three In One Concepts' has a unique way of dealing with wounded spirits which need immediate attention. To bring harmony to our male/control and female/creative sides, we also need to rebalance our Polarity Energy. The polarities of the body are waves of essential energy, the life force itself. They are more directly related to the spirit than either Meridian or Chakra Energy. Each part and particle of our physical body is polarized (has a positive and negative within). If any changes occur in the polarities after an important physical or emotional shock, the whole balance will collapse and the oneness between the body and the mind will disintegrate, leaving the door open to accidents, cancer, infection etc.

All of the information, all the corrections relate directly to disharmonies within the total of being. We are dealing with a wholeness of interaction on every level.

Gordon Stokes.

To preserve a perfect balance between the polarities is crucially important as everything has its opposite - Yin and Yang, solid and hollow, cold and hot, dark and light, moon and sun - and we need to maintain a perfect harmony within ourselves, the world and the universe in order to grow spiritually and progress towards higher levels of awareness.

Diane Piette – kinesiologist, Dronfield, Derbyshire
http://www.dianepiette.co.uk

29

REIKI

Linda McCartney

Linda McCartney entered the world of complementary therapy through her own experience of Reiki healing. Forced to abandon her career of seven years in 1994, due to a progressive illness, she became reliant on a wheelchair. In 1996 her condition was dramatically improved when 'by chance' she met a practitioner of Reiki who totally transformed her life. Linda went on to become a Reiki healer herself which has been her main focus since; giving treatments, introductory talks and training workshops. She finds that, as well as Reiki, Qigong, yoga and meditation were tremendously supportive to her well-being, enabling her to relinquish her wheelchair completely by 1999. She then studied Kinesiology at Harmony College in Glasgow, Scotland, the knowledge from which she finds extremely valuable. In 2001 she opened a Reiki Centre where she treated a wide spectrum of people, including nurses, doctors and carers, many of whom trained in the field of Reiki. This she felt a great honour; to help those who themselves care for others. Linda regards Reiki not as work, but rather as a privilege and educator for life. She now practices from home and is currently writing a book about her experiences with Reiki healing energy.

'The art of medicine consists of amusing the patient while nature cures the disease!'
Voltaire (1694-1778)

Reiki - Introduction

What I could share with you about Reiki would require a series of books and, indeed, this chapter did start off as an epic. Therefore, I have attempted to capture the essence of Reiki in only a few pages, which I trust does it justice. There is much literature already available explaining Reiki; how to work with subtle energies for stress relief and guidelines on how to stimulate and support the body's own inherent healing abilities. Rather than referring to this information, I have chosen to share a few of my own experiences of Reiki, beginning with how I first encountered this 'intelligent', un-intrusive and ancient art of Natural Healing: I will begin by providing a basic introduction for those unfamiliar with Reiki.

Reiki - The Energy

Rei-ki (pronounced ray-kee) is the vital life-force energy that flows through all living beings and matter, being spiritual in nature and holistic in effect. Reiki energy has been recognised by many cultures throughout time; kings and priests utilising it to heal by the power of touch. It has been given various names; Hippocrates called it '*The Healing Power of Nature*'. It is also known as Chi, Ki, Prana, Universal Life Energy, Biocosmic Energy, Orgon and the Light, to name but a few. Jesus connected with Christ Energy, bringing healing to many, harmonising with the purest vibration of Love as did Mikao Usui who connected with Reiki. Both of these men and many others, attuned to the Universal Source, enabling them to channel healing through their energy systems (aura, chakras and meridians). To clarify, no matter how it is described, it is the same basic energy from the same one source, which brings about healing, although healing techniques have numerous titles. Similarly, there are currently many forms of Reiki available, such as Radiance Technique, Kuruna Reiki, Seikhem Reiki – something for everyone I guess.

Mind-body power helps us overcome challenges; exceed limits in countless areas of our lives, but to whom or where do we turn when we experience loss of control in our lives; when we no longer feel the strength to fight our personal battles? We could ask for help from God, angelic beings or loved ones in spirit but sadly we tend to ignore this possibility until we are overcome by fear, have lost hope and are weary from our mounting trials: only then do we recognise there is something beyond mind-body power. With Reiki now widely available, we no longer have to wait until dark times of pain and suffering to seek help. Reiki reaches beyond science and logic; it provides deep peace and is a true constant of life, eternally perfect in its pattern. Love attracts and guides Reiki to harmonise areas of dis-ease and disturbance, be it of environmental, physical, emotional, mental or spiritual origin.

Reiki - The Method

Usui Reiki Ryoho, which translates as 'The Usui Method of Natural Healing', is known as the 'Original Form': it is a simple, pleasant, non-intrusive holistic method of connecting with the Reiki source, transferring appropriate vibrations through our own natural energy systems, for self and others, to reduce stress, promote well-being, support and enhance life in all its forms. The only way to really discover Reiki is to experience it, as it enables you to open up and go with the flow. It is important to choose a Reiki Master or Practitioner whom you trust and with whom you feel comfortable.

This system was structured by Dr Mikao Usui in Japan in early 20th century, along with the Reiki Principals. He rediscovered Reiki after many years of teaching and studying ancient texts, which led him to discover the potential of the healing energies of the Universe. He received the 'first Reiki attunement' whilst meditating and fasting on a 21-day retreat on the sacred Mount Kurama, near Kyoto in Japan. Mikao Usui was born 15th August 1865 and died on 9th March 1926.

The 'Original Form' and 'Principals', which Dr Usui developed and made available to the world has since been modified by succeeding Reiki Masters, mainly to accommodate its use in the West and acceptance in our modern society, which indicates that Reiki has many, perhaps infinite, vibration frequencies and can accommodate our various abilities, no matter what method is used

For more factual information and interesting details about Mikao Usui and Reiki, several books are available by Frank Arjava Petter which are definitely worth a read, especially *Reiki - The Legacy of Dr Usui* and *Reiki Fire*.

This is My Story - Amazing Grace

In March 1994, the pains started in my arms and by September had progressed to my legs. By December, I was mostly housebound and reliant on a wheelchair and both my husband and I were both forced to give up our jobs.

I had stopped seeing the beauty in things, the colour, and the joy, there was none. Vibrations from noise and motion hurt immensely. Any movement attempted had to be contemplated and slow, and each time with dreaded fear of shocks and pain. Only stillness and silence was bliss. I literally could not be touched for over 2 years. God I missed hugs. A hug was one thing I prayed for frequently. I was, at this point, slowly letting go of life and the living; ready to hand over my 'future' to my creator. I felt worthless and useless; abandoned by the medical profession, whose prognosis was guarded and unclear. Medication brought me relief for a while before adding more symptoms to my fight. Doctors' advices, lack of knowledge and understanding of my condition only served to reduce my faith in any chance of recovery.

I prayed for God's help, asking to be useful and worthwhile; to know my purpose or go *home* where I knew the continuous torture would stop. I really meant it, I'd had enough. I'd felt tortured by incredible nerve and muscle pains for so long. I was tired and weak. I guess this is what is termed as surrendering! It did bring me the freedom that I had sought for so long. It was immediately after this 'talk' with God, I met someone who answered my prayers…and more.

By the Grace of God and through the Spirit and Love of a very special man, I experienced a personal miracle on 15th August 1996 which changed my life in a most profound and positive way forever. Far beyond my understanding, this experience realigned me to another part of myself…my spiritual or energy self; I became aware that I *was* aware and, most importantly, recognised clearly just what I was aware *of*. I felt alive and realised that I had accepted 'just existing' before. I was certainly not aware of how spiritually blessed

I was, of the potential within us all to heal ourselves. We all have the ability to read our body's signs for nourishment or change before it's forced to cry out more severely to get our attention. I'd like to share this miracle with you and hope that it inspires love, faith and inner strength, which I believe I gained much of through this experience.

How Reiki Found Me

I knew the birds were singing that day for, apart from brief showers, the sun was shining and the flowers blooming. But I felt only the agonizing vibrations from my chair. My husband pushed me and mother-in law strolled behind, trying to keep my attention from pains, the cause of which was still a mystery. As we travelled the path near our caravan, a silver car pulled up. The driver rolled down his window and asked very respectfully what was wrong with me. He told me he may be able to help me. His eyes beamed optimism in waves of true compassion and genuine faith in his proposal. He told us he practised Reiki and explained it was a simple, non-intrusive method of healing from Japan which involves channelling universal life force energy. I had never heard of such a thing, but his eyes were so bright and sincere, I accepted his kind, unexpected offer. We arranged a treatment for the next morning at his house. Later, he explained that he had, seemingly by coincidence, seen me and my companions three times since late the previous evening: the first time, he had taken his three dogs for a short walk and seen a wheelchair, A rottweiler (Rocky) and a couple of people, in silhouette against the lights at the Lower Station and retreated quickly to avoid the dogs fighting. Secondly, he had observed us walking up through the village the next morning and this was the third time he had seen us, as he returned home to collect his spectacles from his house. He regarded this series of events as an example of synchronicity, (as discussed in chapter 14) which is why he had stopped to ask about my condition.

Next day, severe toothache, on top of the usual distress, made me miserable and pessimistic. I asked my husband to cancel the appointment, partly because my pain was so intense that I couldn't bear to be touched but he returned saying the man asked me to at least let him try as he felt very confident that he could help and he would treat me without touching my body. Rab carried me to the house, close to our caravan. The man's name was John, a very active businessman who played an integral part in his local community and such a gentle, wise and spiritual soul. I did not know what to expect as I knew nothing about Reiki but, after the most relaxing and truly 'awakening' hour I'd ever experienced in my life, I tasted the sweetest fruit of freedom I'd prayed so long for. I saw extraordinary colours, felt intense peace and moved without severe pain. I was as light as a feather. I gave John a hug; the first hug for so long that didn't hurt. I had no words to express my gratitude to this stranger except 'thank you'. I walked, with support from Rab (for balance mainly as my muscles were weak and wasted). I still had a lot of work to put in to regain strength and stability, but I moved free of pain and felt tremendous inner contentment. My husband and mother-in-law stood astonished at my ease of movement. We were all pretty stunned. They too could only thank this man who had just demonstrated to us the miraculous power of Reiki. Our sceptical minds were now full of amazement and gratitude.

I remember hearing laughter, which I now realise was the release of nervous emotion. Not only did I gain mobility and growing self-esteem, I found a deep inner faith which I never knew existed in me; a spiritual side which I never let breathe before. John opened my eyes to aspects of me that I'd stopped nurturing. In this clear state of mind, I discovered some truths about my illness - a physical reflection of repressed energies and emotions. Reiki helped me in a way that no pills could ever do. Even with endless support from my husband, family and friends through my torturous, unfathomable ordeal, Reiki is the key that opened my heart and allowed me to heal properly. I wrote a poem to thank John that says it all. I called it 'My Special Guru' because he introduced me to so much of life's precious and amazing treasures...

My Special Guru

You've shown me a door
And helped me to enter
You've given me strength
When my own was deplete

You've restored in me hope
That so long I'd forgotten
You've triggered my senses
That were for so long asleep

You brought to me Light
And eased all my pain
Like a miracle you appeared
Like a rainbow during rain

All of these things
I owe you so much
All of these things
From only your touch

You've given me direction
And taught me wonderful ways
But most important of all
You've brought back my faith

In that summer of 1996, I met a wonderful man whose unconditional love and healing wisdom opened for me a door, one that helped me renew my faith in life and the living just when I was losing hope. Not only did John enlighten and encourage me to unfold my potential, to bloom in my own way with unconditional support, he also introduced me to friends, many of whom I will always hold dear and cherish having met. Three of whom are very special people: Mary and the late Anu and Alex, thank you from my heart for sharing with me your time and wisdom, the foundations to help me grow in confidence in the healing work I now do with love, pleasure and joy.

John introduced me to another remarkable soul called June Woods, my wonderful Reiki Master, a truly spiritual being for whom I have the utmost respect. I received my Reiki I attunement on 9th March 1997. June took my hand and guided me as I walked through that door to a place I felt was familiar. June's wisdom and love made me feel secure, protected and confident, with a deep inner strength and clarity. It felt like I'd come home after many long years of fighting constant battles, tortured and torn inside and totally disillusioned to the point of surrender. My warm affection and trust for June's simple method of teaching and our clear spiritual connection with each other, assured me she was the prefect teacher for me. I attained my 2nd degree on 29th March 1998 after a year of regular and intense self-healing. Reiki flowed so strongly and I had built up an extra-ordinary amount of case studies during that time which enabled my smooth progress with Reiki. On 21st August 1998, having developed a deeper commitment to working with Reiki, I attained Master Teacher level Usui Reiki Ryoho. Since, I've had the pleasure and privilege of teaching Reiki to many and will always remain in touch with June, my spiritual mother and treasured friend.

With thanks to Reiki, Yoga and Love from precious people who helped me gain improved quality of life, I continue to share Reiki. Every treatment and attunement is still like the first, bringing incites, surprise and wonder of how this amazing energy, with such Divine qualities, can be so simple and accurate, so gentle yet powerful. I've never looked back to regret the 'torture' time, for those hurdles brought renewed faith and purpose to my life. I promised myself always to listen to my body for, as Mary once told me, 'If we ignore the whispers, we hear the shouts, if we ignore the shouts, we'll feel the bangs - and those we can't ignore!': wise words. The choice is always ours.

Reiki Experiences

As a dedicated Reiki teacher and, therefore, full-time channel for Reiki, sometimes we are called to aid souls in need, even if we think we have a day off. Some of my experiences in channelling Reiki are described below.

Lady in Trouble - Reiki Knows Best
Let Thy Will Not My Will Be Done

Having shared Reiki with so many for years, I promised myself and Rab (who was concerned about me 'over-doing it' whilst recovering from such serious health issues!), that I'd refrain from using Reiki for others – just a short break. This was crucial for both of us at the time. We went for a stroll near home.........

A lady collapsed about 20 yards away. Remembering my promise, I exercised my will. 'There are others here who can help', I convinced myself. Four ladies went to her aid. She fell again and they were unable to lift her. Rab ran over to help. This was the perfect opportunity, I thought, to test my will power, to be in control of my time! Enforcing my decision not to get involved, I stayed where I was, as an observer. Once on her feet, the woman appeared strong and steady. Stepping over a metal barrier, she headed in my direction. Two feet in front of me, she collapsed. Straight down hard, her legs completely gave way. I felt challenged, put on the spot. Rab returned and we helped her to a seat in the nearby bus shelter, where a small crowd began to gather. Two ladies comforted her with kind words, but kept their distance. The lady repeated 'I'm alright,' but she was obviously intoxicated and disorientated. I really didn't want to get involved, but noticed her head was bleeding. Reiki started to flow; I could feel the heat coming through my hands and knew instinctively it was primarily to stop the bleeding. To apply Reiki whilst avoiding appearing strange to onlookers (Reiki was not well known at the time), I asked for a tissue, held it over the cut, allowing Reiki to help. Just then, she looked at me, an expression of sorrow in her eyes followed by bewilderment. I knew she felt the energy. She didn't say anything. Reassuring her, I whispered, 'It's okay, it's only Reiki. You cut your head when you fell, Reiki will stop the bleeding'. She asked me who I was. 'I do healing work,' I replied. She placed her hand tightly over mine as Reiki flowed. Her eyes sad, she looked lost. It felt right to help this lady, I now wanted to. She said she needed more healing. I told her to call me, but she pleaded with me 'I need help now, you don't understand, I can't wait'. She seemed alert and desperate for immediate help. The lady repeated her plea, refusing to let me leave! I offered to take her to hospital and see her tomorrow, but she was stern and asked me to help her now! I saw a woman in pain. How could I not at least try? We knew that, rationally, we should take her to hospital to receive proper professional care, but we took her home. The lady felt our inner conflict and continually assured us we were doing right by her; that she needed healing right now or we should let her out of the car. She was adamant that she didn't need a hospital. During an intense Reiki session, her legs and arms flailing about whilst lying on the treatment couch; she released much tension, and then slept deeply for 2 hours. When she awoke, she panicked, thought it was morning and she was late for work. Then she recognised me and her expression calmed. She remembered! She smiled! She looked like a different person. We had a cuppa and a chat. She was a nice lady and began to explain why she was in such a state...After having lost her daughter recently to cancer; she started drinking to ease her pain and lost her job as a result. She was calm and centred now and so grateful. She said 'you are an angel, you saved my life'. I asked her to thank Reiki - it gave her what she needed. 'You don't understand,' she added, 'you really saved my life!' From her handbag she pulled out 2 cans of strong lager and continued, 'When I met you, I was on my way to the park to kill myself....' She pulled out a bottle of pills and shook them, '...with these!' I was stunned, totally amazed by her story and by Reiki's guidance. I now recognised more clearly the Inner Voice of Truth, the Master Within (which I stubbornly argued with before). Reiki came strong for this lady. The urgency in her pleas made sense now. That moment I realised the vastness of the Greater Will through working with Reiki, the connectedness that enables Oneness of which I'd so often heard. Also, I realised the true meaning of being an 'open, trusting channel' from this experience and learned to accept that when Reiki is needed and can support lost souls, it just happens!

Stairs at Oban -
The Supportive Power of Reiki for Self
Where there's a Will, There's Reiki Support

After learning Reiki first degree, whilst driving in Oban, Scotland we passed this wonderful landmark, McCaigs Monument, an open architectural structure built on top of a very steep hill. Countless numbers of stairs led up to a flat, grassy plateau, where, through an array of stone arches, the view is breathtaking. Rab and I were always active prior to my illness; we loved camping, hill-walking. I missed all that and wanted to see the view from the top after hearing how fresh and invigorating it was. As my hips were painful, Rab offered to drive me to the top. But, having experienced the supportive powers of Reiki, I was determined that, with the help of these newly attained skills, I would walk (though Rab was not convinced I should yet). Simply by placing each hand in my back pockets to support my arms, I let Reiki flow to my hips. It eased the pain immediately. I was amazed. As long as I kept my hands at my hips, I could walk, slow but steady! Rab had not the same incentive as I and opted to drive up and meet me at the top. I made it without distress; rather incredible as I still had trouble with many simple things at that time. Reiki also lets you see the colours and beauty of nature in a more intense way. The view, the air and the look of relief on Rab's face, were a picturesque site. This ascent, I have been told since, is found taxing for the fittest of folk!

Freedom of Flow on the Train -
Trust and learn that all things connect
*The Spirit of Love Connects; The Master Within Guides;
Unconditional Love Heals*

Whilst on a train journey, my mind engrossed in a book, I felt Reiki suddenly begin to flow. I knew it wasn't for me; I felt full of energy and had no pain. I wondered where it was going. There were many passengers, so I could not tell. With comfortable, warming energy flowing through me, I simply offered my willingness for Reiki to flow and continued reading. Several minutes later, Reiki just stopped. I became curious to know where the energy had gone. Instantly, a woman with a broad highland accent poked her head between the headrests in front of me and uttered, 'Oh, what a relief, my legs were aching.' She commented on the seats being uncomfortable every time she made this journey as she re-adjusted her position to stretch out on the double seat. With a knowing awareness and smile in my heart, I listened on. What a wonderful gift Reiki is, I thought. I gave quiet thanks for this blessing.

We began to chat for the rest of the journey: she was a strong, kind, caring soul with many difficult charges. When hearts are in need, the ordinary person, stranger or not, can bring support in extra-ordinary ways by simply being a channel for universal love. To quote Mother Teresa:

> *There is a Light in this world —-*
> *A Healing Spirit much stronger than any darkness we may encounter.*
> *We sometimes lose sight of this force where there is suffering, too much pain.*
> *And suddenly the Spirit will emerge through the lives of ordinary people,*
> *And answer in extra-ordinary ways!'*

Car Crash Shocker -
Being in the right place at the right time
When the Student is Ready, the Opportunity is Given

When I had just completed my Reiki second degree, Rab and I were driving near Forres, stopping occasionally to stretch our legs and view the colourful summer scenery. On one such occasion, I was strolling along without a care in the world, observing and savouring as much country atmosphere as possible, pausing at any interesting insect or plant. Soon I realised my sauntering was irritating Rab, who began imploring me to catch up. He was, understandably, bored, having been on his own again while I enhanced my

Reiki skills. He was hungry and his patience wearing thin for yet another slow stroll. So I caught up. On approaching the car, I stopped to tie my lace, much to Rab's annoyance. With Reiki energy flowing I was content, undisturbed by my now very impatient husband. We set off and along the tree-lined road witnessed a car, travelling in the opposite lane, flip over and land on its roof only yards in front of us. The driver, a young photographer, whose cameras and equipment were scattered across the road, looking deeply shaken. He appeared unhurt, apart from a bleeding hand. Rab attended to oncoming vehicles while I reassured the man. Another driver stopped and called an ambulance. Reiki came through. I knew he was in shock, but I felt self-conscious, unsure of his reaction to Reiki. He was trembling, so I put aside my awkwardness and explained I could help him with Reiki. Fortunately, I had just learned to apply an effective trauma-shock treatment. To my delight, the man knew of Reiki and gave permission for me to help re-balance his energies. He was lucky to be alive. He was in a hurry and turned the bend too quickly, causing his wheel to catch the embankment and car to flip twice before landing on its roof. My first chance to use the new Reiki techniques for trauma-shock was a memorable and extremely effective one, both for this man and for my own confidence. My reason for sharing this experience is because it was Rab who noticed the synchronicity and timing on this occasion. He remarked that the delay earlier; when I stopped to tie my laces, ignoring his impatience with me (or words to that effect!), were vital moments that saved us from becoming victims of the crash ourselves. He actually thanked me for not listening to him. How good can it get!

Animals Love Reiki -
Plants Also Benefit
*Sharing Reiki Light, Bringing Peace and Comfort
to the Lost and Fearful*

Every healing thought for an animal will support that animal. Animals receive Reiki without blocking or controlling the process, allowing the energy to flow freely. Animals are honest and instinctive and will always let you know when they've received enough. We cannot force the energy on them. As a channel to bring through healing support, we should remain calm and assertive, gently and confidently offering love, allowing the animal choice to receive of its own freewill.

This story may better convey my point...*A student observing insects in cocoon state breaking free from protective membranes to begin their new life as moths. One, he noticed, was struggling to burst this tough outer shielding. Upset at witnessing this little creature's plight, he could not bear it and went to help it break free. As he reached out, his Master interrupted with stern words, warning him off interfering. The young boy, confused by this, asked why he wasn't allowed to help the poor little insect. The Master explained 'It's all part of the process! The insect has stored energy whilst an infant to transform itself and break free from the sack. It has to build up physical strength to release itself from its confinement. Then it will be strong enough to survive in its new form. If you interfere and set it free before it has had time to strengthen, it will surely die.'* Some afflictions are necessary steps towards one's own development. Our motivation to provide support should not be merely to ease our own distress because we cannot bear another's suffering; their permission is essential. There's a fine line between 'helping' and 'interfering'.

A wonderful place to share Reiki with animals is at Animal Shelters. Often frightened and timid animals find tranquillity and comfort from Reiki. Having lost our own beloved Rocky a few years previously, we decided to look for another at Dog Shelters. On our first visit I met 'No.8', a male German shepherd dog around 6 years old. He was noisy; barking; wouldn't let anyone near him. I was drawn to him right away. He felt lost, frustrated and in a strange, limiting cell. Who wouldn't be upset, I thought. I wandered back and forth to him. It was busy, excited children around, so I was unable to connect with him. Someone noticed my concern and revealed he'd been visiting the past few days and that dog never stopped barking. He said he'd tried to calm him several times as he was beautiful, but decided he was unapproachable. The angry dog was pacing at the back of his pen. I crouched near his cage and sent out loving, comforting thoughts, speaking to him from my quiet heart. I was honest in my thoughts and I told him these people were trying to find a new home with loving people to care for him; that he'd have a better chance if he settled down, as right now no-one wanted to approach because he was so angry. Just then, No.8 became quiet and sat down, watching me from the back of his pen. A worker nearby was surprised at this, he hadn't seen the dog respond since it arrived. I almost convinced myself to take him home, but that wasn't my involvement here. My thoughts became clear on this; I was to do something else for him. At that moment, I saw a bright silver thread-like light at the back of the pen, where No.8 was now sitting quietly, giving me his full attention. For a few moments there was just me, the dog and this shining silver thread. My attention was drawn to the ceiling, where a strong white ball of light appeared with a golden dust-like glow around it. I knew instinctively that I was to reach out in my mind and connect the thread up to the light. As I did so, my heart was filled with peace. It felt like I restored his connection with an angel. Nothing about this seemed strange; it all felt so natural. No.8 came to me. Just then, a third man approached, startling us. No.8 began barking and moving away until the man backed off, then he returned calmly and friendly. I wiped my tear-filled eyes whilst squeezing fingers through the cage to stroke his thick coat. He enjoyed being touched. With great enthusiasm, he assumed awkward positions just to let me caress different areas. He even lay on his back, pressed against the cage, to enjoy a belly rub. The onlooker spoke in a quiet tone that he had not seen anything like that before. For a moment I thought he witnessed what I saw, but realised he was referring to the dog's actions. I remained with No.8 for a while. It felt right but sad to leave. I told him there's an angel with him to protect him. He was quiet when I left. I contacted the shelter a few times to enquire about him and he was fine, much calmer. He will always be in my heart. I had such a clear and profound experience with No.8. I am so thankful to him for his trust. Because of him, I visited so many other dogs in similar situation to share with them quietly and lovingly Reiki Light.

Plants also accept Reiki and some physically 'dance' when receiving. Observing this creates quite a remarkable joy within; to see another element of life respond in such a physical way strengthens the soul and bonds us with nature. These experiences convey the simple and responsive nature of Reiki, which flows, whether or not we're conscious of what's occurring.

Listen to the Whispers

Reiki can be effective for pain relief, but we shouldn't ignore the area of dis-ease being brought to our attention by pain or emotions. Even when a pain eases, something needs attention; to be changed, remembered or loved. Only sincere action towards dealing with root problems can release the disturbance within; then the pain will have served its purpose, having alerted you to respond; like an alarm warning of threat. To clarify, the following is a quote from a wonderful healer and is a great way to remind us of this fact…

> *If you ignore the whispers, you'll hear the shouts…*
> *If you ignore the shouts, you'll feel the bangs…*
> *And that you can't ignore!*

It is a beneficial and wise practice to listen to what our bodies 'talk' to us about. Notice the areas, the physical disturbances, which may be drawing your attention to an emotional issue or unsupportive situation. Pain is our body's way of bringing to light some area that needs harmonized and is the last resort to get your immediate and focused attention. With reference to Edgar Cayce's model, the following should elucidate this also…

> *The Energy (Spirit) flows through the Pattern (Mind), then reflects or projects itself Physically (Body). Physical signs are the body's last attempt to get your attention to attend*

to dis-ease in some aspect of your life. Something does not serve you and needs acknowledged and changed.

When we focus too much on our emotions we give them control over our choices. We have forgotten how to correctly interpret them as the 'I feel' and not 'I am' aspect of ourselves. Emotions, be it anger, sadness or joy, are important tools in determining our well-being. If we learn to view them as such, we can master them. The Emotional Barometer used in the field of kinesiology illustrates this fact very well.

Reiki is a Blessing

This ancient, mysterious energy is spiritual in nature and responds to love, reminding us that ALL things connect at some level. Reiki in its entirety is undeniably far beyond our current logical and scientific understanding (perhaps remaining so until we recognise and honour more consistently our precious relationship with our universe). Nonetheless it is with us; available to us now at this time. With so much stress, change and misguidance dominating our lives, Reiki, being a natural, universal energy, is extremely valuable, supporting re-connection with our instincts and realisation of our true nature. It helps us recognise and develop our inner strengths with clarity of the 'NOW' principle, enabling us to release patterns that no longer support our true needs.

Just as networks of veins and arteries allow blood to flow to and from organs, there's exists the meridian system; connective pathways through which energy flows. These need to remain clear to function effectively and maintain good health and well-being. If meridians are blocked, healthy energy flow would be restricted. Reiki helps clear these blockages and free the energy (just like removing a dam to allow the river to flow again). Reiki also offers tremendous potential for clearing and harmonising energy disturbances in our environment. With the intense suffering, unrest and greed in our world, Reiki is a blessing; a means to encourage peaceful outcomes to feuds that repeatedly shatter lives; a light to transmute suffering, a Divine Light that in merely connecting with, we do so honour. Anything that is constant and unconditional in its support is an expression of Love. Reiki is one of life's wonderful constants. Whilst being adamant in nature, is adaptable, flexible in its effect and use. Reiki is integral to life and should be honoured as a precious gift to all living creations on this earth.

We Are Evolving

I heard announcements that Reiki is changing; getting stronger and increasing in frequency. I wish to impart my contrary opinion, which I trust will serve, at the very least, to bring an open-minded perspective. It is not Reiki which is evolving, we are! We are increasing our frequencies and becoming able to connect with and anchor finer Reiki energies that already exist; they are not 'new' or 'better'. Reiki is whole and of infinite range. All things are in constant motion in our universe. Things change, grow, die, renew. Reiki is not attached to this fixed, sustaining evolutionary development, we are! Reiki is free, it is constant; it is universal and responds to vibrations of Love.

Some assume you need to believe in Reiki for it to work. I disagree. If that were true, plants, animals, children (and indeed me at first) would not feel any benefits. Reiki may appear mystifying; immeasurable and hard to believe. To support so many aspects of our being, leaving us spiritually nourished and energised, it is astonishing – and it is very real! It is healthy practice to be sceptical. Witness Reiki for yourself with someone you trust. It may transform your perceptions of life and awaken dormant senses that have been unrecognised and under-exercised. We cannot always explain the wonders of the Universe - just observe them and love them.

My Inner Joy Sparkles With Reiki

Life teaches us many things, its constant laws, patterns, creations. When we learn from and integrate our experiences, how can we be sure it's the Truth? Reiki has brought me to consider many possibilities. My journey with this life-enhancing energy is ceaseless in enquiry. It fortifies my love and trust in the Universal Laws and in my Self. Reiki comes to Hearts not Minds. Our minds interpret our experiences by utilising information, which is already available. Unconditional Love attracts Reiki, and the quality of that Love may be an element in determining our channelling ability. Observing and trusting Reiki enlightens and is a steady foundation for learning.

Strangers can bring much clarity and insight into our life, indeed a stranger brought me a gift - a life long, perhaps eternal connection to Reiki Source. Reiki brought me renewed and stable faith in myself, and I have chosen to share this gift every day for over 11 years, guiding others in their journey with Reiki and beyond.

30

SATHYA SAI SCHOOL

Lesley-Ann Patrick

Lesley-Ann Patrick holds a BA Honours [University of London] and a PGCE [University of Cambridge]. She is a qualified Montessori teacher for children from birth to twelve years and is trained in Sathya Sai Education in Human Values. She has many years experience of teaching in Cambridgeshire, South Devon, and Hyderabad in India. She is currently Head Teacher of the Casa della Pace Montessori Ecoschool in St.Andrews, and integrates SSEHV throughout the whole school ethos and curriculum. She is working with the British Institute of Sathya Sai Education to promote personal self-development training for teachers and to organise SSEHV activities for children throughout Scotland.

Sathya Sai tells us. *'Children are precious treasures and yours is the great task of rearing them'*. As India's leading social reformer, it is, in my opinion, Sai Baba's work in education which is the most crucial. Our troubled world can only ever be healed by the purification of every individual heart, and the cultivation of love in each and every one of us. Not a love shadowed by emotion and attachment, but a universal love for all, emanating from a greater force than any single human being. The earlier that this work begins the easier it is.

Transforming society through the education of children

is not a new or unique idea- all the inspired holistic educationalists (Froebel, Stemer, Montessori, Dewey, Magaluzzi) have shared the same view But Sai Baba's programme puts forward this idea by offering to children a model of essential human values- these are ancient cross-cultural values which are truly inherent in all people They are not something which can be put into the human being, but are to be drawn out from beneath the layers which so often hide them. So what are these values? They are truth, love, peace, right conduct, all of which culminate in non-violence.

So how is this ideal put forward to the children? These children come to us rising 3 years of age, and already at this age, there are more often than not many layers of conditioning which hide who the child truly is. These children are not empty vessels into which we pour knowledge, ideas, modes of how to be and how to behave, but our role is to begin to peel away these layers one by one in order to free the child so that he/she can reveal who he/she really is, so that the inherent values become visible. But where have these layers, these veils come from? We know that every child has a true spark of divinity within, and the potential to be perfect, but from birth these children have been living in a fast, competitive, chaotic world where so much emphasis is put on success, gain, and consumerism. Can you imagine how it is to be a tiny child with images flashing past your eyes and your delicate aura, be it from television, supermarkets, loud voices, and so on?

And so Sathya Sai tells us that the teacher has the most important role of all professions: *'The teacher has to help the pupil unfold and manifest the skills and qualities inherent in him'*. Are teachers prepared and trained to carry out this task?

Certainly the intent of modern educational policy is noble, and we hear meaningful words spouted- citizenship, personal and social development, a culture of respect, personal learning plans- but why do we not see results in the young people leaving school? Why do we have more racism, more addictions, and more social unrest on the streets than ever? Well, this must surely be because teachers can only deliver this noble policy recommended by our governments if they themselves work on their own self-development: do the teachers themselves live their lives with human values? Do they constantly look into their own being and weed out the qualities which are not wholesome - envy, greed, anger, fear? Of course, as adults we all carry painful wounds from the past and we have a bank of stored experiences which constantly cause us to respond and react emotionally. Don't we call it 'having my buttons pressed", triggers which bring out our negativity. So to be a teacher who can truly support and nurture the child's growth and development we have to be able to look at ourselves honestly, change our old patterns, and aim to become a living model of human values. It is a journey which goes on and on as we constantly aim to improve ourselves and heal our flaws.

So we create an environment in our school which is imbued with values. We know that the children must arrive and be welcomed with values, supported through their work and play by values, and sent off home with values. This does not involve only the teachers in the school, but the treasured people who cook the food, tend the garden, fix the pipes etc. etc. - all adults in the environment must be carefully selected, able to model what we believe we truly are. From this the children absorb the values, in a sense they come to know nothing different, and gradually, (or sometimes quickly) the layers peel away.

We create a simple, pure, aesthetically- pleasing environment an oasis of peace and calm and beauty which the children come into, a place in which they can breathe, they can experiment and risk failure without being judged. Sai Baba tells us: *'Ceiling on desires is a must for leading a peaceful life'* - what does this mean? Help the children find resources within themselves to create their own entertainment - no toys, no material objects, but just props from which they can create their own play (frames, cloths, pegs etc.) This is the first step in helping them to escape from *'the getting and possessing'* society in which one has to earn large sums of money to fund ever- increasing desires, wants becoming needs. Our children must be shown another way. Remove the clutter from their environment, and offer a simple holistic alternative which will feed the soul. Reduce their desires to have, and show them how to care for, how to mend, how to improvise when they do not have. Help them to be self-sufficient. This not only satisfies them, but also offers a very 'green' model of education. Our environment discourages the use of television, video, and computers, instead we include a pool of books, stories which the children can share, and this material becomes the fodder for creative play Instead of the 'soap-opera' conversations which are heard in so many playgrounds, our children have a rich literary source to explore.

Our school motto is *'Love All Serve All'*, and we place a large emphasis on being able to serve others, serve our planet. Sai Baba says: *'The purpose of life is to grow in love— there is no discipline like service for the eradication of ego'* Ego, that consuming monster of peace and contentment. But to be able to serve, children need practical life skills, and so from day one they are given opportunities to develop these skills- how to clean, how to cook, how to garden, how to use tools, how to sew, - a series of activities which enable them to build up and refine large and small muscles, seek independence, be helpful, a truly 'free' man is the one who can meet all his own needs, and to reach this place we work with the theory of 'Help me to do it by myself. When the skills are developing we offer the children opportunities to do 'useful work' each day - prepare the lunch space, washing up etc. Every Friday they clean the school at the end of the morning before going swimming. And they begin to take on community service projects from a very early age.

As the values reveal themselves in the child the aim of education becomes clear - it is not earning a living which is the most important aspect of existence, but learning how to live your life. Sai Baba tells us: *Without character, wealth, education and social status are of no avail.*' To help our children develop good character we must offer them the necessary support. Firstly, we must help them to identify their feelings and learn how to deal with them *'Trouble and turmoil are temporary, like passing clouds - people can and should try to restrain these harmful emotions from outward expression,*' Sai Baba says. When children respond emotionally we have to offer them activities which will help them to process these emotions - creative arts and creative expression are the modes which we choose. Painting, modelling, drama, music and dance - all of these help children to identify their feelings and learn how to manage them in a wholesome way which will not be harmful to themselves or others. We all have files of past experiences and responses to them, and so we want to help the children find the strength to overcome these; only opening hearts can lead to true transformation. Secondly, to support character development we use particular strategies which are effective - mixed aged groups where older children lead the younger ones, a non-competitive ethos where the child progresses on his/her own journey, a weekly democratic meeting where everyone is heard and valued, personal teaming plans where every child is supported individually in all aspects of growth and development - academic, mental, emotional, physical, and spiritual Circle activities and conflict resolution skills are used, and meaningful roles are given to all the children to contribute to the school community. From the age of six we encourage them to write a Journey to Excellence diary - not 'I had a chocolate cake for tea' but rather 'What have I done well this week?'

As they reach the age of six, seven years we begin to explore with the children a journey of self- enquiry: what use is knowledge of scientific and cultural subjects without some relevant meaning? Knowledge for the sake of itself is not education: it is the self-enquiry alongside the academic subjects which is true learning. Sai Baba poses the questions for children to ask themselves as they study all subjects: *'Who am I? From where have I come? What is my purpose for being here?'* This is a truly cosmic education - huge questions to which we are all seeking the answer. And children have great wisdom - they want to know the answers to deep and meaningful questions - it is a privilege for us to share this journey with them.

Just as we use the classroom to offer a holistic, caring,

environment for learning, we also use the natural world. Sai Baba says *'Nature is the best teacher - for in nature there is goodness, simplicity, purity, and selfishness'*, and so we take our children into the trees, the woods, by the river, helping them to grow on all levels by using the stuff of the world - mud, puddles, grass and so on

Diversity is a very popular word now in our society. And it is a word which we employ in two different ways: firstly we recognise that children have many different learning styles and many ways of expressing themselves. It is our job as teachers to give them the resources and skills with which to progress their teaming and implement their ideas - if they are able to be diverse in initiative and express their initiative with conscience and consciousness this can only produce worthy future citizens who can contribute for the good of the whole. Sai Baba says: *'Though living beings appear in the universe in a myriad of forms, all of them are waves that have emerged from the ocean'*. Secondly, through our study of geography, history, zoology, botany, physics, chemistry, and astronomy we see clearly that there are fundamental needs for all living entities which are and always have been the same -the need for food, shelter, and the ability to reproduce the species. We look at the diversity, but what we truly celebrate is the oneness, the similarities, the essence of all life forms emanating from the one source, whatever that may be. It is this second aspect of our working with diversity which is paramount: all the cultures and all the religions have differences and these are to be honoured and respected, but fundamentally the message is the same emanating from all faiths and cultures, and it is this unifying strand of teaching which we focus on. When the teacher's heart truly embraces this unity in diversity then the children are equally touched. When we celebrate our sameness, our oneness, rather than our differences, then can education for peace be seen in action: only then can world peace come?

Can world peace ever come without individual peace being established first? We believe not. And so children have to be helped to access their own inner peace. Beginning with balance games, whisper and tiptoe games for the very young, through yoga and tai chi games as they grow, from a few minutes of quiet time in comfy cushions perhaps listening to a meaningful story each day, the children are gradually introduced to the exercise of silent sitting. This is their opportunity to sit quietly in reflection, gently hum or chant, focus on a candle flame, or absorb the gentle sounds around in their silence. In this place of stillness and quietness they are able to access their own intuition, conscience, higher self, that deep wisdom which has been accumulated since the ascent of man. This sense of pervading peace brings tolerance, equanimity, and a great sense of being at ease with oneself. Sai Baba says: *'Contact your own reality in the silence that is created by quietening the senses and controlling the mind'* One of our five year olds told me the other day, 'I can hear my brain'. This enables the child to be able to send love and light to all. Together we end our silent sitting with the words, 'May all the beings in all the worlds be happy''. From this deep searching and intuition children make wonderful statements. That same five year old made a personal request: following his French class he asked me, 'Lesley can you teach me all the languages in the world so that I can talk to everyone?' This must surely be this child's recognition of the real brotherhood of man, and the true need for us all to be able to communicate. So together we explored his question, and we remembered the same divine spark which is in all. He decided himself that even without the words he can still talk to everyone in the world because there is only one language, as Sai Baba says: 'the language of the heart' and that is called love.'

Appendix

Strathfillan, Scotland - Strathfillan Community Development Trust

Background

Strathfillan is a community located in the rural Central Highlands of Scotland with a population of 385, encompassing the villages of Crianlarich and Tyndrum. This isolated area is 20 miles from the nearest GP and 40 miles from the nearest secondary school.

The Strathfillan Community Development Trust (SCDT) was set up in 1997 in response to local demand as a means of delivering community regeneration initiatives in the area. The project is described as such: 'it is like a community bus... a vehicle that local people can get on to drive to individual project destinations. Often we have partners...which we invite on the bus journey with us; sometimes the community is alone'. Extensive community consultation and significant partnership working informed the first phase regeneration strategy.

Results

The Trust's achievements to date are impressive. It has planted two community woodlands, with a network of paths, designed and built a play-park; bought, renovated and rented out four houses; employed development managers, and funded its office. A working group, chaired by a SCDT director, leads each project. Other partner organisations are involved, as appropriate.

In 2001, priorities were reassessed (through consultation) to inform Phase Two. Current projects within this phase include; a cycleway; the management of affordable housing; further acquisition of community woodlands; a kick-around area for Tyndrum children; redevelopment of the disused station yard in Crianlarich; participation in setting up the Breadalbane Virtual Learning project, including an internet café. This pilot project is seeking to bring broadband into these rural areas and encourage skills development in information communication technology. Also, in partnership with the Stirling Council Youth Team, our youth group has been re-started, after a 2 years absence.

The Trust has also set up the Strathfillan Action Group, which organises social events, evening classes and activities for older people, for example a pensioners luncheon club. In 2003 the community council received a grant to conduct a Rural Voices project. This involved a survey of local opinion in order to support the development of service provision in the area.

The Trust has recently taken over the management of the Tyndrum Village Hall and intends to make it more accessible to the local community. To date the value of completed projects totals around £800,000, although the second phase will see this increase. The Trust has received grants from 35 different funding bodies over seven years. The rental of housing provides a small annual profit, but the Trust is currently looking at further means by which to generate income.

The Trust is fully owned, operated and controlled by the local community. In 2003, 35 people volunteered their time to the work of the group. It is structured as a membership organisation with an elected board of 11 directors.

The Trust has, in effect, been the pioneer for community futures being adopted in all community council areas, throughout the Stirling and Loch Lomond and Trossachs National Park areas. So far, about 20 other community Trusts have been set up or proposed.

The Panel's View

This is a very successful community development trust which has been operating seven years and which has already established itself in the Central Highlands and as an exemplar of community-led regeneration for all rural areas of Scotland. The Trust has begun to tackle apathy and exclusion by developing 'quick win' projects incorporated within a sustainable approach to address issues and challenges defined by local people. The project should be held up as a flagship for rural development, which can be overshadowed by the urban agenda.

Bibliography

1. Exodus 21: 21-27
2. *Jesus Lived in India* Holger Kersten published by Element Books 1986
3. Matthew 7: 7
4. *Other Lives Other Selves* Roger J Woolger published by Crucible
5. *The Works of Omraan Mikhael Aivanhov* published by Editions Prosveta SA, ZA Le Capitou - BP12 , F83601 Frejus, Cedex, France Email: international@prosveta.com www..prosveta.com
   a. You Are Gods
   b. Man's Subtle Bodies and Centres
   c. Daily Meditations: 15th November
   d. Daily Meditations: 15th September
   e. Lecture given 24th April 1983
6. Books by Paramahansa Yogananda Publisher - Self Realisation Society
   a. *The Second Coming of Christ* Volumes 1 and 2
   b. *The Autobiography of a Yogi*
7. *Pendulum Dowsing* Robert Graves published by Element Books
8. *Psychic Protection* William Bloom published by Judy Piatcus
9. John 14: 20
10. *Islam-A Short History* Karen Armstrong published by

Pheonix

11. *The Aquarian Gospel of Jesus The Christ* Levi H Dowling published by Fowler

12. 1 Corinthians 13: 11-12

13. Various books translated or written by Edmond Bordeaux Szekely published by the International Biogenic Society, PO Box 849, Nelson, BC Canada V1L 6A5

    a. *Cosmos Man and Society*

    b. *The Essene Gospel of Peace*

    c. *The Essene Origins of Christianity*

    d. *Search for the Ageless* - Volume One

    e. *The Book of Living Foods*

    f. *The Discovery of the Essene Gospel of Peace*

14. *Gospel of Thomas* Hugh McGregor Ross published by Watkins

15. *The Dead Sea Scrolls Deception* Michael Baigent & Richard Leigh
published by Arrow Books

16. *The Tomb of God* Richard Andrews & Paul Scellenberger published by Little Brown and Company

17. *The Agnostic's Prayer* Lionel MacClelland 1996 - Lionel is a member of the Scottish folk group, 'Black Eyed Biddy'

18. *The God Delusion* Richard Dawkins published by Houghton Mifflin 2006

19. *Love Without End* Glenda Green published by Heartwings Publishing

20. *The New English Bible - New Testament* published by Oxford University Press/Cambridge University Press 1961

21. 1 Corinthians 13: 11-12

22. *Mind Memory and Archetype Morphic Resonance and the Collective Unconscious* paper by Rupert Sheldrake

23. *The Celestine Vision* James Redfield published by Bantam Books

24. *Transmission - A Meditation for The New Age* Benjamin Crème published by The Tara Press

25. Matthew 7: 12

26. *Chambers 20th Century Dictionary* edited by E M Kirkpatrick

27. *Matreya's Mission - Volume One* Benjamin Crème published by Share International Foundation

28. *The Celestial Voice of Diana* channelled by Rita Eide published by Findhorn

29. A paper prepared by ITC (Napier University) *An e-Democracy Model for Communities,* and details of other ITC's projects and publications, can be accessed on http://itc.napier.ac.uk

30. Works by David R Cowan

    a. An article entitled *Ley Lines, Ill-Health and Spirit Lines*

    b. *Safe as Houses?* published by Gateway Press is currently out of print, but available for free download from his website www.leyman.demon.co.uk

    c. *Ley Lines and Earth Energies* co-authored by Chris Arnold published by David Hatcher Childress, USA.

31. *The Revenge of Gaia* James Lovelock published by Allen Lane

32. *The British Medical Association Complete Family Health Guide* edited by Dr Michael Peters & Dr Tony Smith published by Dorling Kindersley

33. *Living without Cruelty* Mark Gold published by Merlin Press 1989

34. *Death by Modern Medicine* Carolyn Dean published by Ash Tree Publishing, PO Box 64, Woodstock, NY12498

35. *Water & Salt* Dr F Batmanghelidj published by Tagman Press

36. *Sathya Sai Education in Human Values - A Curriculum for the Development of Character* Carole Alderman published by The British Institute of Sathya Sai Education in Human Values of the UK, The Glen, Cuckoo Hill, Pinner HA5 2BE, Middlesex, England

37. *The Five Human Values and Human Excellence* Dr. Artong-Jumsai Na Ayudhya BA, MA, DIC, Ph.D published by International Institute of Sathya Sai Education, 108, Sukhumvit 53, Bankok 10110, Thailand. Tel +66-2-2620832, Email ajtech@ksc.th.com

38. *The Slippery Slope* Ann McMail, is extracted from the book *Sathya Sai Education in Human Values, More Lesson Plans, ages 6-8 years* © BISSE Limited

39. *The Encyclopedia of Alternative Health Care* Kristin Olsen published by Piatkus

40. An Ayurvedic doctor can be contacted Skelmersdale on 01695 51008

41. *The TM Technique* Peter Russell published by Routledge, Kegan & Paul